Contents

Acknowledgements

The following friends and colleagues have supported the writing of this book by inviting me to give talks, reading draft chapters or otherwise commenting on its shape and structure, and in numerous other ways: Natalie Adamson, Gavin Alexander, Laura Berchielli, Andrea Brady, Peter Brennan, Tom and Laurie Clark, David Evans, Matt ffytche, David Herd, Gavin Hopps, Mike Hurley, Lorna Hutson, Laurent Jaffro, Simon Jarvis, Chris Jones, Michael Kindellan, James Loxley, Christian Maurer, Tim Morris, Andy Murphy, Chris Murray, Marko Pajevic, Tony Paraskeva, Don Paterson, Mario Petrucci, Malcolm Philips, Robin Purves, Tom Raworth, Rosella Riccobono, Jennifer Richards, Andrew Roberts, Michael Snow, Jane Stabler, Keston Sutherland, Richard Terry, Aliki Varvogli, Matt Welton, and Jonathan Wild. Sam Ladkin has shown immense and wholly characteristic generosity to me, intellectually and socially, throughout the period in which I was working on the book: I am proud to have such a friend and colleague.

I would like to thank the Carnegie Trust for the Universities of Scotland for funding that supported research in the British Library. A draft was completed whilst I was working as a postdoctoral fellow at PHIER (Philosophies et rationalités), the research centre (EA3297) of the Philosophy department of Université Clermont Ferrand II (Blaise Pascal): many thanks to everyone at the centre for their friendship and support.

I would like to thank the following publishers and individuals for permission to reproduce poems. Lines from *The Path to the Sea* used by permission of Thomas A. Clark. 'She Went to Stay' and 'Song (the grit)', from *The Collected Poems of Robert Creeley, 1945–75*, by Robert Creeley, copyright 1982 by the Regents of the University of California, published by the University of California Press, used by permission of the University of California Press and Marion Boyars Publishers Ltd. 'The Secret Name', from W.S. Graham, *New Collected Poems*, used by permission of Michael Snow. 'Mayakovsky' from *The Collected Poems of Frank O'Hara*, used by permission of Grove/Atlantic, Inc. 'Gaslight' from Tom Raworth, *Collected Poems*, copyright 2003, Carcanet Press Ltd. 'Misremembered Lyric' from Denise Riley,

Mop Mop Georgette, copyright 1993 by Denise Riley. 'The Idea of Order at Key West' from *The Collected Poems of Wallace Stevens by Wallace Stevens*, copyright 1954 by Wallace Stevens and renewed 1982 by Holly Stevens, used by permission of Alfred A. Knopf, a division of Random House, Inc. and Faber and Faber Ltd.

How to Use this Book

The book comprises an introduction, eleven chapters and an epilogue. The chapters and the epilogue all address the works of significant poets in the context of contemporary or near contemporary writing on the theory of poetic language. The order of discussion is chronological (by first publication of the focal poem). The poems are selected on the basis of their intrinsic interest, and also because one (or more) of their features exemplifies the issue addressed by the theoretical writers alongside whom the poems are read. The chapters and the epilogue have been organised into two thematic series, slightly overlapping around the middle of the twentieth century: figure, selection, measure, equivalence, spirit, deviance.

The book may be approached in a variety of different ways. Those whose interest is in the poetic theory and practice of a particular period, or of a particular poet, should be able to approach any of the chapters in isolation. Those readers most interested in a particular theme, such as figure, should be able to read the two chapters on that theme next to one another. Those with an interest in poetic theory and its linguistic and philosophical contexts might want to start with the Introduction. Throughout the book I have tried to point the reader to other chapters, and parts of chapters, in which further or related discussion is to be found.

CHAPTER ONE

Introduction

The argument of this book is that poems encourage their readers to experience language as a dual-aspect phenomenon, as something known and understood in two different ways simultaneously. Poems make the language in which they are made appear contingent, and necessary, at once: they make their writers and readers feel a justness or truth in the poem's language, at the same time as making those writers and readers question just how that part of the poem's language (a rhyme, an image, the weight on a syllable, and so on) could produce the reactions it produces. The language in poems seems marked, both attention-seeking and attention-rewarding, but also to raise questions rather than answer them. When reflecting on what a poem or part of a poem means, and how it acquires that meaning, people often engage in mental or verbal thick description, enriching a semantic paraphrase of the passage with thoughts about tone, emphasis or inter-relations with other features of other phrases that appear to participate in its meaning. So, for example, when the word 'difference' is given three syllables by being placed in a certain position in a metrical scheme, it acquires emphatic qualities it might not always have (see 'Measure: William Wordsworth'). The means of assessing these tones, emphases and connections are comparable to the techniques people have for working out what someone means by saying something in a particular context with a particular emphasis ('Was there irony there, or reluctance?' 'Is my interlocutor just saying what she thinks I want to hear?'). The explanations of poetic or other utterances arrived at in this way may be extensive, but they are also necessarily incomplete: the fullness of the context in which something is said, and what it means in that context, can never be stated, remaining always a matter of partial interpretation.

A further set of questions is raised by the markedness of poetic language. In poems, how what is said achieves what it seems to achieve is troubled by contingency as well as incompleteness: there is always something implausible about the manner in which features identified as having a poetic meaning have that meaning, particularly the aspects of language distant from standard semantic content, such as stress, phoneme repetition and so on. How does elaborating the pronunciation of a word from two to three syllables come to mean something? For this and other seemingly arbitrary features mean a lot. On the one hand, the systematic features of the language (word stress, regularised in metrical patterns; a limited range of phonetic material neces-sarily recurring according to certain principles) are contingent, out of the hands of the poet in question, but necessary, as passed down by the devel-opmental history of the particular language. The odd way in which those systematic recurrences and variations come to seem excessively meaningful in the moment of a poem, or, indeed, across a range of poems, is again simply a by-product, one might say, of the systematic efficiency of language, and yet entirely necessary to the production of just that poem and the variety of meanings it has for its writer(s) and readers along the history of its production and reception.

Because language is neither an insignificant nor discrete feature of human life, but to a high degree characteristic of the species and of the intersubjec-tive and institutional worlds people share, poems encourage their writers and readers to think about these intersubjective and institutional worlds in the same kinds of ways as they think about language. Poems demonstrate exactly how we have come to talk in the ways we do about love, justice, solidarity, hate, fear, death and so on, whilst encouraging us to question why we have come to do so. Poems help their writers and readers to see what it is to be a language-using being, inhabiting highly complex institutional and cognitive worlds that are not made by us alone, and yet whose systems we necessarily transform simply by expending the energies of our lives within them; some of our individual detours sadly perishing, others gathering cumulative force; all of them making our history.

That, in brief, is the argument of this book. To make that argument, this book draws on a wide variety of views about poetry, language and poetic language. The purpose of this introduction is to document the main points of contact with previous treatments of the subject, whilst pointing out where my view qualifies them or differs, noting where particular issues or authors are discussed in greater detail. The domains on which I draw are, crudely designated, analytic philosophy of language, cognitive poetics, structuralist and post-structuralist linguistic theory, speech-act theory and pragmatics. I will begin with a consideration of the central claims of structuralist work on poetic language. Structuralists object to characterising poetic language by one or another poetic feature:

> poetic language is not always *ornamental* expression . . . Nor is *beauty* the constant token of the poetic word . . . Nor is poetic language identical with language designated for the expression of feelings, *emotive* language . . . poetic

language is not fully characterized by *concreteness* ('plasticity') ... neither is a *figurative* nature unconditionally characteristic of poetic language ... Finally, not even *individuality*, the emphasized uniqueness of linguistic expression, characterizes poetic language in general ... no single property characterizes poetic language permanently and generally. Poetic language is permanently characterized only by its function[.][1]

Poetic language, as any other language, should be categorised by its ends, its function. Poetic language is language in which the aesthetic or poetic function is dominant: it makes people concentrate on language itself. Yet there is a seeming paradox in the functional definition of poetic language:

aesthetic effect is the goal of poetic expression. However, the aesthetic function, which thus dominates in poetic language (being only a concomitant phenomenon in other functional languages), concentrates attention on the linguistic sign itself – hence it is exactly the opposite of a practical orientation toward a goal which in language is communication.[2]

Poetic language concentrates attention on language itself: an odd goal or function to have. It does not share the character of other goals and functions of language by communicating a particular kind of information (logical, emotional, and so on). Yet Mukařovský, the writer from whose work I have been quoting, goes on to identify a different kind of goal for this reflective language:

Precisely because of its aesthetic 'self-orientation' poetic language is more suited than other functional languages for constantly reviving man's attitude toward language and the relation of language to reality, for constantly revealing in new ways the internal organization of the linguistic sign, and for showing new possibilities of its use.[3]

This aesthetic function proper to poetry makes people think about how language works, and is used: it operates at a meta-linguistic level, being in language and yet reflecting upon it. I will be developing this structuralist view to suggest that attitudes towards language and its relation to reality are revived and reoriented in specific ways by poetic language, to the extent that the contingent and yet necessary relations within language systems and between language and practical life are known and felt. Poems make the merely possible appear necessary, and the necessary appear to be chosen.

The structuralist definition of poetic language by means of function, the poetic or aesthetic function being to focus attention on language itself, has endured in both speech-act theory and cognitive poetics. The assertion that 'poetry becomes a way of drawing attention to acts of human utterance' brings the vocabulary of speech-act theory (in which things said are commonly called 'utterances' and thought of as 'acts') to the central structuralist insight. The utterer of this assertion regards metre as one strong way of the poet marking the aesthetic function, describing it as 'the codal speech act of putting his text on display as a text, his relation through the poem to an audience'.[4] (A codal speech act is one that tells other people what kind of act one is engaging in.) Metre, then, is a way of saying '*whatever else I may be talking about, I am talking also about language itself*',[5] thereby establishing a peculiar kind of relationship between poet and audience. In cognitive poetics, which aims to supersede structuralist poetics, literary language more generally is still thought of as language that seeks attention:

> if there is one thing that is common to many different attempts to describe or characterise literariness, it is the notion that there is a texture to a text, a sense that the materiality of the object is noticeable alongside any content that is communicated through it. Literature draws attention to its own condition of existence, which is its texture.[6]

Peter Stockwell, the author of the last work cited, also agrees with Mukařovský that specific formal features are not to be identified, individually or collectively, with poetic language: 'it has been demonstrated many times that there is nothing inherently different in the form of literary language'.[7] To seek out such formal distinctions is thus a delusion.

Yet some work in speech-act theory suggests that the structuralist approach to poetic language does just that, arguing that structuralism isolates poetic language from ordinary language, and thereby the world of social and ethical obligations in which ordinary language is such an active participant. This work also takes in bad faith the assertion that the poetic function can be found in many kinds of speech, and that what marks poetic language is the dominance of that function.[8] This critique emphasises that literary works have a context, and that such a context involves people (the speaker and audience) in relation to one another,

> that their existence is presupposed by literary works, that they have commitments to one another as they do everywhere else ... Far from being autonomous, self-contained, self-motivating, context-free objects which exist independently from the 'pragmatic' concerns of 'everyday' discourse, literary works take place in a context, and like any other utterance they cannot be described apart from that context.[9]

This speech-act theorist, then, adopts the exaggerated view that structuralist poeticians believed poetic utterances to be hermetic and auto-generated, rather than simply self-reflexive. The sense of a threat posed by structuralist poetics to literature's integration with life has been felt in other critical approaches also. Derek Attridge, one of the principal Anglophone specialists in poetic language of the last fifty years, and one who has pioneered the study of post-structural approaches, has written that

> structuralism on principle leaves out of account those properties of literature, literary criticism, and literary theory which most obviously set them apart from the objects of the physical world: their existence within and determination by a shifting web of socially produced relations, judgments, and distinctions, and their consequent openness to change and cultural variation.[10]

The structuralist view of poetic language, it is alleged, has isolated formal features of language as poetic and alienated poetic language from the messy world of human relations and commitments.

This view is, however, a poor travesty of the positions adopted by structuralist poeticians, who were, for the most part, operating in a part of the world and at a period in political history when social commitment, real or professed, was paramount: eastern Europe in the first half of the twentieth century. Mukařovský could not be more explicit about the participation of poetic language in the full range of human relations, judgements and distinctions: 'linguistics has provided a model for the structural analysis of the *entire* literary work, not just its linguistic aspect'.[11] That is, structural linguistics, particularly its central thesis that values are produced by differences between elements in a system, and not positively and atomically by those elements in isolation, provides a model not just for the operation of the formal features of the language but for all other features also: the position of the speaker and audience in social and economic terms, for example. Mukařovský distinguishes the practice of structuralism from that of formalism in a response to a remark made by the formalist critic Viktor Shklovsky:

> 'In the study of literature I am concerned with the investigation of its inner laws. To give a parallel from industry, I am not interested in the situation on the world cotton market, or in the policy of trusts, but only in the kinds of yarn and the methods of weaving.' The difference between the viewpoint of contemporary structuralism and the formalist thesis cited could be expressed in the following manner: Even today the 'method of weaving' is, of course, the center of interest, but at the same time it is already apparent that we may not disregard the 'situation of the world cotton market' either, since the development of weaving – in the non-figurative sense as well – is governed not only by the progress of textile technology (the internal regularity of a developing series) but at the same time by the requirements of the market, by supply and demand. The same is valid *mutatis mutandis* for literature.[12]

Here Mukařovský identifies as the defining characteristic of structuralist poetics that which its critics seem to think it banishes: a concern for the interrelation of linguistic and literary systems with all other adjoining or otherwise relevant human systems, such as those of economics. Structuralist poetics does not seal its objects off from the world; on the contrary, it regards structural linguistics as having provided the model for the study of the poetic text in the world of human judgements, relations and actions. Structuralists have continued to emphasise the connectedness of the poetic function of texts with the variety of other functions they are very likely to have: 'The unification of the artistic function with the magical, juridical, moral, philosophical, and political constitutes an inalienable feature of the social functioning of the artistic text.'[13] This socially-oriented structuralism is not to be seen in opposition to a contextually focused speech-act theory, but in partnership with it.

Some linguists and philosophers have indeed adapted and developed the combination of structural and pragmatic impulses seen in socially oriented structuralism. One way in which these interests can be drawn together is by acknowledging that 'thematisation', the process whereby an aspect of language becomes the object of attention, is not limited to the formal aspects of language. Thematisation can relate to 'other factors of communication: the role behaviour of the sender, the response experiences of certain groups of addressees, the mechanisms of the art market, and even the thematized segments of reality'.[14] Aspects of the situation beyond the code employed can be thematised, such as the economic conditions that pertain to the objects and agents involved in the scene of communication. Such a view would have been no news to Byron, who at one point or another thematises most of the conceivable aspects of the speaker-audience relationship, including the economic aspect:

> But for the present, gentle reader! and
>   Still gentler purchaser! the bard – that's I –
> Must, with permission, shake you by the hand,
>   And so your humble servant, and good bye![15]

The things about itself that poetic language can make writers and readers attend to include socio-economic, or otherwise institutional and intersubjective facts, that might not be in any simple sense identifiable in language at the formal level, but which are demonstrably in and of the speech situation (where demonstration is a matter of people agreeing they are there).[16]

Speech-act theories of poetic language have been subjected to a range of criticism themselves, such as the reliance of such theories upon a strict sense of the context that is required to make an utterance 'happy' (successful in the circumstances), and their refusal to see the existence of a speech act that is not in the literary text, but is the literary text. I shall come to these criticisms shortly. But perhaps most strangely, approaches to poetic language that draw on speech-act theory themselves have a tendency to remove their object from the world of human relations and commitments. J. L. Austin's work is foundational for speech-act theory. Austin classes the use of language in poetry together with 'etiolations, parasitic uses, etc., various "not serious" and "not full normal" uses' of language.[17] Yet, in the tradition of analytical philosophy of language following on from Austin, literary language has been recognised as providing a particular challenge precisely because it focuses on the performance of acts rather than the telling of truths: 'Literature poses a problem for philosophy of language, for it directly challenges any theory of meaning that makes the assertorial or truth-seeking uses of language primary and pretends that other linguistic performances are in some sense "etiolated" or "parasitical".'[18] More recently, J. Hillis Miller has argued that there is a defining contradiction in Austin's approach to language. The exclusion of literature from the realm of 'real' speech acts, acts that require sincerity in performance, is the basis of Austin's speech-act theory; yet Austin contends that speakers are bound by their words whether they mean them or not.[19] There is uncertainty, then, concerning the degree to which poetic or literary language can constitute a speech act, enjoining the kinds of response and responsibility that some notable examples of 'real' speech acts, such as promises and vows, enjoin.

Mary Louise Pratt, as we saw earlier, argues that aesthetic modes of reception are not without commitments to other people: 'our role in literary works presupposes aesthetic commitment, not detachment; the conventional responsibilities tied to this commitment are exceedingly elaborate; and that commitment and those responsibilities are what define the literary speech situation'.[20] The literary situation itself implies human bonds and commitments. But Pratt later isolates the literary speech act from such commitments, or rather from the failure perfectly to maintain those commitments (the possibility of not keeping a commitment being vital to its being a commitment). The way in which literature, according to Pratt, becomes isolated from ordinary speech relates to a principle identified by the philosopher Paul Grice as governing conversation with its own fuzzy logic, the co-operation principle.[21] When we speak, we co-operate with other people by not imparting needless, redundant information. If such information is provided in a 'real' speech situation, Grice contends, someone has flouted a maxim of conversation, and may be doing so for a reason. If there is no reason, then the person is not really communicating by imparting the information: it is meaningless. In literature, there is no possibility, Pratt contends, of flouting the maxims of conversation so: if there is redundancy, for example, it must be there for a reason.[22] Such a view of literature would make it impossible for an author to let a reader down, to talk irrelevantly, or in such a way as to hinder rather than promote understanding. Why should a poet not be able to disappoint their audience just as any other speaker? To suggest that a poem is closed to such possibilities on account of its being an artefact rather than an ordinary or natural phenomenon, is to do just what Pratt accused structuralist poetics of doing: isolating poetic language from ordinary language, and closing it off from response and responsibility.[23] Speech-act theories of literature seem internally riven, unsure if the kind of speaking that takes place in poetry is binding or not.

Literature can disappoint and fail in many ways, but its failure is not simply that of leaving unfulfilled some conditions for the performance of the act that seems superficially to be taking place in the language used (promising, for example).[24] Austin talks about successful or happy performances and per-formances that misfire because something is inappropriate about what is said or the circumstances in which it is said. Grice's co-operation principle is an attempt to devise guidelines for describing how performances that look like they are pretty unhappy are actually quite happy. One reason that poetry is so often isolated from ordinary language is that poems do not have contexts in the same way that some other kinds of speech genres have contexts – reliable, repeatable contexts:

> all other, normative and socially sanctioned discourses are founded in some degree on the assumption of relevance as a function of the congruence of inten-tion and interpretation, and . . . this depends on the *reconstitution* and not the *creation* of context.

Poems ask that contexts for their utterance are created rather than sup-plied. I would add the qualification here that all acts require the creation of context, but it is poetry that makes readers particularly aware of the creative, contingent yet necessary nature of such creation. This same writer goes on to allege something rather drastic about the nature of language, thought and belief: 'What literature brings home to us with especial force is the ultimate instability and arbitrariness of all language, and all systems of thought and belief which it expresses'.[25] This is an aggressive way of formulating the idea that human social systems derive their essence from no other source than the history of human interactions themselves, an idea that David Hume formulated as their being artificial and yet 'not *arbitrary*', a formulation less dramatic, but more accurate.[26]

The impossibility of tying the act of literature to specific contexts that will make it a happy act is a topic I will return to shortly when discussing Jacques Derrida. This impossibility is one ground for the post-structural critique of speech-act theories of literary language. Shoshana Felman, in a study of Austin and the Don Juan character, provides one of the most sustained engagements with the theory of the literary speech act from a post-structural point of view. She argues that Grice's attempt to rein in misfires is a failure to understand the spirit of Austin's text, itself a very witty piece of writing that seems not just to tolerate but even to welcome misfiring acts.[27] Felman suggests that Don Juan's frequent promises are taken by him to be mere transient performances, yet taken by others to be constative descriptions of his state of mind.[28] Promises have, for obvious reasons, provided much material for philosophers of speech acts, such as John Searle, who provides conditions for the act of promising, and includes the possibility of insincere promising in his account.[29] But there seems to be a fundamental misconception in Felman's characterisation of the speech situation in the case of literature, and therefore the circumstances to which reference has to be made in order to understand whether or not an act is happy. Characters in a play do not perform speech acts. They are made, in a complex, composite speech act, to say things. The circumstances of the theatre are not forgotten or ignored. Felman's treating Don Juan's promise as a promise and not part of a play suggests that an audience might be unaware of the fact that they are an audience. Yet, as Samuel Johnson says,

> spectators are always in their senses, and know, from the first act to the last, that the stage is only a stage, and that the players are only players. They come to hear a certain number of lines recited with just gesture and elegant modulation.

They do not hear these lines, for example, to be made promises; not, at least, the promises the characters make, or pretend to make, to one another.[30]

What Juan says has the form of a promise, and is taken by his interlocutors on stage for a promise, but is taken by the audience off stage, the 'real' audience, as an insincere promise; or rather, is taken by them as the creation of a dramatic artist probably intending certain effects upon an audience to be achieved by the production of words having the form of a promise and yet evidently being insincere. The speech situation is not one in which Juan and his fictional interlocutor are concerned, but one in which Molière and his audiences are concerned.[31] To think that Juan's promise is an act is precisely the same misconception as to regard the things said in poems as pale or parasitical versions of real speech acts. An effort needs to be made to reintroduce the pragmatics of poetic composition into the discussion of poetic art, in the sense suggested by Kenneth Burke:

> The general approach to the poem might be called 'pragmatic' in this sense: It assumes that a poem's structure is to be described most accurately by

thinking always of the poem's function. It assumes that the poem is designed to 'do something' for the poet and his readers, and that we can make the most relevant observations about its design by considering the poem as the embodiment of this act.[32]

But I would qualify Burke by adding that not all things, indeed, one might argue, very few things, are done by design. And in this sense, the pragmatics of poetry requires the close socio-historical, even anthropological study, that takes place in good literary scholarship all the time, study that helps to show what might have been done by a poem, whether or not it was done by design.[33]

Austin may have left a door open for the kind of act that has no specific happy context. Amongst various classes of act, Austin identifies the class he calls 'perlocutionary acts', acts that 'produce certain consequential effects upon the feelings, thoughts, or actions of the audience, or of the speaker, or of other persons'.[34] In the introduction to Felman's book, Stanley Cavell, the philosopher and cultural critic, notes that Austin had shied away from writing about this class of speech acts, saying it is 'not governed by the conventions or conditions or rituals Austin invokes, but represents the complementary field occupied by or calling for improvisation and passion and aggression'.[35] The kinds of rituals and conventions Cavell is talking about are the conventions that are susceptible to enough definition to enable people to say that a certain act has occurred, and to identify recurrences. Cavell points out elsewhere that for people to be able to say that certain things are the kinds of things that are said (when one marries, for example) there need to be 'standing recurrent when's [sic]' for the situation to be of a determinable type.[36] What he contends of the perlocutionary, however, is that there may be no ultimate regularity in the circumstances that are repeated in different instances of comparable actions. And what Cavell says of the perlocutionary realm may also be true of the supposedly more convention-bound illocutionary realm.

Another way of stating and extending Cavell's realisation is to say that the genres of speech are open and variable: there cannot be hard and fast distinctions between the kinds of things that are or can be said. Such a reading of Austin is in direct contradiction to that proposed by Hillis Miller, who suggests that Austin believes speech acts require precisely defined conventions in order to be happy, and that it is the job of the philosopher to police, or to sanction the policing, of those conventions. Hillis Miller adopts this reading despite his recognition that Austin's own work is revolutionary (in the sense of being the kind of act that looks a little like other previous acts, but which nonetheless radically changes the conventions for its own happy performance) and despite his high estimation of Austin's ironical playfulness, and determined self-undermining.[37] There has been a tendency amongst post-structuralist theorists of language in general to rigidify the resemblances of genre into laws, as if prior utterances entirely and precisely determine the shape of utterances to come.[38] Cavell's recognition that, in certain genres of speech at least, the conventions are always open to change, pre-empts the post-structuralist critique of speech-act theories of literature.

The preceding pages on structuralist and speech-act theories of poetic language might be summarised as follows: if speech acts are of particular types, but those types are open to continual revision through the interaction of utterances and speakers with one another; and if acts are taken to be part of the world, then a kind of language that encourages us to reflect upon the nature of our (verbal) actions, in all their aspects (formal/grammatical, pragmatic, and so on) might reasonably be said to change our world, to be part of the project of critical reflection upon the way in which we make and inhabit our world, and to be part of self-consciousness in general. One could say poetry is the sign of a changing world. Many previous theorists of poetic or literary language have contended similar things. The poet-critic Veronica Forrest-Thomson, still often thought of as a proponent of a poetry sealed off from the practical world, argued that 'the world is not something static, irredeemably given by a natural language. When language is re-imagined the world expands with it.'[39] Emphasising the fact that the representative function of language, that by which it posits an external or empirical world, is merely one of its functions, and not necessarily the predominant function in poetry, Forrest-Thomson argued against the idea 'that poems act as surrogates for their empirical situation', suggesting instead that 'they use their empirical situation (extension of meaning into the external world) in such a way as to change the meaning of "empirical situation"'.[40] Poetry's role is to transcend the languages that describe and delimit a current reality, and Forrest-Thomson identifies 'the true function of poetry: that it must create a middle area where Artifice can open up imaginative possibilities in both the forms and contents of other languages, and thus transcend the world these impose'.[41]

The assertion that poetry changes languages or worlds takes many different forms in other approaches to poetic language. Cognitive poetics suggests literary texts have the capacity to alter our realities by bringing together and modifying the tiny narratives or parables by means of which sense is attributed to events. The drawing together of different parables is called a blend, and 'blends can be inputs to further blends, where emergent structure can again potentially offer modifications of the original cognitive models. This is the mechanism by which, through parable, literature alters our perspective, knowledge, and way of thinking.'[42] In Derek Attridge's more recent work, change is said to occur for the reader of literature through an encounter with an 'other' represented by the text, a way of talking that is not the same as our own, and which, by performing itself through our reading of it, changes the organisation of our linguistic-conceptual world.[43] In various ways, then, the act of reading is recognised as a world-changing act because worlds are themselves to a significant degree made up of linguistic performances. Poetic language, as I am suggesting in this book, is an incitement to such world-changing reflection. My specific contention is that poetry changes our world by making us realise its peculiar status as both free and determined. It is not just the case that poetry allows for the transcendence of the worlds imposed by languages, but that the worlds these languages impose become open to our transcending them because we have been enabled to see them as stages in a series of evolving utterances. Such utterances, seen from the perspective of the past, are dependent upon what has been said before; seen from the perspective of the present they must be different from that past; and seen from the perspective of the future they can be no other than they were.

Poetic language, then, makes the institution of language appear at once both contingent and necessary. Poetry rewards attention because it exploits the simultaneous contingency and necessity of its own construction: 'the play of intersecting regularities gives rise to that "accidentalness in conditionedness" which guarantees poetry its high information content'. It is this high information load of poetry that makes the poetic text 'a powerful and deeply dialectical mechanism of the search for truth, for understanding the surrounding world and our orientation in it'.[44] Poetry opens up the institution of language to those willing to engage critically with it. It makes its writers and readers rethink the relation of their singular acts of creation and interpretation to the history of all such acts in such a way as to make palpable the liberty and the vertigo of being the producers of our own values. Such a description of poetic language is close to Derrida's thinking on the nature of the institution of literature, characterised as a 'peculiar institution which sheds light on institutionality, as a site of resistance to the philosophical tradition of conceptual thought, as a series of singular (but repeatable) acts that demand singular (but responsible) responses'.[45] In this characterisation, the role of the institution of literature is libertarian; it is to be an institution without precedent or future. This role is also one that is regarded as vital to a criticism of the bases of philosophical thought, the reproducibility and repeatability of concepts:

> I am certainly not the only one to have this dream, the dream of a new institution to be precise, of an institution without precedent, without pre-institution. You will say, and quite rightly, that this is the dream of every literary work. Every literary work 'betrays' the dream of a new institution of literature. It betrays it first by revealing it: each work is unique and is a new institution unto itself.[46]

Here the relation between the preceding acts and the new act, necessarily alike yet different, is seen as one of betrayal: it is a betrayal to solidify the necessity of the past, rather than persist in promising an open future. My objection to Derrida's position is not that such an institution is impossible because it would have no grounds, would establish no kind, but rather that every institution has this character: every application of the law is an innovation at the same time as a preservation; every recursion is a variation. Nor is the revelation of the new institution each work initiates rightly seen as a betrayal. The work seen outside its institutional history is an abstraction: all the psychic potentialities of the work are in or triggered by that work, not by something always beyond the work. The idea that literary works inaugurate their own institutions and thereby cease to be singular (in an impossibly abstract sense) is ontologically neutral: it may be a good description, but it implies no necessary emotional nor political values.

The group of tendencies in philosophy normally referred to as 'analytical' has also produced attempts to conceptualise language as the kind of institution being described here, one that exists only in transition, as event rather than state, amongst which the work of Donald Davidson is prominent. Yet Davidson's thinking about language is firmly grounded in a set of irreducible conceptual certainties: he presumes a triangular relation between speakers and world in which speakers share what he calls a 'mature set of concepts' and also know what communication is.[47] Sharing mature concepts, however, is not at all the same as sharing the total structure of a language, if that is to be understood as a set of rules by which utterances are interpreted (semantic and grammatical knowledge). Davidson says that speakers always come to one another with 'prior theories' of communication, which are then modified in any actual exchange, by means of a 'passing theory' of what someone else means by their words. The passing theory may help the speakers get by on that occasion, but there is no guarantee the same theory will help them in the future:

> the theory we actually use to interpret an utterance is geared to the occasion . . . but this does not mean (necessarily) that we now have a better theory for the next occasion. The reason for this is, as we have seen, perfectly obvious: a speaker may provide us with information relevant to interpreting an utterance in the course of making the utterance . . . For the hearer, the prior theory expresses how he is prepared in advance to interpret an utterance of the speaker, while the passing theory is how he *does* interpret the utterance. For the speaker, the prior theory is what he *believes* the interpreter's prior theory to be, while his passing theory is the theory he *intends* the interpreter to use . . . Every deviation from ordinary usage, as long as it is agreed on for the moment (knowingly deviant, or not, on one, or both, sides), is in the passing theory as a feature of what the words mean on that occasion.[48]

Words here certainly have meanings, concepts they signify, but the precise nature of that relation is not determined in advance of any particular speech situation. Davidson suggests that, if his theory were correct, concepts of language would need to be radically revised:

> what interpreter and speaker share, to the extent that communication succeeds, is not learned and so is not a language governed by rules or conventions known to speaker and interpreter in advance ... What two people need, if they are to understand one another through speech, is the ability to converge on passing theories from utterance to utterance.[49]

Such convergences are new institutions, quite like those of the new institution of literature: new with every occasion, solidifying into a prior theory in the moment of use. They are the kinds of theories arrived at when reading poems that are new, or reading them in new ways.

There are, however, reasons to be a little sceptical about Davidson's radical argument. It might well be that passing theories are not given in advance, but formed by various rough and ready principles speakers develop over time. But if there are principles that guide deviations from standard use (I will look at a variety of these in 'Deviance: W. S. Graham' and 'Epilogue: Deviance: Robert Creeley'), are these not just as much rules as the kind of complex rule recognised in modern grammatical study? That is, are prior theories not just congealed passing theories, and are not grammars descriptions of family resemblances between prior theories? The more or less shared ideas of norm and deviance that develop in ever-varying speech situations simply are grammar. Knowing a rule is never more than knowing more or less how assorted and sometimes anomalous phenomena can be arranged for practical benefit.

Davidson and Derrida have been compared and contrasted: they both work from the deviation to the standard, inverting traditions of linguistic investigation; but whereas for Derrida it is language itself that antagonises grammatical and pragmatic conventions, for Davidson it is the individual speaker, intentionally or otherwise, who antagonises these conventions.[50] Derrida locates the deviant energy of the literary in language itself, Davidson in speakers. It will be one of the contentions of 'Spirit: Frank O'Hara' that what is produced by poetry is not produced exclusively by language nor by a speaker, that the conditions of possibility for speech cannot be satisfied by reference to an individual agent nor a linguistic system alone.[51] Indeed, to try to think of language without speakers, or speakers without language leads to two equally absurd scenarios: either the language fully and perfectly existent before and beyond speakers, who come to it and activate it somehow, or speakers (specifically as speakers, and not just beings theoretically capable of speech) fully and perfectly existent before the language. Language and the psychic energy that activates it are inseparable, whatever analytical convenience is possible from treating them discretely. Poetic language is one place where speaker and language take the measure of each other, and, like all measures, have that measure only in the relation they are in (see 'Measure: Robert Creeley'). Poems are between speakers and languages. They are a means of being taught that the world we have on account of being language users is a world that is like it is, but which could have been quite otherwise, and that both of these facts follow necessarily from language being a social and historical institution. The rest of this book will pursue this argument in a series of readings of poetic and theoretical texts.

Notes

1. Jan Mukařovský, 'On Poetic Language' (1940), in *The Word and Verbal Art: Selected Essays by Jan Mukařovský*, trans. and ed. John Burbank and Peter Steiner, foreword by René Wellek (New Haven and London: Yale University Press, 1977), pp. 1–64 (pp. 1–3).
2. Ibid. p. 4
3. Ibid. p. 6.
4. John Haynes, 'Metre and Discourse', in *Language, Discourse and Literature: An Introductory Reader in Discourse Stylistics*, ed. Ronald Carter and Paul Simpson (London: Unwin Hyman, 1989), pp. 235–56 (pp. 242, 237).
5. John Thompson, 'Linguistic Structure and the Poetic Line', in *Linguistics and Literary Style*, ed. Donald C. Freeman (New York: Holt, Rinehart and Winston, 1970), pp. 336–46 (p. 343). A more extensive formulation of the codal speech act that inaugurates poetry has been provided by Samuel R. Levin, 'Concerning What Kind of Speech Act a Poem Is', in *Pragmatics of Language and Literature*, ed. Teun A. van Dijk (Amsterdam and Oxford: North-Holland; New York: Elsevier, 1976), pp. 141–60 (pp. 149–50):

   > The sentence that I propose as the implicit higher sentence for poems, the one that expresses the kind of illocutionary force that the poem is taken as having, is the following: (1) *I imagine myself in and invite you to conceive a world in which* . . . The assumption is that the deep structure of every poem contain (1) as its topmost sentence, and that that sentence is deleted in going from the deep to the surface structure of the poem.

   Levin's sentence, however, works as well for any fiction, whether or not it is poetic, and does not imply a poetic function.
6. Peter Stockwell, *Cognitive Poetics: An Introduction* (London: Routledge, 2002), p. 167.
7. Ibid. p. 7.
8. Mary Louise Pratt, *Toward a Speech Act Theory of Literary Discourse*

(Bloomington and London: Indiana University Press, 1977), pp. xi–xii, 5, 24–5, 35–6.

9. Ibid. p. 115.
10. Derek Attridge, *Peculiar Language: Literature as Difference from the Renaissance to James Joyce* (London: Routledge, 2004 [1988]), p. 6.
11. Mukařovský, 'On Poetic Language', p. 19.
12. Mukařovský, 'A Note on the Czech Translation of Sklovskij's *Theory of Prose*' (1934), in *The Word and Verbal Art*, pp. 134–42 (p. 139).
13. Yury Lotman, *Analysis of the Poetic Text*, ed. and trans. D. Barton Johnson (Ann Arbor: Ardis, 1976), p. 7.
14. Roland Posner, *Rational Discourse and Poetic Communication: Methods of Linguistic, Literary, and Philosophical Analysis* (Berlin, New York, Amsterdam: Mouton, 1982), p. 122.
15. Lord Byron, *Don Juan* (1819–24), I.1761–4 in *The Complete Poetical Works*, V (1986), ed. Jerome J. McGann (Oxford: Clarendon Press, 1986), pp. 79–80.
16. My approach here is influenced by Charles Altieri, *Act and Quality: A Theory of Literary Meaning and Humanistic Understanding* (Brighton: Harvester, 1981), who recommends a 'dramatistic' attitude to the language of literature.
17. *How to Do Things with Words: The William James Lectures Delivered at Harvard University in 1955*, 2nd edn, ed. J. O. Urmson and Marina Sbisà (Oxford: Oxford University Press, 1975), p. 104.
18. Donald Davidson, 'Locating Literary Language (1993)', in *Truth, Language, and History* (Oxford: Clarendon Press, 2005), pp. 167–81 (p. 167).
19. J. Hillis Miller, *Speech Acts in Literature* (Stanford: Stanford University Press, 2001), pp. 27–8.
20. Pratt, *Toward a Speech Act Theory of Literary Discourse*, p. 99.
21. Paul Grice, *Studies in the Way of Words* (Cambridge and London: Harvard University Press, 1989), pp. 26–9.
22. Pratt, *Toward a Speech Act Theory of Literary Discourse*, p. 215.
23. Jürgen Habermas, 'On the Distinction Between Poetic and Communicative Uses of Language', in *On the Pragmatics of Communication*, ed. Maeve Cook (Cambridge: Polity, 1999), pp. 383–401 (p. 392), notes precisely this tension in Pratt's work. Habermas regards world-disclosure as characteristic of poetic language, but associates the poetic most strongly with fiction (pp. 397–8).
24. I attempt to address some of these issues in '"Poetry's a Public Act by Long Engagement": Geoffrey Hill and the Eighteenth Century', in *The Salt Companion to Geoffrey Hill*, ed. Andrew Roberts (Cambridge: Salt, forthcoming).
25. H. G. Widdowson, 'Old Song That Will Not Declare Itself: On Poetry and the Imprecision of Meaning', in *Literature and the New Interdisciplinarity: Poetics, Linguistics, History*, ed. Roger D. Sell and Peter Verdonk (Amsterdam: Rodopi, 1994), pp. 31–43 (p. 40). A similar view, but one which is taken as supporting a view of the literary speech act as of a distinctive aesthetic kind

at one remove from 'truly' practical speech acts, is found in Teun A. Van Dijk, 'Pragmatics and Poetics', in *Pragmatics of Language and Literature*, pp. 23–57 (p. 50).

26. David Hume, *A Treatise of Human Nature* (1739–40), ed. L.A. Selby-Bigge and P.H. Nidditch (Oxford: Clarendon Press, 1978), p. 484.

27. Shoshana Felman, *The Scandal of the Speaking Body: Don Juan with J. L. Austin or Seduction in Two Languages*, trans. Catherine Porter, foreword by Stanley Cavell, afterword by Judith Butler (Stanford: Stanford University Press, 2003), p. 96.

28. Ibid. p. 19.

29. John R. Searle, *Speech Acts: An Essay in the Philosophy of Language* (Cambridge: Cambridge University Press, 1969), pp. 57–62.

30. 'Preface' to *The Plays of William Shakespeare* (1765), in *Samuel Johnson: A Critical Edition of the Major Works*, ed. Donald Greene (Oxford: Oxford University Press, 1984), pp. 419–56 (p. 431).

31. On these points see Nils Erik Enkvist, 'Context', in *Literature and the New Interdisciplinarity*, pp. 45–60 (p. 52) and Roger Sell, 'Literary Gossip, Literary Theory, Literary Pragmatics', in the same volume, pp. 221–41 (p. 232).

32. Kenneth Burke, *The Philosophy of Literary Form: Studies in Symbolic Action* (Baton Rouge: Louisiana State University Press, 1941), p. 89.

33. One model for socio-historically nuanced analyses of poetic performance are J. H. Prynne's three book-length commentaries on individual poems: *They That have Power to Hurt* (Cambridge: privately printed, 2001); *Field Notes: 'The Solitary Reaper' and Others* (Cambridge: privately printed, 2007); *George Herbert, 'Love' [III]: A Discursive Commentary* (Cambridge: privately printed, 2011).

34. Austin, *How to do Things with Words*, p. 101.

35. Felman, *The Scandal of the Speaking Body*, introduction, p. xx.

36. Stanley Cavell, *Philosophical Passages: Wittgenstein, Emerson, Austin, Derrida* (Oxford: Blackwell, 1995), p. 153.

37. Hillis Miller, *Speech Acts in Literature*, pp. 55, 27.

38. James Loxley, *Performativity* (London: Routledge, 2007), p. 55 suggests that John Searle might place a greater emphasis on law and convention, and so present writers such as Hillis Miller with an easily travestied variety of speech-act theory.

39. Veronica Forrest-Thomson, *Poetic Artifice: A Theory of Twentieth-Century Poetry* (Manchester: Manchester University Press, 1978), p. 20. See Keston Sutherland, 'Veronica Forrest-Thomson for Readers', in *Veronica Forrest-Thomson: A Retrospective (Kenyon Review Online)*. Available at <http://www.kenyonreview.org/kro/vft/Sutherland.php> (last accessed 11 July 2011).

40. Forrest-Thomson, *Poetic Artifice: A Theory of Twentieth-Century Poetry*, p. 133.

41. Ibid. p. 151.

42. Stockwell, *Cognitive Poetics*, p. 127.
43. Derek Attridge, *The Singularity of Literature* (London: Routledge, 2004), pp. 27, 93, 98.
44. Lotman, *Analysis of the Poetic Text*, pp. 55, 132.
45. Derek Attridge, 'Introduction: Derrida and the Questioning of Literature', in Jacques Derrida, *Acts of Literature*, ed. Derek Attridge (London: Routledge, 1992), pp. 1–29 (p. 25).
46. '"This Strange Institution Called Literature": An Interview with Jacques Derrida', in *Acts of Literature*, pp. 33–75 (pp. 73–4).
47. Donald Davidson, 'A Nice Derangement of Epitaphs', in *The Essential Davidson*, intro. by Ernie Lepore and Kirk Ludwig (Oxford: Clarendon Press, 2006), pp. 251–65 (p. 259).
48. Ibid. pp. 260–1.
49. Ibid. p. 264.
50. Reed Way Dasenbrock, 'Philosophy after Joyce: Derrida and Davidson', *Philosophy and Literature* 26:2 (2002), 334–5 (pp. 340–1, 343).
51. The grounds for Martin Heidegger's argument that 'language speaks' and 'Man speaks in that he responds to language', 'Language' (1950), in *Poetry, Language, Thought*, trans. and intro. by Albert Hofstadter (New York: Harper & Row, 1971), pp. 187–210 (p. 210), are clearly relevant to this topic, but would require too extensive a treatment to be fairly introduced here.

CHAPTER TWO

Figure: Walter Ralegh

Walter Ralegh's 'Farewell to False Love' is a poem of eighteen lines and around twenty metaphors describing the nature of false love. False love is an 'oracle of lies', 'A way of error, a temple full of treason', 'a nest of deep deceit', 'A fortress', 'A siren song', 'A ranging cloud that runs before the wind, / A substance like the shadow of the sun'. The metaphorical elaboration of the nature of false love is, by the end of the poem, reduced to comparisons that are themselves only approximate (like) to ephemeral and insubstantial things (shadows). When Thomas Heneage replies to Ralegh's poem he parallels and varies Ralegh's repertoire of images. Welcome love is a 'mortal foe to lies', 'A way to fasten fancy most to reason', 'a nest of sweet conceit', 'A fortress', 'A hopeful toil', 'To ranging thoughts a gentle reining hand; / A substance such as will not be undone'.[1] Heneage's reply is somehow self-defeating: love (welcome love at least) is a point of reference, a means by which the ranging fancy can be grounded and guided, a source of sweet thoughts and expressions, a means of combining the imagination, or fancy, with reason. But his poem depends upon Ralegh's poem. It depends upon it in the basic sense of being a reply, but is also modelled upon Ralegh's poem, in metre, stanza, syntax, diction and, notably, figure. Ralegh's poem must at least be a legible description of love if Heneage's reply is to be a legible re-description. And so a reader of the pair of poems sees that love, false or welcome, can be talked about in a variety of different ways: it is not just that figures for love may be elaborated within the same poem, but that different poems from radically different points of view can both make sense of what love is; different kinds of love, certainly, but love nonetheless. This dialogue between the two poets on how love should be talked about demonstrates that what we decide to call love, how we figure it, is part of its nature, just as it demonstrates that there can be more than one way of figuring the same essence.

Ralegh's longer poem 'The 21th: and last booke of the Ocean to Scinthia' leaves no doubt that he, as many other writers of his era, considered figures, the substitution of one term or concept for another, central to the rhetorical strategies and purposes of poetic composition. Simile and metaphor, despite sometimes being grouped as 'imagery', are not always imagistic and often contribute to poetic texts in other ways than by picturing. Ralegh's figures frequently create no image, or, alternatively, create so many images that they cannot be sustained pictorially by a reader. Ralegh's poem causes its readers to reflect upon what is figurative and what is literal, to ask what the relation between these two orders of meaning is; in doing so it engages with questions of what is natural and what is artificial in language that also occupy literary critics and theorists, of the Renaissance, and today.

I will turn to George Puttenham, an Elizabethan poet-critic, to see how he relates figuration in poetic language to the delimitation of the artificial from the natural. The chapter closes with a consideration of essences in Ralegh's poem, and observes that the essences Ralegh evokes are not entirely or simply a distillation of an organism or property. The essence can sometimes be external to a thing, and in being the essence, it demonstrates that things are permeable (just as the loved object is both within and without the lover); in a parallel manner, the figural can sometimes participate in the literal. The reading of Ralegh complements other chapters in this book that argue that the language of poetic texts is poetic because it encourages readers to reflect on the very means by which the texts are constructed, pointing to the unnervingly arbitrary way in which meanings are made at the same time as making those meanings seem right, intuitive, natural.

Figuration operates in all kinds of manners in Ralegh's poem. The title indicates its being governed by an overarching metaphor, in which Queen Elizabeth I is identified with Diana, the Roman goddess associated with hunting, chastity and the moon, by means of an epithet (Cynthia) sometimes applied to Artemis, the Greek goddess who is the near equivalent of Diana. Ralegh himself is identified with the ocean. Ralegh was involved in sea-faring colonial enterprises and privateering (a form of governmentally authorised piracy), and was also, at various stages in his life, a significant person in Elizabeth's court. Thus, in as much as Elizabeth's will largely influenced the actions of her courtiers, and as Ralegh worked with the sea, the title refers to their public connection. It also refers to the formalised love between the two, as an element of their public, political connection, which was disrupted by Ralegh's marriage, and the consequent imprisonment of him and his wife. The poem probably dates from this period in Ralegh's life, and so relates to the public love, the rupture of which costs Ralegh personally as well as publicly and politically. Thus with every image of the sea and its environs, or the moon and associated terms, this complex of personal and political relations is evoked. The image appears in fairly direct form within the poem, as the queen is said to have 'sent her memory / more strong than weare tenthowsand shipps of warr / to call mee back'.[2] The poet presents his current state as one of seeking 'faire floures amidd the brinish sand' (l. 24), notes that there are no longer 'pleasinge streames fast to the ocean wendinge' (l. 33) to distract him, compares his heart and mind to one 'forsaken, frind-less onn the shore' who 'writes in the dust as onn that could no more' (ll. 89, 91, with 'dust' for 'sand'), feels overcome by 'seas of wo' (l. 140). The target of address in the poem, hovering between the queen, love, the muse, is 'shee that from the soonn reves poure and light' (l. 250), that is, the moon. If the highly involuted nature of the poem's images produces a sense of the precarity of the poet and poem, the material history of the poem itself goes some way to justify that sense: it survived in one manuscript copy, given by Ralegh to Sir Robert Cecil, and probably never presented to the Queen.[3]

In addition to this titular conceit, and the trains of imagery to which it gives rise, the poem contains explicitly marked figures of comparison, such as this simile:

> Yet as the eayre in deip caves under ground
> is strongly drawne when violent heat hath rent
> great clefts therin, till moysture do abound
> and then the same imprisoned, and uppent,
> breakes out in yearthquakes teringe all asunder,
> So in the Center of my cloven hart,
> my hart, to whom her bewties wear such wounder
> lyes the sharpe poysoned heade of that loves dart
> which till all breake and all desolve to dust
> thence drawne it cannot bee, or therin knowne[.] (ll. 450–9)

These figures are over-elaborate. The geological process is closely described in a manner that is difficult to read into the features of the love that is pent up in the poet's heart. Furthermore, as the simile is concluded, the poem resorts to several further metaphorical levels, from the banal equation of emotional dis-turbance to the piercing of the heart by an arrow, to the much more abstract suggestion that this arrow cannot be withdrawn until an unspecified 'all' is broken and dissolved to dust. How one takes the breaking and dissolution into dust is significant: if the body that contains the heart is taken for 'all', then it will more or less literally break and dissolve into dust upon death. But this is a rather physical reading of an abstract passage that promotes figural rather than literal readings of its terms.

Levels of figuration are developed relentlessly and serially in this text. Verb choice often indicates a semantic domain that is applied to a subject, sometimes with a clear metaphor, sometimes bordering on lexicalised meta-phor (one that has become a standard expression): beauty breeds a fancy in the mind, the heart-blood nourishes desire, sweetness feeds an affection and affection flourishes (ll. 376–9). Such trains of image are particularly difficult to sort into the lexicalised and the 'real' metaphors. When the poet refers to his 'harts internall heat, and livinge fier' (l. 302), is that fire to be taken as part of the series of terms concerning temperature to which states of the heart are compared, or is it an expansion on a non-metaphorical notion of the heart as a part of the body transmitting vital heat, as seems possible from contemporary medical literature?[4] The mode of the poem's composition calls into question the delimitation of literal and figurative meanings, risking the failure of its metaphorical language by pointing to the very porosity of the border that separates it from the literal.[5] The poem also calls into question the boundaries between categories within Renaissance rhetorical arts. One rhetorician divides the ornamental part of rhetoric, which he calls 'Brauerie', into tropes and figures:

> a Trope or turning is when a word is turned from his naturall signification, to some other, so conuenientlie, as that it seeme rather willinglie ledd, than driu[en] by force . . . A figure is a certeine decking of speech, whereby the vsual and simple fashion thereof is altered and changed to that which is more elegant and conceipted.[6]

Figures include metre, rhyme, the use of exclamation, rhetorical questions and so on, as well as a cultivated patterning of syntax. The temptation to take 'my hart', for example, as a trope, giving 'hart' a spiritual rather than a physical sense, is increased by the term echoing 'my cloven hart'. The figure (patterning) helps to make the trope (metaphor).

The poet describes his poem as a conceit. The entries in the Oxford English Dictionary (OED) for 'conceit' begin with the power of conception, run through neutral acts of conceiving, through evaluative or subjective conceptions, to the conception of ideas or devices, and finally to the sense of a developed, witty, possibly stretched comparison. It is one of the standing puns of poetry in this period that the poet's conceit or understanding might be identified with her conceit or poetic comparisons. When the pastoral scene is evoked, and the poet laments the lack of 'sheapherds cumpunye / that might renew my dollorus consayte' (ll. 29–30), the conceit might be a frame of mind or process of conceiving (OED, I, 2.c and I, 3), or fancy and witty expression (OED III, 7b and III, 8). Conceit is explicitly linked to writing in the poem when the poet describes his mental state in his abandonment:

> sumetyme I died sumetyme I was distract
> my sowle the stage of fancies tragedye
> then furious madness wher trew reason lackt
> wrate what it would, and scurgde myne own consayte. (ll. 143–6)

Madness, figured as a tragedian, overwrites the poet's conceit, either by altering the poet's conceptions, or by commanding his writing: at such moments

the two are inseparable. The poet's understanding and invention are thus tied
to his writing, and that writing is understood as the process of searching out
figures or likenesses. The poet reflects on the way in which he had previously
described Elizabeth as

> "Th'Idea remayninge of thos golden ages
> "that bewtye bravinge heavens, and yearth imbaulminge
> "which after worthless worlds but play onn stages,
> "such diddst thow her longe since discribe, yet sythinge,
> "that thy unabell spirrit could not fynde ought
> "in heavens bewties, or in yearths delighte
> "for likeness, fitt to satisfy thy thought
> Butt what hath it avayl'd thee so to write? (ll. 348–55)

The poet acknowledges that his writing is, or at least was, the search after
likeness, prompted by desire (ideal, though clearly not unrelated to physical desire), but that the search after likeness avails neither in poetic nor in
personal and political terms.[7] There is a realisation here of the unlikeness
of all the likenesses that the poem searches after, and a recognition of the
futility to which such a realisation testifies. There is a difference as well as an
identity to every comparison (see 'Figure: Tom Raworth'). One could present
the psychological drama of the poem as the shifting between two views of
the world, of cognitive life, and of writing, in the first of which things are
naturally comparable to and associated with one another, whereas in the
second they are only temporarily, disappointingly connected by an artificial,
searched out comparison.

The third book of George Puttenham's *Art of English Poesy*, 'Of Ornament',
moves in similar terrain to Ralegh's poem, questioning the status of ornament in speech and writing. Puttenham's text may not have been particularly widely known or used in Elizabethan England, but his concerns are the
central concerns of rhetorical theory found, for example, in Quintilian: the
orator should understand that there can be no ornament without propriety,
and that ornament must be suited to the matter of a discourse.[8] Puttenham's
emphasis on figurative language departing from ordinary or plain meaning
may be connected to courtly habits of self-presentation, where art is hidden,
and an easy grace is taken to imply real or pretended strengths, a style of
behaviour Ralegh may have cultivated.[9] Puttenham arrives at his discussion
of ornament after having dealt with proportion, in metre and stanzaic form,
noting that there is

> yet requisite to the perfection of this art another manner of exornation, which
> resteth in the fashioning of our maker's language and style to such purpose as
> may delight and allure as well the mind as the ear of the hearers with a certain

novelty and strange manner of conveyance, disguising it no little from the ordinary and accustomed, nevertheless making it nothing the more unseemly or misbecoming but rather decenter and more agreeable to any civil ear and understanding.[10]

The discussion of ornament, principally as figure, in terms of transport or 'conveyance' and as a matter of civic decency is central. Puttenham names 'figures and figurative speeches' as some of the ornamental means of concealing poetic language from 'the common course of ordinary speech and capacity of the vulgar judgement', distinguishing between ornaments for the ear and ornaments for the mind, between *energeia* and *enargeia*.[11] One surprising assertion that Puttenham makes in the course of his discussion is that 'Speech is not natural to man', an assertion that may make it unsurprising that figure should be considered an unnatural ornament in language; or, on the contrary, surprising, given that one could hardly expect a phenomenon in an unnatural medium to be itself natural.[12] The artificiality of figure is first presented as a matter of language abuse:

> As figures be the instruments of ornament in every language, so be they also in a sort abuses, or rather trespasses, in speech, because they pass the ordinary limits of common utterance, and be occupied of purpose to deceive the ear and also the mind, drawing it from plainness and simplicity to a certain doubleness, whereby our talk is the more guileful and abusing.

Athenian judges are said to have banished figurative ornaments 'as mere illusions to the mind and wresters of upright judgement', as 'foreign and coloured talk'.[13] The artificiality of ornamented language is seen in its difference from normal speech and writing, a difference that is established to some purpose:

> Figurative speech is a novelty of language evidently (and yet not absurdly) estranged from the ordinary habit and manner of our daily talk and writing; and figure itself is a certain lively or good grace set upon words, speeches and sentences to some purpose and not in vain, giving them ornament or efficacy by many manner of alterations in shape, in sound and also in sense: sometime by way of surplusage, sometime by defect, sometime by disorder or mutation, and also by putting into our speeches more pith and substance, subtlety, quickness, efficacy or moderation, in this or that sort tuning and tempering them by amplification, abridgement, opening, closing, enforcing, meekening or otherwise disposing them to the best purpose.[14]

Puttenham distinguishes the 'sensable' from the 'auricular' ornaments, the former working more upon the mind, the latter the ear, the sensable figures working by 'alteration of intendments'. The conception of figure as transport, as movement, is evident in the translations of Greek terms for tropes that Puttenham provides, calling mesozeugma 'the middlemarcher', hypozeugma 'the rearwarder', hyperbaton 'the trespasser', and periphrasis the *figure of ambage*.[15] These figures are exemplary ways of transporting sense, of leaving the common path of ordinary speech, but to some particular purpose.

Derek Attridge has found a great strain in Puttenham's statement of the relationship between the natural and the artificial in ornamented language. Attridge criticises Puttenham's presentation by scrutinising the terms 'nature' and 'decorum' that are notionally held in distinction, but which tend to converge. Decorum is said to be an unstable concept in Puttenham, presenting itself by means of a varied terminology. This instability is a mark of the concept's convergence with that from which it is supposed to be distinguished: 'decorum is precisely that aspect of the poet's art which is not reducible to rule. And human activity that is not reducible to rule is usually called "natural".' Attridge conceives of Puttenham's position as a 'problem':

> the problem for Puttenham . . . is that he is writing a *manual* whose only conceivable user is the individual who does *not* possess the natural decorum of the few: the would-be poet, who is eager to acquire the necessary learning and experience.

Attridge claims to have identified a relationship of occlusion operating in Puttenham's text, whereby everything in art that is not the product of nature can be attributed to decorum, itself a natural (non-rule governed, free) quality:

> The Renaissance emphasis on art's distance from nature gave rise . . . to an uncontainable oscillation between contradictory apprehensions of the meaning and ideological function of the concept of nature, as that which art is defined both by and against. To put it another way, an inherent instability in the set of ideological functions performed by the term 'nature' resulted in a concept of art which both emphasized and denied its natural origins and subservience. All attempts to pin down the difference between nature and art, or more specifically between ordinary language and the language of poetry, produce further instabilities. Every characteristic of poetic language which is claimed as peculiar to it suffers the same double bind, because it is an instance either of a superior language, in which case the foundation of an ordinary language is discredited, or of an inferior language, in which case the defense of poetry as a special human achievement collapses.

Poetic language claims to be natural, and yet excludes nature. This diagnosis of the status of poetic language, simultaneously incorporating and excluding the natural, in the form of ordinary language, is not in my view a 'problem':

what is poetic in language is a consciousness of the contingency of the manner in which speech departs from the natural into the artificial, and of the possibility of those departures being reincorporated into the natural. Attridge, earlier in his discussion of Puttenham, makes reference to Derrida's conception of the supplementary in order to proceed with his analysis, noting that this conception occupies a place in between rhetoric and philosophy:

> Derrida . . . is using a rhetorical and not a logical or dialectical method: we are not being shown a previously veiled 'truth' but by a certain kind of persuasive language are being freed from the narrow paths we have hitherto traveled [sic].[16]

A writer such as Derrida is recognised as challenging the boundary between philosophy and rhetoric, in a manner that will also be relevant to the discussion of Paul de Man on figure (see 'Figure: Tom Raworth'). But Attridge strikingly refuses to note the way in which his own description of Derrida's practice picks up on Puttenham's terms, whereby language is taken out of its ordinary role in the service of a persuasive strategy, changing the perceptions that the reader might have. The porous boundary between the concepts of nature and art that Attridge makes the limiting opposition of *The Art of English Poesy*, is, I am suggesting, Puttenham's point of departure, and one shared by many poets of his generation.

As is evident in Puttenham's text, the status of the figurative is somewhere between the natural and the artificial:

> So, albeit we before alleged that all our figures be but transgressions of our daily speech, yet if they fall out decently, to the good liking of the mind or ear and to the beautifying of the matter or language, all is well[.][17]

On what grounds does Puttenham make this sudden inclusion of the deviant and figurative within the order of the natural? He argues that poets take ordinary or natural speech and make it appear as strange as it is, for indeed nature is strange:

> In that he [the poet] speaks figuratively, or argues subtly, or persuades copiously and vehemently, he doth as the cunning gardener, that, using nature as a coadjutor, furthers her conclusions, and many times makes her effects more absolute and strange.[18]

Puttenham writes from a position in which nature is not to be considered self-sufficient, self-evident, patent, given, known without effort of familiarisation or study. The complexities of this position can be seen in the final phrase cited. 'Strange' might perhaps be taken in its sense of quantitative emphasis, as in OED 9.a: 'Exceptionally great (in degree, intensity, amount, etc.), extreme.' But this is the only definition of the word that excludes the sense of foreignness. Twice in passages that I have quoted, Puttenham aligns the strange with novelty, and not extremity. Nature is not natural: it is alien. There is also a grammatical ambiguity: either the works of nature when supplemented by art would be 'more absolute' and therefore 'strange', or 'more absolute' and 'more strange', the latter reading suggesting that nature is already strange, and becomes more so through the work of art.[19] In the second reading one would find a concept of nature that already incorporates the figurative transpositions and substitutions noted in Puttenham's analysis, a conception of nature very close to the world of Ralegh's 'Ocean to Scinthia' that was discussed in the earlier part of this chapter, and to which I now return.

Ralegh's poem, with its various levels of figuration and its close consideration of its own manner of conceiving, presents a world in which the natural already incorporates something of the artificial, and the literal something of the figurative. Perhaps that is one reason for its being at once an absorbing and disorienting poem to read. Donald Davie has remarked on the disorienting effects of the modulating series of images in the poem:

> throughout the poem, images are turning over, double-edged; one whole binding sequence of imagery from water, for instance, appears to be deployed with just this in view – no sooner have we grasped an image of the queen as a ruinous inundation flooding the poet's pastures, than we have to adjust ourselves into seeing her as rain which falls too grudgingly upon his thirsty acres. ... one emerges from one of Ralegh's images (not just from his metaphors and similes), or from a train of such images, at a different door from the one we went in by.[20]

The poem presents nature constantly transforming itself into other natures, figuring itself in various guises. Love enters into the poet's mind and becomes its essence, where essence is sometimes understood as the vital, characteristic element of a thing, something internal to it, and at other times, that which sustains its life from without:

> But in my minde so is her love inclosde
> and is thereof not only the best parte
> but into it the essence is disposde ...
> "Oh love (the more my wo) to it thow art
> "yeven as the moysture in each plant that growes
> "yeven as the soonn unto the frosen ground
> "yeven as the sweetness, to th'incarnate rose
> "yeven as the Center in each perfait rounde,
> "as water to the fyshe, to men as ayre

"as heat to fier, as light unto the soonn
"Oh love it is but vayne, to say thow weare,
"ages, and tymes, cannot thy poure outrun. (ll. 426–41)

The poet's mind has had love's essence transposed into it: it is not of its own nature exclusively, but shares its nature with another. This sharing of essences is figured in a serial simile that might itself be regarded as a sharing of essences, as each of the things used to figure mind shares its essence with mind, each of those to figure love with love. Yet there is also an unlikeness in these likenesses, each of the essences standing in a slightly different relation-ship to its object: the moisture in the plant is drawn from its environment, but becomes part of the plant, incorporated into it; the sun causes the gen-eration of things in the earth, it has an effect upon the ground, but is not in the ground; the sweetness of the rose is an incorporated property, but one not known until it is distilled from the rose; circles have a centre, but these do not cause the circles, nor could they be ascribed the same generative potential as the other essences; water to the fish and air to men are both necessary envi-ronments for life that transgress borders between the inside and outside of the organism; heat is produced by fire, light is produced by the sun. The poet blends the categories of contemporary logic, confusing material causes with subjects, and with adjoints of those subjects.[21] In this array of causal, meto-nymical, microcosmic relations however, there are common necessary condi-tions of interdependence, of one essence entering into another in order for that essence to be what it naturally is. So the poem describes and enacts the sharing of essences amongst things, the supplementation of what is natural to a thing by what is external to it and beyond it, in its figurative language.

The poet states that love is that with which his essence has become unified, adding weight to the suggestion that desire impels figurative language to search after likenesses that will always remain partially unlike. Such a desire might be understood psychoanalytically,[22] but one might with more purchase on Ralegh's time refer to the opening of the Latin poet Lucretius' *De rerum natura*, where the goddess of love is evoked, and her aid requested

Whose vital power, air, earth, and sea supplies,
And breeds whate'er is born beneath the rolling skies;
For every kind, by thy prolific might,
Springs, and beholds the regions of the light. . . .
Be thou my aid, my tuneful song inspire,
And kindle with thy own productive fire (I.3–6, 32–3)[23]

It is love, understood as the implementation and expenditure of vital energy, that sets the world in motion by making its essences participate in one another, and which gives birth to a poetic world also. Ralegh's series of images in which literal and figural senses interpenetrate, whose essence is in what is alien to them, tease away at the boundary between the artificial and the natural in language, a boundary that becomes less clear the more closely it is approached. Puttenham too, in his account of the strange yet natural ornaments of poetic speech, its deviations that get straight to the point, demonstrates the permeability of whatever boundary there may be between the natural and the artificial in poetic language. In both the theory and practice of figuration, the suspicion of artifice that attaches itself to the most natural seeming modes of expression is characteristic of the peculiar reflectiveness created by encounters with poetic language.

Notes

1. Sir Walter Ralegh, *The Poems, with other Verse from the Court of Elizabeth I*, ed. Martin Dodsworth (London: Dent, 1999), pp. 4–5.
2. *The Penguin Book of Renaissance Verse, 1509–1659*, selection and intro. David Norbrook, ed. H. R. Woudhuysen (Harmondsworth: Penguin, 1992), pp. 102–16, ll. 63–5. Further references to this poem are given by line number in the text. The poem was probably composed in 1592.
3. Steven W. May, *The Elizabethan Courtier Poets: The Poems and Their Contexts* (Columbia and London: University of Missouri Press, 1991), p. 132.
4. See for example Levius Lemnius, *The Touchstone of Complexions Generallye Appliable, Expedient and Profitable For All Such, As Be Desirous & Carefull of their Bodylye Health*, trans. Thomas Newton (London: Thomas Marsh, 1576), p. 8.
5. Brian Cummings, 'Metalepsis: The Boundaries of Metaphor', in *Renaissance Figures of Speech*, ed. Sylvia Adamson, Gavin Alexander and Katrin Ettenhuber (Cambridge: Cambridge University Press, 2007), pp. 217–33 (pp. 220, 226) notes the danger of failure in the trains of metaphors in metalepsis, and also the figure's tendency to question the division between the figural and literal, the natural and artificial, and does so in a broader argument that language itself requires unlikeness within its representational functions.
6. Abraham Fraunce, *The Arcadian Rhetoric [1588]* (London: Thomas Orwin, [N.D. 1588]/Menston: Scolar Press, 1969), sigs.A2v, B8r.
7. Robert E. Stillman, '"Words Cannot Knytt": Language and Desire in Ralegh's The Ocean to Cynthia', *SEL: Studies in English Literature, 1500–1900*, 27:1 (Winter 1987), 35–51, notes the association between language and desire in the poem, describes it as recording a process of symbolic exhaustion, and suggests that it represents Ralegh's abandonment of an attempt to find a transcendent symbolic order, pp. 39, 36, 49.
8. *The Institutio Oratoria of Quintilian* (c. 95–6 CE), trans. H. E. Butler, 4 vols (London: Heinemann, 1922), III, 219, 217
9. Daniel Javitch, *Poetry and Courtliness in Renaissance England* (Princeton:

Princeton University Press, 1978), Chapter II, pp. 50–75 (pp. 52–4, 62, 69–75).

10. George Puttenham, *The Art of English Poesy* (1589), in Gavin Alexander (ed.) *Sidney's 'The Defence of Poetry' and Selected Renaissance Literary Criticism* (Harmondsworth: Penguin, 2004), pp. 55–203 (p. 133).

11. Ibid. pp. 134–5. Linda Galyon, 'Puttenham's "Enargeia" and "Energeia": New Twists for Old Terms', *Philological Quarterly* 60:1 (Winter 1981), 29–40, esp. p. 37, suggests that Puttenham identifies musical/pre-cognitive and imagistic/cognitive levels in the perception of figurative language.

12. Ibid. p. 136.

13. Ibid. pp. 143–4.

14. Ibid. p. 148.

15. Ibid. pp. 148–9, 154, 151–2, 163.

16. Derek Attridge, *Peculiar Language: Literature as Difference from the Renaissance to James Joyce* (London: Routledge, 2004 [1988]), pp. 29, 30, 35, 46, 22–3.

17. Puttenham, *The Art of English Poesy*, p. 197.

18. Ibid. p. 201.

19. Emma Smith, '"Signes of a Stranger": The English Language and the English Nation in the Late Sixteenth Century', in Philip Schwyzer and Simon Mealor (eds), *Archipelagic Identities: Literature and Identity in the Atlantic Archipelago, 1550–1800* (Aldershot: Ashgate, 2004), pp. 169–79 (pp. 179, 171), notes the tendency of writers of Puttenham's era to consider English as 'a language incorporating its own other, at once foreign and native', and presents Puttenham as an author who derives his idea of 'the standard language fit for the poet's use by a process of deduction of various sites of non-standard use, defined variously by distance from London, demography, social status and education'.

20. Donald Davie, 'A Reading of *The Ocean's Love to Cynthia*', in John Russell Brown and Bernard Harris (eds), *Elizabethan Poetry* (London: Edward Arnold, 1960), pp. 71–89 (pp. 82, 88–9). Davie is interested in the temporal aspect of this disorientation.

21. For these categories see, for example, *The Logike of the Moste Excellent Philosopher P. Ramus, Martyr* (London: Vautrollier, 1574), *passim*. Such logical categories leave their mark on rhetoric, as when Fraunce defines various kinds of metonym by reference to their substitution of cause for effect, adjoint for subject and so on, *Arcadian Rhetoric*, sigs. A3r-A6v.

22. See Stillman, '"Words Cannot Knytt"', *passim*.

23. John Dryden, *John Dryden: A Critical Edition of the Major Works*, ed. Keith Walker (Oxford: Oxford University Press, 1987 [1685]), pp. 271–2.

CHAPTER THREE

Selection: William Cowper

The previous chapter suggested that some poetic choices of figure can question the boundary between figurative and literal meaning. This chapter will explore a comparable phenomenon within the vocabulary of poetry more broadly considered. Even when poets are not being metaphorical, they still make choices of vocabulary, they still engage in acts of selection. One of the great pleasures poetry sometimes offers is exhilarating correctness, the use of exactly the right form of words. There are also pleasures, or interesting effects, at least, associated with incorrect or peculiar or unsettling choices of words. This chapter will ask what such effects achieve, and how. As human experience is incomplete (not least as there is more of it to come), the vocabularies of natural languages are incomplete: they are imperfect taxonomies. It follows that descriptions are always partial, descriptions of something seen by someone from a particular point of view. Every description, then, has a register, pertains to a person or kind of person with a socio-cultural position. To choose amongst possible descriptions, to select the words that seem poetically adequate to an occasion, an action or a thing, is also, necessarily, to align oneself with or distance oneself from other people conceived of as socially and culturally positioned. This chapter, then, will explore the 'rightness' and 'wrongness' of poetic vocabulary in relation to the question of social register and social allegiance.

The main focus of the chapter will be the work of William Cowper, seen as a response to Alexander Pope and other eighteenth-century writers, but a brief discussion of John Milton will provide some historical connection between this chapter and the preceding one. Milton's position in the history of English poetry has from time to time been controversial, largely because he has been seen to do things with and to the English language that are not natural to it. In the early eighteenth century, some of Milton's conjunctions of terms were taken to be so unusual they were revised by editorial intervention, as when Richard Bentley revised the celebrated phrase describing the lighting of Hell, 'darkness visible' (*Paradise Lost*, I.63), to 'a transpicuous Gloom'.[1] Twenty-five years later, towards the middle of the century, such

phrases were recognised by Edmund Burke as being vital to the sublime effects
Milton achieves in his poetry, forcing the mind to bring together concepts
that cannot in reality be found together. Burke suggests that the phrase 'the
universe of death' is particularly strong because it presents two concepts 'not
presentible but by language; and an union of them great and amazing beyond
conception'. Burke distinguishes between a clear and a strong expression: 'the
one describes a thing as it is; the other describes it as it is felt'.[2] Burke recognises that Milton is attempting to give a certain view of things, one that takes
account of their impact on a person, and not a view from nowhere.

A still greater peculiarity in Milton's English is evident in his tendency
to allow English to become the register of his immense learning in other
languages, particularly Latin, so that the vernacular language is inflected
by those other languages.[3] Terms in Milton with which modern readers are
unfamiliar or uncomfortable often have a close connection with another
language. So, when the editor Bentley introduced the term 'transpicuous',
he was using a Latinate form of language (the word comes directly from the
Latin verb *transpicere*, to see through). Milton uses this word elsewhere in the
poem (VIII.141), and also the (no less Latinate) form that is more familiar,
'transparent' (VII.265). Milton sometimes uses the connection between
Latin and English to relatively light effect. In composing an early poem
for an entertainment at his college, he hails English as his native language,
the earlier parts of the entertainment having been in Latin. He notes that
English 'mad'st imperfect words with childish trips, / Half unpronounced,
slide through my infant lips, / Driving dumb silence from the portal door'
('At a Vacation Exercise in the College, part Latin, part English', ll. 3–5).
There are two bad jokes here, deriving from the connection between Latin
and English words. Infant lips cannot really speak: 'infant' means 'young' in
English, but *infans* is Latin for 'unspeaking'. The contradiction implies that
Milton's lips were unspeaking until that moment, or that they spoke only
feebly. 'Portal' is derived from Latin *portalis*, like a gate or door, and so a
'portal door' is a 'doory door': the Latinism is amusingly redundant. In this
poem at least Milton is having a little fun with the interrelation of English
and Latin. There is less humour in Samson's report of falling upon the 'choic-
est youth' of the Philistines and felling them 'with a trivial weapon' (*Samson
Agonistes*, ll. 264, 263). 'Trivial' is now much more common in OED sense
6 ('Of small account, little esteemed, paltry, poor; trifling, inconsiderable,
unimportant, slight') than sense 5 ('Such as may be met with anywhere;
common, commonplace, ordinary, everyday, familiar, trite'). Samson makes
a heroic boast in claiming that the ass's jawbone, the common weapon he
picked up from the ground, is poor, but that nonetheless he killed a thousand
men with it. Milton's deviations from English norms relate to word order
as well as word choice, and he often compresses the grammar of an English

sentence. When announcing that he has created and decided to elevate his son above the rest of the angels, God says 'your head I Him appoint' (*Paradise Lost* V.606), meaning 'I appoint him [as] your head'; and again that 'him who disobeyes / Mee disobeyes' (V.610–11), meaning 'he who disobeys him [my son] [thereby] disobeys me'. Milton makes English pronouns perform twice their normal work, being both personal and relative at once.[4]

These features of Milton's language have not always been regarded as achievements. Critics of the early twentieth century see a threat to the language itself in Milton's work. In an early essay, T. S. Eliot writes that Milton 'may still be considered as having done damage to the English language from which it has not wholly recovered'.[5] Softening his view somewhat later, Eliot still thinks of Milton as a deviant writer, locating the 'peculiar greatness' of Milton in his deviation from ordinary language:

> Every distortion of construction, the foreign idiom, the use of a word in a foreign way or with the meaning of the foreign word from which it is derived rather than the accepted meaning in English, every idiosyncrasy is a particular act of violence which Milton has been the first to commit. There is no cliché, no poetic diction in the derogatory sense, but a perpetual sequence of original acts of lawlessness.[6]

F. R. Leavis believes Eliot to have allowed his attitude to peculiarity to soften too much, and demonstrates a stronger dislike of the strange from a demotic point of view than Eliot from his rather judicial perspective:

> I find it hard to believe that salutary lessons in 'verse structure' or in the avoidance of '*servitude* to colloquial speech' are likely to be learnt from a master in whom 'there is always the maximal, never the minimal, alteration of ordinary language' – who departs so consistently and so far from speech that the sensitiveness and subtlety of rhythm that depend on an appeal to our sense of the natural run are forbidden him.[7]

To follow such a master in his deviations from the common tongue is necrophilia: 'Milton invented a medium the distinction of which is to have denied itself the life of the living language.'[8] Milton's English has, for Leavis, become too distant from the ordinary and common speech that is the life of the language: he has adopted a distant social register.

Leavis's sensitivity to the social register of speech is comparable to that displayed by participants in the important debate on the nature of poetic diction in the eighteenth century. If students of English poetry are familiar with this debate, it is most likely to be through the criticisms levelled by Wordsworth and Coleridge at eighteenth-century poetry. Samuel Taylor Coleridge identified Alexander Pope's translation of Homer as a storehouse of poetic diction, characterised by its opponents as borrowing word meanings or phrase structures from Latin both frequently and obtrusively.[9] This chapter will explore the nature of the socio-cultural and political implications of the kind of selection from language for poetry that becomes known as 'poetic diction'. I will be suggesting that interesting poems take a highly self-critical attitude towards their own vocabulary, and that this critical attitude consists in acknowledging the necessary connection between vocabularies and certain social and historical facts; facts about the nature of economic divisions within society and the social position of the poet and poetry. Whilst much of this chapter deals with fairly concrete matters such as the rank of social life from which vocabulary is drawn, it will relate to topics addressed in other chapters, such as the shared social nature of all utterances and the relationship between individual creative acts and linguistic structures (see 'Spirit: Frank O'Hara', 'Deviance: W. S. Graham', 'Selection: Denise Riley' and 'Epilogue: Deviance: Robert Creeley'). The discussion will focus on the work of William Cowper as poet and translator, approaching him by means of a comparison with Pope.

Poets who use a poetic diction characterise it positively. Here is Pope's description of Homer's diction from the preface to his translation:

> We acknowledge him the father of poetical diction, the first who taught that *Language of the Gods* to men. His expression is like the colouring of some great masters, which discovers itself to be laid on boldly, and executed with rapidity. It is indeed the strongest and most glowing imaginable, and touch'd with the greatest spirit. *Aristotle* had reason to say, He was the only Poet who had found out *living words*; there are in him more daring figures and metaphors than in any good author whatever. An arrow is *impatient* to be on the wing, a weapon *thirsts* to drink the blood of an enemy, and the like. Yet his expression is never too big for the sense, but justly great in proportion to it. 'Tis the sentiment that swells and fills out the diction, which rises with it, and forms itself about it: And in the same degree that a *thought* is warmer, an *expression* will be brighter; as that is more strong, this will become more perspicuous: Like glass in the furnace, which grows to a greater magnitude and refines to a greater clearness, only as the *breath* within is more powerful, and the *heat* more intense.
>
>   To throw his language more out of prose, Homer seems to have affected the *compound-epithets*. This was a sort of composition peculiarly proper to poetry, not only as it heighten'd the *diction*, but as it assisted and fill'd the *numbers* with greater sound and pomp, and likewise conduced in some measure to thicken the *images*.[10]

Pope here identifies diction with the totality of the poetic art.[11] Diction is responsible for adding expression to poetry, as the use of colour in a painting; it is closely related to figure, as the choice of words describing particular objects or actions creates animating metaphors (the arrow is a bird; the weapon is an animal/person). Homer's diction is a product of thought, and also of a desire to remove his language from prose, the latter through the use of compound epithets, which also lend grandeur to the metre of the poem. Diction, then, as Pope sees it, is not a selection from a certain set of phrases artfully distinct from some more ordinary register of speech, nor an oppressive Latinate reworking of English, but a vital principle animating poetic composition on all its levels.

Pope was, however, accused of elevating Homer's diction. His elevation was not necessarily a matter of using one word rather than another though. Pope describes the Trojan Helenus meeting the Greek prince Menelaus in battle, and Helenus' arrow bouncing off Menelaus' armour:

> Full on his breast the *Trojan* arrow fell,
> But harmless bounded from the plated steel.
> As on some ample barn's well-harden'd floor,
> (The winds collected at each open door)
> While the broad fan with force is whirl'd around,
> Light leaps the golden grain, resulting from the ground:
> So from the steel that guards *Atrides*' heart,
> Repell'd to distance flies the bounding dart. (XIII.737–45)

Here diction elevates labour. Winds cannot really be collected at barn doors: they can be admitted, but the word choice here suggests either a mastery of nature, or the co-operation of nature in a human purpose. The use of 'resulting' to mean 'jumping or bouncing back' is Latinate, and whilst Pope does not use this verb often, he does use it in its now more familiar sense (as in *An Essay on Criticism*, l. 248). The Latinate yet concrete sense is shaded by the more abstract, intellectual sense, so that the laboriousness of the activity is masked. The line's elongation to twelve syllables, with at least six stresses, including two on the first two syllables of the line, attempts to capture the activity of the scene, but the active verb applied to the grain ('leaps') and the passive to the fan ('is whirl'd') again mask the labour that produces the activity. And whilst a 'fan' is exactly the instrument used in winnowing grain, it is also many other things, the broad scope of the term again occluding the kind of labour taking place in the simile. Pope's note on the simile suggests he might have felt some distancing effects necessary:

> We ought not to be shock'd at the frequency of these similes taken from the ideas of a rural life. In early times, before politeness had rais'd the esteem of arts subservient to luxury, above those necessary to the subsistence of mankind, agriculture was the employment of persons of the greatest esteem and distinction: We see in sacred history Princes busy at sheep-shearing; and in the Time

of the *Roman* common-wealth, a Dictator taken from the plough. Wherefore it ought not to be wonder'd at that allusions and comparisons of this kind are frequently used by ancient heroic writers, as well to raise, as illustrate their descriptions. But since these arts are fallen from their ancient dignity, and become the drudgery of the lowest people, the images of them are likewise sunk into meanness, and without this consideration, must appear to common readers unworthy to have place in Epic poems.[12]

Pope knows that this question of seemingly inappropriate registers is one of historical disjunction, of social and historical difference. Yet he is careful to attribute the fault for that perceived disjunction with 'common readers': it is the reader's lack of distinction that will make the agricultural language appear inappropriate.

Cowper's diction, by contrast, in his translation of the same passage, acknowledges more fully the labour that produces the scene:

> The arrow of the son of Priam struck
> Atrides' hollow corselet, but the reed
> Glanced wide. As vetches or as swarthy beans
> Leap from the van and fly athwart the floor,
> By sharp winds driven, and by the winnower's force,
> So from the corselet of the glorious Greek
> Wide-wandering flew the bitter shaft away. (XIII.713–19)

The grains leap as a result of the 'winnower's force', and they are not golden grains, but 'vetches' or 'swarthy beans', much less idealised agricultural products. The winds here are sharp, suggesting the discomfort they are likely to produce, rather than harmonising with human labour. The 'van' is precisely a raised surface in a barn used for winnowing. Cowper's selection of terms can seem over-precise, even to the point of lowering the scene by admitting the drudgery involved: it is a precision that is born of a consciousness of the socio-cultural implications of selecting a particular poetic vocabulary. Cowper conceived of his own translation of Homer at least in part as a corrective to Pope's. He claims that his own 'diction is plain and unelevated', but acknowledges the difficulty of reproducing the range of activities described by Homer without violating the rather decorous limits of eighteenth-century poetry:

> It is difficult to kill a sheep with dignity in a modern language, to flay and to prepare it for the table, detailing every circumstance of the process. Difficult also, without sinking below the level of poetry, to harness mules to a waggon, particularizing every article of their furniture, straps, rings, staples, and even the tying of the knots that kept all together.[13]

Homer might be the greatest poet with the most vivid yet plain diction, but he poses nonetheless a serious challenge to the translator wishing to remain within the register of the poetic as it was conceived in the eighteenth century.

Cowper's remarks clarify the connection between standards of poetic language, the desire to be precise and memorable, and the use of registers of language associated with what were understood to be menial habits and professions. Many poets between the end of the seventeenth and the end of the eighteenth centuries were highly conscious of a need to be polite in verse, where politeness means in part that diction should refuse any close association with professional jargon. The language of poetry should be a separate, urbane, genteel, standard, literary language, as John Dryden notes in the preface to his translation of the *Aeneid*:

> I will not give the reasons why I writ not always in the proper terms of navigation, land-service, or in the cant of any profession. I will only say, that Virgil has avoided those properties, because he writ not to mariners, soldiers, astronomers, gardeners, peasants, etc., but to all in general, and in particular to men and ladies of the first quality, who have been better bred than to be too nicely knowing in the terms.[14]

The avoidance of the specialist languages of the professions is a question of social propriety, recognising the probable social identity of the target audience, and employing a vocabulary that will be familiar to them. Knowledge of a specialist vocabulary is a sign of poor breeding, of having to earn one's living by engaging in labour, and politeness is one way for an elevated, aristocratic world to escape from the socially fractious world of competing interest groups.

Poets such as Dryden are attempting to counteract the linguistic effects of the division of labour, a subject that was frequently discussed in sociological and economic theory in the eighteenth century. Some theorists argued that in the early stages of social development every member of a community participated in all the activities necessary to the maintenance of life. Every person was a farmer, soldier, politician, priest and so on. An important stage in social development is arrived at when specific groups of people come to concentrate on one of these life-sustaining activities, realising it is more efficient for one person to farm and others to labour in other areas. Gradually specialist communities emerge and become entrenched, and there are advanced, complex professions, such as soldiery or the law. This phenomenon is mixed: it is at once progressive and corrupting. If a separate class of soldiers emerges, paid to defend a particular country, then all other members of the community may lose an important part of their personal commitment to defending their society. Adam Smith's biographer Dugald Stewart notes the 'melancholy conclusion' to Smith's scattered thoughts on the division of labour: 'the same causes which promote the progress of the arts, tend to degrade the mind of the artist; and, of consequence, . . . the growth of national wealth implies a sacrifice of the character of the people'.[15] That is, the transition to being a modern, commercial society is both wealth-creating and soul-destroying, as a people are alienated from various life-sustaining activities. When a class of people loses its contact with those activities, it also loses touch with the vocabulary that sustains and supports those activities; and as those activities become more isolated and complex, the harder it is for anyone outside the caste to understand and appreciate it, so that in 'advanced' societies it is impossible for people in different professions to understand one another's activities and concerns.

There are some indirect yet very important consequences for poetry and poetic diction here. Poetry that comes from a community in which people have not been alienated from the total range of human activities will be more robust, and more likely to inculcate public spirit and civic virtues, because it will draw on the vocabulary of all possible forms of life, and make them palpable to all. Adam Ferguson, theorising the place of the arts in the history of civil society in 1767, relates the virtues of ancient poetry to this connection between primitive states of social life and a comprehensive poetry:

> In rude ages men are not separated by distinctions of rank or profession. They live in one manner, and speak one dialect. The bard is not to chuse his expression among the singular accents of different conditions. He has not to guard his language from the peculiar errors of the mechanic, the peasant, the scholar or the courtier, in order to find that elegant propriety, and just elevation, which is free from the vulgar of one class, the pedantic of the second, or the flippant of the third. The name of every object, and of every sentiment, is fixed; and if his conception has the dignity of nature, his expression will have a purity which does not depend on his choice.

Good literature, Ferguson says, has 'a reference to mankind', it is imbued with the activity of public life, and not separated off from human activities in the way Dryden suggests his translation of the *Aeneid* will be. Ferguson's editor has pointed out that the questions Ferguson raises are highly relevant to his time, when the work of poets such as Robert Burns was testing poetical register, and the kinds of language that could be included in poetry, particularly in relation to notions of public belonging and empowerment.[16]

Such a literature that has reference to all social life avoids the separation of poetic language from the quotidian. James Beattie, a poet and philosopher, explains in an essay of 1776 how a poetic diction comes to separate itself from ordinary speech over time:

poetry is better remembered than prose, especially by poetical authors; who will be always apt to imitate the phraseology of those they have been accustomed to read and admire: and thus, in the works of poets, down through successive generations, certain phrases may have been conveyed, which, though originally perhaps in common use, are now confined to poetical composition.[17]

The memorability of poetry here is both curse and blessing, dignifying poetry through its diction, yet thereby removing it from the language of ordinary life and instruction. Seeing poetic diction in relation to the division of labour and certain ways of understanding social development puts the politics of poetic selection into sharper focus. Making claim to or refusing the vocabulary of certain forms of life, certain classes and castes, is implicitly political, an assertion of the value of particular registers and their public relevance. The selection of particular registers is also a means of indicating the alienation that a poet might feel from a supposedly integrated prior state of social organisation (regardless of whether such an integrated society is any more than a myth, or interest in it anything more than nostalgia).

Cowper exemplifies the crisis into which labour forces diction. One of the most famous passages of his long poem *The Task* concerns growing cucumbers out of season:

> To raise the prickly and green-coated gourd
> So grateful to the palate, and when rare
> So coveted, else base and disesteem'd, –
> Food for the vulgar merely, – is an art
> That toiling ages have but just matured,
> And at this moment unessay'd in song.
> (III.446–51)[18]

Cowper asks pardon from the 'sage dispensers of poetic fame' (III.457) for broaching this theme, mentioning mock epic poems on the subjects of gnats, frogs, mice, and a shilling (III.452–7). At the same time, he introduces the idea that his mock-epic subject (which is also a georgic subject, a matter of agricultural instruction) bears comparison to his own activity as a poet, producing goods for a 'critic appetite' (III.461).

Cowper begins his instructions with an audacious Latinism, a most refined reference to a pile of dung:

> The stable yields a stercorarious heap
> Impregnated with quick fermenting salts,
> And potent to resist the freezing blast.
> (III.463–5)

It is around this manure that the cultivator builds a frame in such a position that it 'may front / The sun's meridian disk' (III.472–3). The reader receives instruction, in implausibly over-refined and yet distinctly accurate language, on spreading hay, building a sloped shelter for the fruit, placing the frame at an angle that drains off rainwater, and so on. Scientific-sounding Latinisms that raise the subject to a form of nobility and permanence, and yet also practise a form of poetic self-criticism abound: the vapours that accumulate under the frame ask 'egress' (III.497), from the Latin verb *egredi*, to step out; there is 'fermentation' under the frame (III.510, 519), along with a large number of other abstract nouns; the earth is genial (III.519), meaning that it has generative power, rather than that it is friendly; fruit are 'apparent' (III.536), using the Latinate form of the present participle as if it had the meaning of the English form 'appearing'.

These Latinisms can seem to mock or ironise themselves, and one of their effects is certainly to make the trouble of the cucumber grower and the poet who describes that activity appear ridiculous. At the same time they have a pathos that prevents them from being entirely self-abnegating.[19] These Latinisms are one part of the poet's skill, the careful selection of accurate, scientifically precise, historically durable terms for particular things and phenomena, and the very difficulty of the task Cowper has set himself, its implausibility, its tendency not to appear worth the effort, allies it to the productions of agricultural art he has been describing. These two practices, and all other practices that aim to produce luxury items for a class that is wealthy without having to labour, are united in appearing futilely over-refined to those very people for whom they are produced:

> Grudge not, ye rich, (since luxury must have
> His dainties, and the world's more numerous half
> Lives by contriving delicates for you,)
> Grudge not the cost. Ye little know the cares,
> The vigilance, the labour, and the skill
> That day and night are exercised, and hang
> Upon the ticklish balance of suspense,
> That ye may garnish your profuse regales
> With summer fruits brought forth by wintry suns. [...]
>   It were long,
> Too long to tell the expedients and the shifts
> Which he that fights a season so severe
> Devises, while he guards his tender trust,
> And oft, at last, in vain. The learn'd and wise
> Sarcastic would exclaim, and judge the song
> Cold as its theme, and like its theme, the fruit
> Of too much labour, worthless when produced.
>   (III.544–52, 558–65)

Cowper realises that art production is tied to the habits of consumption of a leisured class that is now so entirely divorced from active engagement with productive life, that they scorn the very efforts required to furnish them with luxuries they feel obliged to consume. Poetry is one of these products, winter cucumbers another. Refined poetry then is one of the victims of the division of labour, inheriting a vocabulary distinct from that of daily life, practised by a group of people who are losing touch with the totality of the lives of their communities because those communities themselves are fragmented and alienated internally. Such poetry mocks and mourns its own position in an economy that is at once materially beneficial and morally destitute. Cowper's verse engages directly with the socio-political questions raised by the theory of poetic diction. Wordsworth and Coleridge's responses to these questions will provide a starting point for the next chapter.

Notes

1. John Milton, *Paradise Lost* (1667/1674), ed. Richard Bentley (London: Jacob Tonson, 1732), p. 4, I.63n.
2. Edmund Burke, *A Philosophical Enquiry into the Origin of our Ideas of the Sublime and the Beautiful and Other Pre-Revolutionary Writings*, ed. David Womersley (Harmondsworth: Penguin, 1998 [1757]), p. 198.
3. John K. Hale, *Milton's Languages: The Impact of Multilingualism on Style* (Cambridge: Cambridge University Press, 1997), p. 13.
4. References are to John Milton, *Paradise Lost*, ed. Christopher Ricks (Harmondsworth: Penguin, 1989) and John Milton, *Complete Shorter Poems*, ed. John Carey (Harlow: Longman, 1968).
5. T. S. Eliot, *Selected Prose*, ed. John Hayward (Harmondsworth: Penguin, 1953), p. 131.
6. Ibid. pp. 141–2.
7. F. R. Leavis, 'Mr Eliot and Milton', in *The Common Pursuit* (Harmondsworth: Penguin, 1993; first publ. London: Chatto and Windus, 1962), pp. 1–32 (p. 32).
8. Ibid. 'In Defence of Milton', pp. 33–43 (p. 42).
9. Geoffrey Tillotson, *On the Poetry of Pope*, 2nd edn (Oxford: Clarendon Press, 1950), pp. 71–2.
10. *The Iliad of Homer Translated by Alexander Pope* (1715–20), ed. Stephen Shankman (Harmondsworth: Penguin, 1996), 'Preface', p. 9.
11. There is a tradition in twentieth-century criticism of identifying diction with the entirety of poetic art. See, for example, Owen Barfield, *Poetic Diction: A Study in Meaning*, foreword by Howard Nemerov, afterword by the author (Middletown, CT: Wesleyan University Press, 1973; first publ. London: Faber and Gwyer, 1928), p. 41, and Emerson R. Marks, *Taming the Chaos: English*

Poetic Diction Theory Since the Renaissance (Detroit: Wayne State University Press, 1998), p. 13.

12. *The Iliad of Homer translated by Alexander Pope*, pp. 646–7.

13. *The Iliad and Odyssey of Homer*, trans. William Cowper, 4 vols (London: J. Johnson, 3rd edn, 1809), I, xxiii, xxx–xxxi.

14. John Dryden, *Essays*, ed. W. P. Ker, 2 vols (Oxford: Clarendon Press, 1900 [1697]), II, 236.

15. Adam Smith, *Essays on Philosophical Subjects with Dugald Stewart's Account of Adam Smith*, ed. W. P. D. Wightman, J. C. Bryce and I. S. Ross (Indianapolis: Liberty Fund, 1982), p. 315.

16. Adam Ferguson, *An Essay on the History of Civil Society*, ed. Duncan Forbes (Edinburgh: Edinburgh University Press, 1966), pp. 174, 177 and 'Introduction', p. xxxv.

17. James Beattie, *Essays: On Poetry and Music*, intro. by Roger J. Robinson (Edinburgh: W. Creech, 1779/London: Routledge/Thoemmes, 1996), 'An Essay on Poetry and Music as they Affect the Mind', p. 213.

18. *The Poems of William Cowper II: 1782–1785*, ed. John D. Baird and Charles Ryskamp (Oxford: Clarendon Press, 1995).

19. Ritchie Robertson, *Mock-Epic Poetry from Pope to Heine* (Oxford: Oxford University Press, 2009), pp. 230–4 considers Cowper's Latinism in relation to mock-epic and georgic and also suggests the phrases are not entirely self-mocking.

CHAPTER FOUR

Measure: William Wordsworth

This chapter follows on from the last by offering an account of the differences between Wordsworth and Coleridge's thinking on poetic diction and measure. Wordsworth's well-known objections to poetic diction were made just before the death of Cowper, whose work Wordsworth read and admired. Wordsworth understands poetic diction as a strictly delimited and historically sanctioned set of words found frequently in poetry and infrequently in prose, and therefore an artificial deformation of language, like metre and rhyme. Unlike those deformations, however, poetic diction is unpredictable:

> the distinction [from prose] of rhyme and metre is regular and uniform, and not, like that which is produced by what is usually called poetic diction, arbitrary and subject to infinite caprices upon which no calculation whatever can be made.

Wordsworth's vocabulary here is politically inflected, 'arbitrary' and 'capricious' being terms often applied to absolute monarchs. Indeed, his argument in general is socio-political. Wordsworth thinks poets should employ a selection from the real language of men, with 'men' restricted to those having simple rural occupations, because they 'hourly communicate with the best objects from which the best part of language is originally derived'.[1] The language of this class of people is timeless, because, as one perhaps unwittingly witty critic has noted, 'the peasant . . . changed neither his clothes nor his diction, after the manner of the sophisticated'.[2]

Wordsworth's solution to the crisis of socially divided and over-refined diction, then, is to valorise the register he regards as superior precisely because it is common. Wordsworth emphasises that he recommends selection from this language, but, as he argues his way through the 'Preface', he becomes increasingly distanced from the idea that the poet should use the words that a simple rural person would use:

> in these Poems I propose to myself to imitate, and, as far as possible, to adopt the very language of men, and I do not find that . . . personifications make any

regular or natural part of that language . . . the language of such Poetry as I am
recommending is, as far as is possible, a selection of the language really spoken
by men . . . the dramatic parts of composition are defective, in proportion as
they deviate from the real language of nature, and are coloured by a diction
of the Poet's own, either peculiar to him as an individual Poet, or belonging
simply to Poets in general, to a body of men who, from the circumstance of their
compositions being in metre, it is expected will employ a particular language[.]

Later the poet is a sage selecting from the real language of men 'or, which
amounts to the same thing, composing accurately in the spirit of such selection'; and finally Wordsworth says he has 'endeavoured to bring my language
near to the real language of men'.[3] This sequence of ever-weaker positions
raises a complex question of the relationship between the language selected
on a particular occasion and the totality of the language a speaker has.

Wordsworth has been strongly criticised for a variety of selective poeticising that exploits the association between particular dictions and particular
social positions, despite (even, to a degree, because of) this very claim to
compose in the real language of men. The criticism reaches to the heart of
Wordsworth's conception of art as related to nature:

art is grounded in the nature in which all participate, but its existence as art
depends on its difference from nature, and that difference is in the hands of the
minority who possess the leisure to cultivate, promote, and safeguard it.[4]

Wordsworth, according to this criticism, is only able to make his claims to
select from the language of the rural poor because he is not a member of that
class, but of a leisured elite: his claims to a demotic vocabulary, with all its
political potential, are false; or rather, his being sufficiently leisured to select
from this language places him outside the group of users for whom it is a real
language. Grounds for this criticism are easy to identify. In 'The Idiot Boy'
the narrator, a poet bound to the Muses for fourteen years (ll. 337–8), uses
various means to show that the real language of ordinary people has been
selected for the poem.[5] Betty Foy has sent her son, the 'Idiot Boy' of the title,
to fetch a doctor from town to attend a sick neighbour. His failure to return
in good time distresses his mother:

And Susan's growing worse and worse,
And Betty's in a sad *quandary*;
And then there's nobody to say
If she must go, or she must stay!
– She's in a sad *quandary*. (ll. 167–71)

The italicisation of this word, an English noun derived from a Latin verb
itself formed from an adverb, suggests it is being drawn from an identifiable

source, possibly Betty's own vocabulary. That this is Betty's word, and what is more, a word with which she might not be fully comfortable, is confirmed by the uncertainty and ungainliness of the intonation of the word within the form of the stanza. The word is now routinely pronounced disyllabically, but in this stanza, rhyming only with itself, and unable, even with considerable manipulation, to provide the number of stresses normally provided by the final line of the poem's stanza, it is entirely unclear how to say the word, or unclear how the speaker from whom the poet borrows it knows how to say it. (I will be returning to stress in intonational and metrical patterns shortly.) The poem closes by quoting Johnny's rehearsal of the night's experiences in which he calls owls 'cocks' and the moon 'the sun' (ll. 450–1). A felt linguistic superiority is part of this poem's mode. But it is, I would suggest, a mock-heroic mode like Cowper's (see 'Selection: William Cowper') that questions its own status: the distance between poet and protagonists, the chilliness of the mockery, are an important part of the uneasiness of reading this poem.

The criticism of Wordsworth's aforementioned exploitation of the vocabulary of the labouring classes shares something with one aspect of Coleridge's complex response to Wordsworth. There is an ostensible similarity in the positions of Wordsworth and Coleridge: both are opposed to artificial diction. Coleridge cites Pope's translation of the *Iliad* and notes that

> the language from 'Pope's translation of Homer', to 'Darwin's Temple of Nature', may, notwithstanding some illustrious exceptions, be too faithfully characterized, as claiming to be poetical for no better reason, than that it would be intolerable in conversation or in prose.[6]

But Coleridge opposes the theory that poetic language should be a selection from the real language of men, as Wordsworth suggests, on three grounds: that 'real' language is simply what is common to all kinds of users, and not a particular class; that the best language is not that of rural, labouring life, but the life of the mind; that any language the poet uses is the poet's language, and not that of some other group. I will take these in turn. Coleridge suggests that when Wordsworth says 'real' he means 'common': 'Omit the peculiarities of each, and the result of course must be common to all.'[7] The operative part of the language, Coleridge suggests, is that which all classes share, and not the vocabulary of any one particular social group. This is not, in itself, an objection to using the real language of men, but a redefinition of where that language is to be found. Coleridge's second objection is comparable, but rather undermines the first: the best language is not necessarily that of the rural labouring classes. Coleridge rejects common forms of psychological associationism, the idea that strong feelings are connected with particular natural objects by means of a recurrent experience of those objects in a variety of mental states. He is more interested in vocabulary that relates to the reflective powers of the mind:

> The best part of human language, properly so called, is derived from reflection on the acts of the mind itself. It is formed by a voluntary appropriation of fixed symbols to internal acts, to processes and results of imagination, the greater part of which have no place in the consciousness of uneducated man; though in civilized society, by imitation and passive remembrance of what they hear from their religious instructors and other superiors, the most uneducated share in the harvest which they neither sowed nor reaped.[8]

For Coleridge, the 'best part of . . . language' is reflexive, concerned with the operations of the mind; for Wordsworth, it is concerned with natural objects. There is evidently an implication for the class status of the truly imaginative person in Coleridge's description. The person whose intellectual capacities are not buffeted around by fancy, but whose imagination takes a strong role in forming the phenomenal world, also forms the best part of language, and does not merely imitate the language of instructors and social superiors. Coleridge's employment of the vocabulary of rural labour ('harvest . . . sowed . . . reaped') appropriates the role of active producer to the intelligentsia on the metaphorical level also. And indeed much of Wordsworth's writing might be more Coleridgean in spirit. He singles Coleridge out as a person of peculiar intellectual penetration, someone to whom 'The unity of all has been revealed', and who regards science

> Not as our glory and our absolute boast,
> But as a succedaneum, and a prop
> To our infirmity.   (II. 226, II.218–20)[9]

Even in a poem that traces the growth of the poet's mind from its earliest interactions with other people and the forms of nature, Wordsworth searches out a rare term to describe the role of human intellection: there is no injunction to avoid all consciously selected Latinate terms.

The last of Coleridge's objections is logical, and restates a problem raised above:

> the very power of making the selection implies the previous possession of the language selected. Or where can the poet have lived? And by what rules could he direct his choice, which would not have enabled him to select and arrange his words by the light of his own judgement?[10]

Such selections are caught in a double bind. If the language I use is selected from the language a different person or group of people uses, in using it I have made it my language: it is no longer the language of a different class of people, but my language. And yet if I am choosing an item even from my own language, I am not using an entire language but only a selection from it: my utterance is an artificial selection, not a real language. All language uses, then, are selections, but they must be selections from a language already our own; they are selections based on an idea of how other people speak, even when attempting the expressive act of composing a poem in the confessional voice. Coleridge argues that the principle of selection (Wordsworth never argues for simple reproduction) is in itself enough to invalidate the claim to the kinds of reality, naturalness and ordinariness that Wordsworth makes for 'the language of men', as any kind of selection is the result of the powers of the mind, of judgement. If the poet has chosen from the 'real language of men', then that selection is guided more by powers of poetic judgement than any intrinsic property of the selected language, such as its realness or ordinariness. Coleridge identifies the double bind into which Wordsworth's theory of selection leads him.

Differences between the programmes these two poet-critics pursued, or retrospectively imposed upon their practice, again masked by a superficial similarity, can also be seen in their thinking about the psychological origins and aesthetic functions of metre. They agree that poetical composition is metrical, and that its being metrical is related to its being a kind of composition that is particularly exciting and excitable, attention-seeking and attention-rewarding. But the purposes this feature of poetic language is taken to serve, though closely associated, are also distinct. Coleridge is concerned with the subordination of differences to a unified end in the aesthetic object (and in other kinds of objects), Wordsworth with the continual interplay of identity and difference.[11] I will now look at the elision of syllables in one of Wordsworth's poems in the context of Wordsworth and Coleridge's differences on the subject of the unifying and diversifying function of metre, whilst continuing to engage with the questions of social difference and the position of the poet raised above in this and the previous chapter, but reading them through the interplay of emphases found when metre and other pressures in a poem purposefully interact.

The fact of metre is taken by Coleridge to represent an agreement with readers that certain kinds of excitement are to be produced. Poetry, which need not be metrical, does not continue evenly throughout a work of any length, but those parts that are not strictly speaking poetry must preserve their coherence by means of a 'studied selection and artificial arrangement' in order to produce the general poetic property of 'exciting a more continuous and equal attention, than the language of prose aims at, whether colloquial or written'.[12] There are, then, several artificial and studied means by which poetic language distinguishes itself from the language of prose, and metre is prominent amongst them. Coleridge is convinced that metrical compositions are not prose with verse 'superadded', but must be metrical in their entire conception. He traces the origin of metre

> to the balance in the mind effected by that spontaneous effort which strives to hold in check the workings of passion . . . this balance of antagonists became organized into *metre* (in the usual acceptation of that term) by a superven- ing act of the will and judgment, consciously and for the foreseen purpose of pleasure.

Two things follow from this origin: being the product of excitement, 'the metre itself should be accompanied by the natural language of excitement'; being the product of artifice, 'the traces of present *volition* should through- out the metrical language be proportionately discernible'. The experience of reading poetry involves 'a previous and well understood, though tacit, *compact* between the poet and his reader, that the latter is entitled to expect, and the former bound to supply this species and degree of pleasurable excite- ment'.[13] Poetry is exciting and excited, it attends to its own features by acts of the poet's will, and attracts the attention of its readers to a peculiar degree. It does these things by prior, tacit agreement with its readers.

Wordsworth is more sceptical about the kinds of agreement that may subsist between writer and reader in the production of metrical compositions:

> it is supposed, that by the act of writing in verse an Author makes a formal engagement that he will gratify certain known habits of association, that he not only apprizes the Reader that certain classes of ideas and expressions will be found in his book, but that others will be carefully excluded[.]

He is however 'certain it will appear to many persons that [he has] not fulfilled the terms of an engagement thus voluntarily contracted' in *Lyrical Ballads*.[14] It is not primarily in relation to metre that Wordsworth fears he has broken this agreement, if his proceeding to discuss his treatment of themes from common life can be taken as any indication. But Wordsworth's think- ing about metre also relates it to the excitement inherent to poetic compo- sition, that 'spontaneous overflow of powerful feelings' that proceeds from the thoughtful individual: 'The end of Poetry is to produce excitement in coexistence with an overbalance of pleasure.' Excitement is an irregular state, necessarily involving a disordering of the mind, a disorder that can go beyond its bounds and hamper poetical pleasure.

> Now the co-presence of something regular, something to which the mind has been accustomed when in an unexcited or a less excited state, cannot but have

great efficacy in tempering and restraining the passion by an intertexture of
ordinary feeling.

Metre is such a regularity, and it makes the emotionally affecting scenes of
Shakespeare a source of continual pleasure in a way that the emotionally
affecting scenes of Samuel Richardson's *Clarissa*, a long, episodic novel,
are not, a phenomenon 'in a great degree to be ascribed to small, but
continual and regular impulses of pleasurable surprise from the metrical
arrangement'.[15] The opposite effect can also be produced by metre, with a
deficiency of passion in the words of the poet compensated by the pleasure
of regularity.

Wordsworth's view of metre is complex, not to mention contradictory.
At some points it appears to be an extrinsic theory of the value of metre,
whereby its chief operative quality is its ordinariness, its not participating
in the disorder of the excitement of the incidents described in the composition. At others, the value of metre is intrinsic, found in its continual and
regular impulses. Yet these impulses, despite their regularity, or seemingly, in
Wordsworth's construction, because of it, are surprising, and cause pleasure
by surprising. It seems deeply odd that something can regulate excitement
in situations where excitement is in surplus or deficit by means of being
associated with other situations that are more or less exciting: for there to be
an association between the metre and a particular level of excitement, one
might have thought that the association should be characteristic, or exclusive of other levels of excitement. But it seems not: metre is effective just
by being common to all metrical compositions. The ordinariness of metre,
then, its commonness to various forms of poetic composition, is not related
to its regularity: its ordinariness regulates excitement purely by association;
its regularity draws on the intrinsically pleasurable alternation of security and
surprise that is characteristic of metre.

The arbitrariness of the association of metre with more or less excitement, and the intrinsic pleasure of regular yet surprising rhythm characterise
Wordsworth's broader aesthetic theory in opposition to Coleridge's. Both
poet-theorists make the principle of finding similarity, of finding identity
within difference, a species-defining principle for humans, and one with
aesthetic implications. For Coleridge, differences and identities are to be
reconciled by their subservience to a particular determining end:

I adduce the high spiritual instinct of the human being impelling us to seek
unity by harmonious adjustment, and thus establishing the principle, that *all*
the parts of an organized whole must be assimilated to the more *important* and
essential parts. This [argument] may be strengthened by the reflection, that
the composition of a poem is amongst the *imitative* arts; and that imitation, as

opposed to copying, consists either in the interfusion of the SAME throughout the radically DIFFERENT, or of the different throughout a base radically the same.[16]

Coleridge's reconciliation of the same and the different is to be in the service of the important or essential parts of a thing. His supplementary reflection suggests that imitation consists not in being the same, but in being the same at the same time as being different: an imitation of a person in a painting or statue is not that person, or another person, but something of a radically different nature into which sameness, here understood as visual resemblance, has been interfused.

Wordsworth is interested in a slightly different notion of the identical within the different. Picking up on the vocabulary of a range of eighteenth-century writers on beauty, he uses the terms similitude and dissimilitude to describe the play between identity and difference in poetic metre:

> If I had undertaken a systematic defence of the theory upon which these poems are written, it would have been my duty to develope [sic] the various causes upon which the pleasure received from metrical language depends. Among the chief of these causes is to be reckoned a principle which must be well known to those who have made any of the Arts the object of accurate reflection; I mean the pleasure which the mind derives from the perception of similitude in dissimilitude. This principle is the great spring of the activity of our minds and their chief feeder. From this principle the direction of the sexual appetite, and all the passions connected with it take their origin: it is the life of our ordinary conversation; and upon the accuracy with which similitude in dissimilitude, and dissimilitude in similitude are perceived, depend our taste and our moral feelings.[17]

Here similitude and dissimilitude are general without being subordinate to ends or essential or important parts. Differences subsist between the sexes, between objects of taste, between moral categories, and whilst there may well be implicit valuations within the sets of discriminations made between similar yet different objects of this pleasurable perception, there is no particular sense that each distinct perception (of the male, of the ugly, of the vicious, for example) needs to be subordinate to a dominant characteristic of an object. Wordsworth takes on precisely the subject that Derek Attridge, in his reading of the 'Preface' discussed above, finds lurking beneath the distinction of nature and art, ordinary and poetic language.[18] Wordsworth engages more clearly and openly with the ideas of identity and difference, and their regulation through measured language in a physical and poetic economy than Attridge's reading suggests. Wordsworth is vitally aware of what difference is, and what it means for the practising poet; he knows that relations of identity and difference have serious ethical consequences, and he believes he is engaging with those consequences in the 'Preface' and in his poems.

I would like to offer a reading of a famous poem by Wordsworth to demonstrate how he works with the word 'difference', making the tensions between the rhythmical and other systems of language productive.[19]

> She dwelt among the untrodden ways
>   Beside the springs of Dove,
> A Maid whom there were none to praise
>   And very few to love:
>
> A violet by a mossy stone
>   Half hidden from the eye!
> – Fair as a star, when only one
>   Is shining in the sky.
>
> She lived unknown, and few could know
>   When Lucy ceased to be;
> But she is in her grave, and, oh,
>   The difference to me!

The poem is characterised by a disarming simplicity from which statements of tonal complexity emerge. It opens by telling us where the maid, Lucy, who is the subject of the poem, lived: 'among the untrodden ways / Beside the springs of Dove'. Did Lucy dwell there in the sense of inhabiting a particular residence, or did she haunt these ways, as so many female characters haunt isolated rural places in later eighteenth-century literature (Cowper's Kate in Book I of *The Task*, Sterne's Maria in *Tristram Shandy* and *A Sentimental Journey*)? Even though the ways being 'untrodden' must be a hyperbole meaning 'seldom trodden', the surface texture of the poem retains the uncanny exaggeration: the kind of living that Lucy did is made to appear liminal or transient before her death is mentioned. Her qualities are also profoundly uncertain: were there none to praise her because she did nothing praiseworthy? Were there few to love her because she was not loveable? Is she only like a star when that star's light is unchallenged by others? Would her fairness be at all evident if there were more stars in the firmament? Wordsworth here is employing a form of equivocal praise that might, in a different context, correct its equivocations with evident ironies, as Shakespeare does when writing that a mistress's eyes are nothing like the sun, but in this poem the equivocations persist. The poem makes for uncomfortable reading because it raises the possibility of its subject not being a subject of sufficient interest, a possibility that is belittling, and adds to the danger of poetical exploitation, of the poet seeing little in the life and death of a woman other than an occasion for a poem, a danger to which Wordsworth might be thought liable in other poems also.

But the little differences in this poem are marks of serious thought and consideration. I will focus on just one feature of the poem, the relation between its metrical and intonational scheme (a subject that will also be discussed in 'Measure: Robert Creeley'), in particular considering conditions for elision common in English. Some English words and phrases can be pronounced with a varying number of syllables depending on context and emphasis, most commonly words containing diphthongs or medial vowels, and phrases in which vowels occur at the end of one word and the beginning of the next. Elision does not remove a syllable altogether from the scheme of the poem, but it makes the reader aware of the inter-relationship of phonetic and metrical systems: a poetic line containing an elision becomes 'a locus or intersection of two different systems of organisation'.[20] Elision, then, is one way in which different forces can be felt operating in a reading of a poem. This poem presents several opportunities for elision, only three of which I would argue are strong, and only two of those likely to figure in a performance of the poem: 'the untrodden' (l. 1), 'violet' (l. 5), 'the eye' (l. 6), 'she is' (l. 11), 'difference' (l. 12). The principal factor in determining whether an elision in this poem should be performed or not is metrical. To conform to the ballad metre in which this poem announces itself as participating, just by its presentation on the page and even before commencing a performance, 'the untrodden' needs to be regarded as occupying just three syllables in the metrical scheme, and 'violet' just two. No such metrical obligation is placed on 'the eye' and 'she is', and so, without any typographical prompting, both phrases retain two syllables rather than being slurred into one. 'Violet' and 'difference' can always be pronounced as words of just two syllables, but in this poem one is elided into two, the other not, because there is an obligation to regard 'difference' as occupying three syllables in the metrical scheme.

It is this last refused elision that is the most significant of the candidates in the poem, particularly when it is heard against the earlier elisions. Brennan O'Donnell notes that 'difference' would in most places in Wordsworth's poetry be elided to two syllables, that its taking three syllables here 'cuts against the metrical set' of the poem when compared to the earlier elisions that are taken, and that Wordsworth, in a late manuscript copy of the poem, underlined the first 'e' of the word, presumably to indicate the necessity of pronouncing it. Another reader, on the contrary, has found the final line of the poem 'almost dimeter', as the stress on the third syllable of 'difference' is weak.[21] But this second reading ignores both the metrical and the intonational schemes that produce a particularly emphasised trisyllabic reading of 'difference'. 'Difference', then, takes its full three syllables, and in doing so marks out its difference from other candidates for elision in the poem. In fact, the frequency of eliding 'difference' into two syllables lends the word the appearance of having gained a syllable here. And it seems probable that Wordsworth heard these effects clearly. In 'Lucy Gray; or, Solitude' (*The Poems*, I, 392–4 and notes), a poem that Wordsworth later said was designed to 'exhibit poetically entire *solitude*', the adjective 'solitary' appears twice (ll. 4, 63), in both instances given its full four syllables by the metre, whereas other possible elisions ('powdery', l. 27, and one of two in 'In heaven we all shall meet', l. 42) are demanded by the metre.

The word 'difference' becomes, by registering the interaction between two schemes, a focal point of the poem. It is a word that continues the tendency of the poem to present complexities with unsettling directness. The primary sense of the final line is that the death of Lucy has made a great difference to the poet: things are not the same since she died. But the grammatical form of the preceding lines of the poem, almost all of which describe the qualities or characteristics of Lucy, tempt the reader to continue the pattern: Lucy herself is the difference, 'she is in her grave and, oh, (she is) the difference to me'. Lucy could be the difference to the speaker by being different from, being the 'other' to, the poet; or she could be the difference to him by being that which made the difference in some abstract sense, perhaps that which made an existence qualitatively distinct, interesting or just bearable. By being different, she marked the life of the speaker, and has marked the speech of the speaker in the poem as a whole, and in this elongation of 'difference' itself. In this choice between different differences, the poem makes evident the importance of the metrical in relation to the other systems operating in the language of the poem. One of the big differences, that between life and death, is registering itself in this word and the tension between systems that is manifested in it. The question of the exploitation of the death of this young woman might not be solved, but one of the reasons Wordsworth is an interesting poet is that in their uncanniness, his poems recognise the impossibility of entirely resolving the question of having exploited a subject for a poem just by making it a subject for a poem.

Tension in 'difference', its openness to the systematic energies of the language and the poem, is one of the factors that demonstrate a complexity of attention to questions of identity and difference in Wordsworth's poems, as in his critical thinking. 'She Dwelt Among the Untrodden Ways' is a poem in which social difference figures, marking out the difference of the speaker from his subject. But that speaker, in registering the difference Lucy's death makes, recognises her challenge, the challenge of any other person, the ultimate undesirability of subordinating her to him as a subject of his utterance: she shapes and differentiates him. The different schemes that measure the poem out, intonationally, metrically, are the means of recording the play of identity and difference.

Notes

1. William Wordsworth and Samuel Taylor Coleridge, *Lyrical Ballads* (1798/1800), ed. W. J. B. Owen, 2nd edn (Oxford: Oxford University Press, 1969), 'Preface', pp. 164–70, 156.
2. Edwin Berry Burgum, 'Wordsworth's Reform in Poetic Diction', *College English* 2:3 (December 1940), 207–16 (p. 210).
3. Wordsworth, 'Preface', pp. 161, 164, 169, 170, 175.
4. Derek Attridge, *Peculiar Language: Literature as Difference from the Renaissance to James Joyce* (London: Routledge, 2004, first published 1988), p. 89; see also Chapter 3, 'Romanticism and the Language of Nature: The Project of Wordsworth's Preface', *passim*. Similar issues are raised in 'Figure: Walter Ralegh'.
5. William Wordsworth, *The Poems*, ed. John O. Hayden, 2 vols (Harmondsworth: Penguin, 1977), I, 281–95.
6. Samuel Taylor Coleridge, *Biographia Literaria* (1817), ed. Nigel Leask (London: Dent, 1997), p. 194.
7. Ibid. p. 211.
8. Ibid. p. 210.
9. William Wordsworth, *The Prelude: The 1805 Text*, ed. Ernest de Selincourt and Stephen Gill (Oxford: Oxford University Press, 1970).
10. Coleridge, *Biographia Literaria*, p. 214.
11. Two recent articles note the importance of identity and difference in repetitive language in Wordsworth: Corrina Russell, 'A Defence of Tautology: Repetition and Difference in Wordsworth's Note to "The Thorn"', *Paragraph Special Issue: The Idea of the Literary* 28:2 (July 2005), 104–14; Alexander Regier, 'Words Worth Repeating: Language and Repetition in Wordsworth's Poetic Theory', in Alexander Regier and Stephan H. Uhlig, ed., *Wordsworth's Poetic Theory: Knowledge, Language and Experience* (Houndmills: Palgrave, 2010), pp. 61–80.
12. Coleridge, *Biographia Literaria*, p. 184.
13. Ibid. pp. 182, 219–20.
14. 'Preface', *Lyrical Ballads*, p. 155.
15. Ibid. pp. 157, 171–2.
16. Coleridge, *Biographia Literaria*, p. 225.
17. 'Preface', p. 173. Yury Lotman, *Analysis of the Poetic Text*, ed. and trans. D. Barton Johnson (Ann Arbor: Ardis, 1976), p. 42, makes a remarkably similar characterisation of poetic rhythm:

    The rhythmicity of poetry is the cyclical repetition of different elements in identical positions with the aim of equating the unequal or revealing similarity in difference, or the repetition of the identical with the aim of revealing the false character of this identity, of establishing differences in similarity.

18. Attridge, *Peculiar Language*, pp. 46–89.

19. Wordsworth, *The Poems*, I, 366. Hayden's editorial choices provide me with the clearest opportunity to discuss elision. For a version of the poem which marks the elision in the first line with an apostrophe see William Wordsworth and Samuel Taylor Coleridge, *Lyrical Ballads*, ed. Michael Mason (Harlow: Pearson, 1992, 2nd edn 2007), p. 245.

20. Brennan O'Donnell, *The Passion of Meter: A Study of Wordsworth's Metrical Art* (Kent, OH, and London: Kent State University Press, 1995), p. 31. O'Donnell also suggests that one can see in Wordsworth's employment of elision 'signals of tension between metrical and phonetic systems', p. 81. Simon Jarvis, *Wordsworth's Philosophic Song* (Cambridge: Cambridge University Press, 2007), pp. 10–12 remarks on the importance of syllabically ambiguous words in Wordsworth's metrical practice in the establishment of large philosophical tensions in his work.

21. O'Donnell, *The Passion of Meter*, p. 152; Roger L. Slakey, 'At Zero: A Reading of Wordsworth's "She Dwelt among the Untrodden Ways"', *Studies in English Literature, 1500–1900* 12:4 (Autumn, 1972), 629–38 (p. 637).

CHAPTER FIVE

Equivalence: Gerard Manley Hopkins

Poetry can be a reflection upon what it is to be the kind of being that uses language, a reflection upon how humanity is characterised by being linguistic. This reflection, in the form it takes in several of the poems read in this book, is critical, in as much as it emanates from a crisis, a deeply unnerving realisation about the nature of being a language-using being. This unnerving realisation, I suggest, is the realisation that the language people use, and which can feel to its users so deeply intertwined with the natures of the objects it refers to, the operations and situations it describes, is constituted by a set of entirely contingent relations between the material elements of sound-pattern and orthography that share no necessary properties with objects, operations or situations in the world. This part of the realisation can make the conceptual world people inhabit appear worryingly arbitrary. There can be a further stage to this same reflection, in the realisation that once in use, the contingent relations between the parts of a language that allow it to operate become necessary: they cannot simply be altered and adopted at will by an individual or a legislative body of some kind. The history of the language demands that everyone operate within its course, even if every intervention in that course of events is new and unique. The essence of the objects to which words refer has no necessary or natural determining effect on the material form of the words themselves. Nonetheless, it is natural and necessary, with regard to the historical development of particular languages, that any given referring word, and no other, is the word used to make that reference in the given language.

Certain thinkers about language, and human institutions more generally, present this historical or retrospective necessity of initially contingent relations as a consolation demanded by how unnerving it is to think that justice, say, just as much as language, is a contingent product of human interaction, rather than being an attribute measurable against a permanent underlying standard. But there is no necessary reason that this second stage of realisation should or should always be consoling. One might find that the contingency of language relations rings through a particular utterance with a hollow note of absurdity; and that rather than being consoling, the necessity of speaking in that way adds nothing more or less than an aura of fatalism to the utterance. In this way the creative potential of language, and of poetic utterances in particular, can appear under the aspect of a terrifying dilemma between the contingent and the necessary, the absurd and the tragic, with very little sense of the excitement of the auto-genesis of the speaking subject that is evident in some other instances studied in this book.

In this chapter I will look at a poem by Gerard Manley Hopkins, and suggest that it reflects upon the contingency of its own language. J. Hillis Miller has said that 'the fundamental method of Hopkins' poetry is to carry as far as it will go, into every aspect of his verse, the principle of rhyme', and that 'The basic method of poetry as of music is repetition, the repetition of different forms of the same inscape.'[1] ('Inscape' is a technical term in Hopkins' vocabulary relating to the paradigmatic features of an object and also to their tendency towards 'design' or 'pattern'.)[2] In this chapter the term 'equivalence' will be preferred as a means of describing the intense interrelations of objects in Hopkins' poetic language, as it captures the sense of the partial identity and partial difference of the elements bound together. Whilst being a highly distinctive poet, Hopkins' thinking about equivalence in verse structure has precedents, and is cited by later writers. Edgar Allen Poe, for example, identifies equality as the origin of verse, and locates it in the systematic interrelation of equivalents:

> *Verse* originates in the human enjoyment of equality, fitness. To this enjoyment, also, all the moods of verse – rhythm, metre, stanza, rhyme, alliteration, the *refrain*, and other analogous effects – are to be referred . . . [equality's] idea embraces those of similarity, proportion, identity, repetition, and adaptation or fitness . . . Various systems of equalization are appreciated at once (or nearly so) in their respective values and in the value of each system with reference to all the others.[3]

Equivalence is also the term preferred by Roman Jakobson, the linguist and poetician who worked in both the Moscow and Prague Linguistic Circles, and who recognised in Hopkins' writings on poetry an important precursor for his own methods of poetic analysis and his theoretical conception of poetic processes. There may seem to be a great distance between the kinds of meaningfulness that are possible in the worlds of Hopkins and of Jakobson. Hopkins was a Jesuit, and, as is evident from his journals as much as his poems, experienced the world as a continual yet ever-varying struggle towards the differentiation of things through the expression of their interior properties. Jakobson scrutinises phenomena for evidence of their participation in systems, for signs of their dominating or being dominated by the phenomena of other related systems. But, as I shall try to show in the

course of this discussion, the very coincidence of the interior and the superficial, the individuated and the structural is the subject with which both are
dealing, and Hopkins' verse demonstrates as richly critical an attitude to it as
Jakobson's texts.

I will concentrate on one poem by Hopkins. 'Spelt from Sibyl's Leaves' is
an extended Italian sonnet, that divides each of its lines into two hemistichs,
themselves containing four stresses, with no fixed number of unstressed syllables between them (ranging easily between none and four).[4] There is an
extreme concentration of effects of equivalence (alliteration, consonance,
assonance, syntactic parallelism, internal rhyme and so on) that has been
associated with the trauma of the vision reported in the poem: a mundane
evening is seen as the end of the world, a glimpse of hell, as imagined in the
Jesuit tradition. All human actions are divided into two kinds, the good and
the bad, as the sheep are divided from the goats in the image of the last judg-
ment (Matthew 25:31–3).[5] The poem, then, imagines an extreme form of differentiation, between the good and bad, those welcomed into the kingdom of
God, and those rejected; it does so by presenting a series of equivalences that
are value-bearing precisely because they are not identities, because no matter
how much they approach one another they remain distinct. If the contingent
relations between the various elements of the language of the poem create a
bewildering degree of interconnectedness, it is counterbalanced by the stark-
ness of the negative conception of equivalence as a degree of difference, not a
degree of identity. This degree of difference is inescapable and fatal in that it
renders the contingency of the equivalences absurd (despite all my efforts and
all appearances, I may be one of the damned). There is a terror in the poem
that differences will endure even after the final dissolution.

> EARNEST, earthless, equal, attuneable, | vaulty, voluminous, . . . stupendous
> Evening strains to be tíme's vást, | womb-of-all, home-of-all, hearse-of-all night.
> Her fond yellow hornlight wound to the west, | her wild hollow hoarlight
>   hung to the height
> Waste; her earliest stars, earl-stars, | stárs principal, overbend us,
> Fíre-féaturing heaven. For earth | her being has unbound, her dapple is at an
>   end, as-
> tray or aswarm, all throughther, in throngs; | self ín self steepèd and páshed
>   – qúite
> Disremembering, dísmémbering | áll now. Heart, you round me right
> With: Óur évening is over us; óur night | whélms, whélms, ánd will end us.
> Only the beak-leaved boughs dragonish | damask the tool-smooth bleak light;
>   black,
> Ever so black on it. Óur tale, O óur oracle! | Lét life, wáned, ah lét life wind
> Off hér once skéined stained véined variety | upon, áll on twó spools; párt,
>   pen, páck

Now her áll in twó flocks, twó folds – black, white; [|] right, wrong; reckon but,
    reck but, mind
But thése two; wáre of a wórld where bút these [|] twó tell, each off the óther;
    of a rack
Where, selfwrung, selfstrung, sheathe- and shelterless, [|] thóughts agaínst
    thoughts ín groans grínd.[6]

The poem exhibits the traditional turn in subject, with the octave focusing on the dissolution of individuality in the evening seen as a type of the end of the individual life, and the end of life altogether. The sestet then imagines that the variety of life can be polarised, so that 'bút these [|] twó tell, each off the óther', and this very differentiation seems as terrifying if not more so than the preceding dissolution. The poem shares its concerns for the preservation of a meaningful set of differentiations with other poems, such as 'That Nature is a Heraclitean Fire and of the comfort of the Resurrection', in which the humble physical world is replete with differentiation, seen in the patterning of drying mud, but in which nothing in man is to be found 'so stark / But vastness blurs and time [|] beats level.'[7]

Equivalence, identity and difference are central to Hopkins' thoughts on beauty, in verse and prose. Beauty is a good for people because perceiving the similarities and differences that produce it is a form of mental activity of value in itself: beauty 'keeps warm / Men's wits to the things that are'.[8] Differentiation between comparable elements is beautiful even when it becomes eccentric: 'All things counter, original, spare, strange . . . He [God] fathers-forth'.[9] In a Platonic dialogue on beauty, the professorial speaker asks his interlocutors to

> remember I wished beauty to be considered as regularity or likeness tempered by irregularity or difference . . . The accentual sequence (which we call a trochee) in odours is the same as in when sweet or in sicken, but the foot is not exactly like them simply because it is made of a different word . . . Rhythm therefore is likeness tempered with difference, is it not?[10]

Rhythm is just one possible variety of equivalence between the elements of language. In another prose piece Hopkins offers a categorisation of the 'kinds of resemblance possible between syllables':

(1) Musical *pitch*, to which belongs tonic accent
(2) Length or time or *quantity* so called
(3) Stress or emphatic accent; αρσις and θεσις
(4) Likeness or sameness of letters and this some or all and these vowels or consonants and initial or final. This may be called the *lettering* of syllables
(5) *Holding*, to which belong break and circumflexion, slurs, glides, slides etc.[11]

Clearly, all of these effects are evident in the poem, although the explanations which Hopkins goes on to provide for the kinds of resemblance, particularly kinds one and three, are not perfectly clear. He makes a distinction
between emphatic and tonic accent, coming close to identifying tonic accent
with word stress, the most accented syllable of a word in a 'neutral' pronunciation of it.[12] It is difficult to provide contrastive examples of tonic accent
and emphatic accent, as Hopkins is interested in harnessing the stress already
in the words, rather than imposing stress upon words through metre. But in
some of Hopkins' more audacious coinages, or borrowings from vernacular
idiom, tonic and emphatic accent can be distinguished. So with 'overbend'
and 'Disremembering', stress is heard in 'o' and 'dis' as well as in the 'natural'
positions 'bend' and 'mem', as an emphasis produced by metre or pronunciation is competing with them. But these are not necessarily words with which
the reader will be familiar enough readily to attribute to them a tonic accent.

Quantity can be understood here simply as the time taken by a particular
syllable, without any closer comparison to the system of ancient Greek and
Latin quantitative metrics. So 'throngs', 'boughs' and 'spools' occupy more
time than 'night', 'life', 'flocks' and 'rack', although they are all monosyllabic.
Arsis and thesis, the stress produced in a phrasal arrangement of words, rather
than the tonic accent, can also mark out syllables as like or unlike, even when
the syllable is the 'same' syllable. Thus in the trilogy of qualifiers for the stars
of the fourth line, 'earliest stars, earl-stars, | stárs principal', the first and third
occurrence of 'stars' are stressed, the second unstressed. A great variety of
interrelationships are being established by these equivalences and differences
of one sort and another, so that the same word, 'stars', can at once be like
and unlike itself. The resemblances Hopkins points out are complex, some of
them depending on one another, some of them perhaps not being evident at
all, unless great interpretive care is taken in the reading of the poem (silent
or voiced).

The fourth of Hopkins' modes of resemblance, the lettering of words, is
perhaps the most prominent in the poem.[13] The series of initial, terminal
and medial echoes of phonemes, syllables and groups of syllables begins
immediately and soon reaches extreme complexity. The opening line consists
entirely of adjectives that qualify the evening: 'EARNEST, earthless, equal,
attuneable, | vaulty, voluminous, . . . stupendous'. Their lettering creates
relations among them, the equivalences in the first syllables of the first two
terms ('ea', 'ea'), the final syllables of the second pair of terms (sounding 'ul'),
the alliteration of the third pair, and then the shared adjectival ending of the
'voluminous' and 'stupendous' creating the illusion that these properties are
in some sense related to one another, if it is indeed an illusion, when they are
all simultaneously characteristic of the evening. The terms are in some sense
equal to one another, attuned to one another, announcing a running parallel

of the poem's subject and its technical procedure that continues throughout. Such an effect is aided by the interplay of systems, as Poe recognised: the tonic accent makes trochees of the first three terms, so that they also have a commonality.[14] Each of these equivalences of lettering is perceived as contributing to a sequence that continues throughout the poem. Hopkins' final category of 'holding' is perhaps more oblique, closer to musical phrasing in which values can be performed in attenuated or accented fashion. In lines 10–11 'on' occurs twice, three times if one includes its occurrence within 'upon'. In the first of these occurrences it is followed by an unstressed syllable, in the other(s) by a stressed syllable. The first occurrence is, as a consequence, half swallowed, whereas the other occurrences are performed more completely (at least in my attempts to vocalise the poem). Hopkins' scheme of syllabic resemblance indicates the seriousness with which he took the phonological and prosodic arrangement of a text.[15]

It is unsurprising that a poet's thinking about poetry should bear some relation to her or his practice, but I have done little so far to relate Hopkins' views on equivalence to the argument of the poem as I have characterised it. The poem concerns the evening becoming the night, and the dissolution of identity that occurs at this moment. So the run of equivalences between the letterings of the adjectives in the first line, and the continuing trains of equivalences throughout the poem perform this elision of difference in identity. Such processes are ubiquitous in the poem. The evening is straining 'to be tíme's vást, ǀ womb-of-all, home-of-all, hearse-of-all night', and the sequence womb-home-hearse is felt as much in the half rhyme and alliteration that link the three parallel terms as in the temporal sequence (birth, life, death) that their referents suggest. The second sentence continues to conjure the threat of eliding difference whilst refusing complete identity in equivalent parts. The syntactic parallel has the 'yellow hornlight wound to the west' and the 'hollow hoarlight hung to the height', doubled by equivalences in alliteration and internal rhyme, yet although 'height' answers 'west' as the place where the light hangs, there is a second answer to 'west' across the line break in the main verb of the clause 'Waste', so that a difference emerges from the identity even as the wasting effect of the coming night is evoked. The poem is evoking the moment at which objects lose their edges, the moment when 'being' is 'unbound' (l. 5) and selves are absorbed in one another 'quite / Disremembering, dísmémbering ǀ áll now' (ll. 6–7). The term 'unbound' recalls the stars that 'overbend us' in the heaven where the coming of evening threatens. The disremembering and dismembering of selves is played out in the disremembering and dismembering of words, whose parts come to participate in one another so intensively that a near universal equivalence between all linguistic elements threatens, a situation of non-differentiation, of forgetting. This is the vision of a common death that concludes the octave, or, as Hillis Miller puts it a presentation of 'the symbol of that nonbeing which will overtake all mortal things'.[16]

The sestet goes on to present the vision of the octave as a dissolution to be wished for, as the speaker employs the optative: 'Lét life, wáned, ah lét life wind / Off hér once skéined stained véined variety ¦ upon, áll on twó spools' (ll. 10–11). Yet this loss of variety still seems terrifying: the addressee is told to 'wáre of a wórld where bút these ¦ twó [right and wrong] tell, each off the óther' (l. 13), a world where 'thóughts agaínst thoughts ín groans grínd' (l. 14). The world is not becoming undifferentiated, but more starkly differentiated. If the vision of the octave was one of terrifying dissolution of the difference of equivalences in their identities, the sestet fears that the differences within those equivalences will be polarised, and with extreme consequences. The same effects as employed in the octave, the pairs and triplets of terms sharing some features and being distinguished in others ('párt, pen, páck', l. 11), the syntactic parallels running in counterpoint to other modes of resemblance ('Lét life, wáned, ah lét life wind / Off', ll. 10–11), are seen as it were from the other side. They are simply elements that differ from one another in a more or less arbitrary fashion, but their difference is nonetheless vital, or even fatal, determining everything that can be conceived of as humanly meaningful.

Is it fanciful to think that the equivalences embedded in a vocabulary and syntax can contribute to the meaning of a poem in this way, supplementing its argument and evoking its values? That a word happens to be made of some of the same or indeed exactly the same sound patterns or orthography as another need not imply the conceptual relation of their referents. Hopkins, however, is willing to entertain the possibility of such relations: speech must take certain historical forms and incarnations, a certain character or inscape, and so it is impossible for the material forms of words, and therefore their reference also, not to be in one way or another related.[17] In an earlier essay, 'Poetic Diction', he remarks on the importance, indeed the necessity of parallelism to poetry:

> The artificial part of poetry, perhaps we shall be right to say all artifice, reduces itself to the principle of parallelism. The structure of poetry is that of continuous parallelism, ranging from the technical so-called Parallelisms of Hebrew poetry and the antiphons of Church music up to the intricacy of Greek or Italian or English verse. But parallelism is of two kinds necessarily – where the opposition is clearly marked, and where it is transitional rather or chromatic . . . And moreover parallelism in expression tends to beget or passes into parallelism in thought.[18]

One can approach the question of how parallelism in expression begets parallelism in thought by studying the reception of Hopkins in the work of

Roman Jakobson on poetic language. Jakobson argues that the equivalences evident in poetic language are a fact of the genre of discourse in which poetry participates, with its specific calibration of the various elements involved in any speech situation. Hopkins shares this idea of poetry as a certain kind of speech situation.

Several times, and in strong terms, Jakobson promotes Hopkins' statements on parallelism: 'Gerard Manley Hopkins, an outstanding searcher in the science of poetic language, defined verse as "speech wholly or partially repeating the same figure of sound."'[19] Rhyme is instantiated as only one manifestation of the principle: 'Rhyme is only a particular, condensed case of a much more general, we may even say the fundamental, problem of poetry, namely *parallelism*.' The suggestion that sonic and semantic equivalence are interrelated also comes through in Jakobson's adoption of Hopkins:

> Briefly, equivalence in sound, projected into the sequence as its constitutive principle, inevitably involves semantic equivalence, and on any linguistic level any constituent of such a sequence prompts one of the two correlative experiences which Hopkins neatly defines as 'comparison for likeness' sake' and 'comparison for unlikeness' sake.' . . . In poetry not only the phonological sequence but, in the same way, any sequence of semantic units strives to build an equation. Similarity superimposed on contiguity imparts to poetry its thoroughgoing symbolic, multiplex, polysemantic essence . . . anything sequent is a simile.[20]

These concepts perhaps require a little interpretation with reference to the rest of the essay from which they are cited. Similarity and sequentiality are important aspects of an utterance for Jakobson, and he develops his definition of them from Ferdinand de Saussure, often regarded as the founder of structural linguistics. Saussure had suggested that there are two ways of looking at the relations between signs: as sequences unfolding over time, or as associations with other terms. These two kinds of relation he calls the 'syntagmatic' and the 'paradigmatic': 'Syntagmatic relations hold *in praesentia*. They hold between two or more terms co-present in a sequence. Associative relations, on the contrary, hold *in absentia*. They hold between terms constituting a mnemonic group.'[21]

Jakobson suggests an empirical criterion for what he calls the 'poetic function' of language may be found in the interference of syntagmatic with paradigmatic relations:

> What is the empirical linguistic criterion of the poetic function? In particular, what is the indispensable feature in any piece of poetry? To answer this question we must recall the two basic modes of arrangement used in verbal behavior, *selection* and *combination*. If 'child' is the topic of the message, the speaker selects one among the extant, more or less similar nouns like child, kid, youngster, tot,

> all of them equivalent in a certain respect, and then, to comment on this topic,
> he may select one of the semantically cognate verbs – sleeps, dozes, nods, naps.
> Both chosen words combine in the speech chain. The selection is produced on
> the basis of equivalence, similarity and dissimilarity, synonymy and antonymy,
> while the combination, the build-up of the sequence is based on contiguity. *The
> poetic function projects the principle of equivalence from the axis of selection into the
> axis of combination.* Equivalence is promoted to the constitutive device of the
> sequence. In poetry one syllable is equalized with any other syllable of the same
> sequence; word stress is assumed to equal word stress, as unstress equals unstress;
> prosodic long is matched with long, and short with short; word boundary equals
> word boundary, no boundary equals no boundary; syntactic pause equals syn-
> tactic pause, no pause equals no pause. Syllables are converted into units of
> measure, and so are morae or stresses.[22]

The equivalences (specifically contrasted identities and differences) of poetic
speech take the principle of synonymy that operates in selectional or associative relations, and apply it to combinatorial or syntagmatic relations.[23] So,
to work with Jakobson's example, the poetic function can be seen in the
utterance 'the kid kips'. Synonymy has been protected here on the selective/
associative level: 'kid' is synonymous with 'child', 'kips' with 'sleeps'. But the
principle of equivalence is also evident in the syntagmatic/combinatorial
relations, in the phonological repetition 'ki', 'ki'. Although no particular
deformation on the semantic level is caused here, it is clear that one form
of equivalence might challenge the other. Here, then, is a remarkably bold
empirical criterion for the poetic function. But the poetic function itself has
not yet been defined.

Poetic function is a disposition of the entire speech situation, however,
and not just the empirical criterion defined above. Jakobson analyses speech
situations into various components, such as the speaker, addressee, message,
and so on:

> The ADDRESSER sends a MESSAGE to the ADDRESSEE. To be operative
> the message requires a CONTEXT referred to (the 'referent' in another, some-
> what ambiguous, nomenclature), graspable by the addressee, and either verbal
> or capable of being verbalized; a CODE fully, or at least partially, common to
> the addresser and addressee (or in other words, to the encoder and decoder of
> the message); and, finally, a CONTACT, a physical channel and psychological
> connection between the addresser and the addressee, enabling both of them to
> enter and stay in communication.[24]

Within this set of variables, various genres of discourse define themselves
by making one element dominant over others, not to their exclusion, but to
their potential deformation: 'The diversity [of language functions] lies not in

a monopoly of some one of these several functions but in a different hierar-chical order of functions.' The particular calibration of the speech situation in the poetic function is a concentration on the message itself, rather than the addresser, the addressee, the context etc.: 'The set (*Einstellung*) toward the message as such, focus on the message for its own sake, is the POETIC function of language.'[25] Focusing on the message itself does not mean that the addresser and addressee, the context or the code become insignificant, but that they are dominated by concentration upon the message itself: poems are written by people, and do refer to things, but the mark of their being poems is that they attract attention to themselves more than to any other feature of the speech situation.

This crucial suggestion of Jakobson's has a parallel in Hopkins, but not one that Jakobson himself notes. Hopkins states that 'Poetry is in fact speech only employed to carry the inscape of speech for the inscape's sake – and therefore the inscape must be dwelt on.'[26] The poem is characterised by a dwelling on the interior character of speech for its own sake, the kind of dwelling provoked by the intensity of coincident features amongst contigu-ous terms in poems such as 'Spelt from Sibyl's Leaves'. One might ask if there is not a considerable difference between Hopkins' notion of dwelling on the inscape of speech for the inscape's sake, and Jakobson's of the set towards the message itself? After all, inscape is the interior essence of an object, that which marks it out as having been made by God for a particular purpose ('The world is charged with the grandeur of God', Hopkins says), whereas the message implies no privileged relations to a context.[27] Jakobson's read-ings of the systems of equivalence operating in poetic messages can appear dry and superficial: their accounting for the grammatical and phonological equivalences of poems are so complete that they appear to have little interest in larger, super-segmental equivalences of theme or attitude or argument. Yet these catalogues of equivalence support readings of the value of particular terms, such as 'cat', in the work of a particular poet.[28] One might see this kind of reading sharing an interest with Hopkins in poems such as 'As Kingfishers Catch Fire', in which Hopkins initially suggests that

Each mortal thing does one thing and the same:
  Deals out that being indoors each one dwells;
  Selves – goes itself; *myself* it speaks and spells,
Crying *What I do is me: for that I came.* (ll. 5–8)[29]

Is there really such a difference between the essence, the interior quality, the inscape of a thing, and the characteristics of the language that is used to represent or evoke it? Jakobson is convinced otherwise, that grammatical and phonological features are vital to semantics: the 'deepest semantic effects' of Shakespeare's Sonnet 129, are, he claims, 'achieved by a nearly exclusive use of constituents which . . . have been labeled mere "linguistic fictions" and which are relegated to "surface" structures by linguists of today'.[30] One might note a distinction between the expression of the essence of a thing in words, and the expression of the essence of a verbal argument in the material features of words, but this distinction is ultimately illusory. Things distinguish themselves from one another by means of superficial formal differences, just as words do: the essence of a particular variety is that it is formally distinct from the other varieties, just as in language, as Saussure noted '*there are only differences*':

> although in general a difference presupposes positive terms between which the difference holds, in a language there are only differences, *and no positive terms*. Whether we take the signification or the signal, the language includes neither ideas nor sounds existing prior to the linguistic system, but only conceptual and phonetic differences arising out of that system. In a sign, what matters more than any idea or sound associated with it is what other signs surround it.[31]

This statement may induce a vertiginous effect, with languages losing any apparent purchase upon their referential contents, and being constantly in danger of slippage. But that would be to imagine that the world of referents lies behind the world of language, untouched by it. A 'bough', for example, may seem a relatively mind-independent thing to name. But the term represents a certain set of distinctions in how trees are seen whereby their various limbs are divided by size as boughs and then branches, shoots and so on. That such an English word exists, and yet is only meaningful because it can be distinguished from near synonyms (branch) and homonyms (plough), speaks to the simultaneous contingency and necessity of human language systems, historically considered. That the essence of a bough is caught up with its being named by the English noun 'bough', and further, by that noun's appearance in Hopkins' poem, damasked by beak-like leaves, persisting against the coming night that seems to be eliding all other differences, also speaks to this simultaneous contingency and necessity. Being a human speaking subject means being dependent upon the most haphazard of constructions in order to be able to speak at all, constructions that can be so absurd they lose their purchase upon reality; those constructions, their equivalences in identity and difference, persist and endure and force us to speak through them, no matter how historically contingent they, and we, have come to seem.

Notes

1. J. Hillis Miller, *The Disappearance of God: Five Nineteenth-Century Writers* (Cambridge and London: The Belknap Press of Harvard University Press,

1975 [1963]), pp. 281–2. James I. Wimsatt, *Hopkins's Poetics of Speech Sound: Sprung Rhythm, Lettering, Inscape* (Toronto: University of Toronto Press, 2006), p. 6, believes Hillis Miller and others, including Jakobson, to be mistaken in identifying parallelism or rhyme with inscape: inscape, he contends, is a matter of speech sound, and rhythm.

2. *The Letters of Gerard Manley Hopkins to Robert Bridges*, ed. Claude Colleer Abbot (London: Oxford University Press, 1935), p. 66, 15 February 1879. Throughout this chapter I am deeply indebted to Mike Hurley for his help in directing me towards the most pertinent passages in Hopkins' work, and for generous critical attention.

3. Edgar Allen Poe, 'The Rationale of Verse' (1848), in *Literary Theory and Criticism*, ed. Leonard Cassuto (Mineola, NY: Dover, 1999), pp. 125–61 (pp. 131, 135).

4. In a letter to Robert Bridges of 11 December 1886 Hopkins calls it 'the longest [sonnet] . . . ever made', and remarks that it should be read 'loud, leisurely, poetical (not rhetorical) . . . with long rests, long dwells on the rhyme and other marked syllables, and so on. This sonnet shd. be almost sung: it is most carefully timed in *tempo rubato*.' *Letters*, p. 246.

5. See *The Poems of Gerard Manley Hopkins*, ed. Alice Jenkins (London: Routledge, 2006), pp. 154–6.

6. *The Poems of Gerard Manley Hopkins*, ed. W. H. Gardner and N. H. MacKenzie, 4th edn (Oxford: Oxford University Press, 1967), pp. 97–8.

7. Ibid. p. 105.

8. Ibid. 'To What Serves Mortal Beauty', p. 98.

9. Ibid. 'Pied Beauty', p. 70.

10. *The Journals and Papers of Gerard Manley Hopkins*, ed. Humphry House, completed by Graham Storey (London: Oxford University Press, 1959), 'On the Origin of Beauty: A Platonic Dialogue', p. 101. See the discussion of the 'Preface' to *Lyrical Ballads* in 'Measure: William Wordsworth' for similar views.

11. Ibid. 'Rhythm and the Other Structural Parts of Rhetoric – Verse', p. 268.

12. Ibid. pp. 269–70.

13. Wimsatt, pp. 76–9, analyses parts of the poem in terms of its lettering, but with a view to demonstrating the 'independent significance of the sounds of poetry' (p. 95) in Hopkins's theory. I do not wish to contest the accuracy of Wimsatt's reading of Hopkins, but the argument of this book challenges notions of the independent significance of sound imagined separable from the referential, pragmatic and other functions of language.

14. Yury Lotman, *Analysis of the Poetic Text*, ed. and trans. D. Barton Johnson (Ann Arbor: Ardis, 1976), p. 64, has suggested that non-coincidence might be more musical than coincidence: 'The greater the extent of the non-coincidences (semantic, grammatical, intonational, etc.) falling upon coinciding phonemes, the more palpable the rupture between the recurrences on

the phonemic level and the difference on the levels of any of its meanings, the more musical, the more sonorous, the text seems to the reader.'

15. Christopher R. Wilson, 'Nineteenth-Century Musical Agogics as an Element in Gerard Manley Hopkins's Prosody', *Comparative Literature* 51:1 (Winter 2000), 72–86 (pp. 77–9), describes the role of rubato, a temporary deviation from the beat made up at a later point in the phrase, in the performance of 'Spelt from Sibyl's Leaves', as Hopkins conceived it.

16. Miller, *The Disappearance of God*, p. 325.

17. See the diary entries for 24 September 1863, in *Journals and Papers*, pp. 4–5, for Hopkins considering various words in relation to the properties of their referents and saying that 'the onomatopoetic theory has not had a fair chance' (p. 5). My own view is that onomatopoetic, motivated or iconic features in languages occur against the background of systematic arbitrary relations. People might make connections between certain phonemes (such as 'gr') and certain phenomena (grinding, grit, greeting). There is no sense in which the phenomena are in the phoneme, as sounds or letters do not have in them particles of matter, or meetings, or anything other than speech sound or writing. But the human association of the phoneme with the phenomena is perfectly real and objective. It takes place in language, not outside it. It is part of the ordering of the world and orientation in it that language performs. It is not the key to the internal structure of languages, but one of their features.

18. Ibid. pp. 84–5.

19. Roman Jakobson, *Language in Literature*, ed. Krystyna Pomorska and Stephen Rudy (London and Cambridge: The Belknap Press of Harvard University Press, 1987 [1980]), p. 72. Wimsatt, pp. 30–2, makes some connections between Hopkins and Jakobson, but focuses more on speech sounds than parallelism.

20. Jakobson, *Language in Literature*, pp. 82, 83, 85.

21. F. de Saussure, *Course in General Linguistics* (1915), ed. Charles Bally and Albert Sechehaye, with Albert Riedlinger, trans. Roy Harris (London: Duckworth, 1983), p. 122. It should also be noted in this particular context that Saussure's later research concerned anagrammatical methods of verse composition in Latin, developing highly intricate models of phonic interrelation. See Jean Starobinski, *Words Upon Words: The Anagrams of Ferdinand de Saussure*, trans. Olivia Emmet (New Haven and London: Yale University Press, 1979).

22. Jakobson, *Language in Literature*, p. 71.

23. Samuel R. Levin, *Linguistic Structures in Poetry* ('s-Gravenhage: Mouton, 1962), p. 30, notes the peculiar exploitation of equivalence in poetic language: 'the exploitation of these equivalences, which may derive from phonic and/or semantic features, is not adventitious, but is carried out systematically in a poem. This systematic exploitation takes the form of placing naturally equivalent linguistic elements in equivalent positions or, put the other way,

of using equivalent positions as settings for equivalent phonic and/or semantic elements.'

24. Jakobson, *Language in Literature*, p. 66.
25. Ibid. pp. 66, 69.
26. Hopkins, 'Poetry and Verse', in *Journals and Papers*, p. 289. I am here developing points made by James Milroy, *The Language of Gerard Manley Hopkins* (London: Deutsch, 1977), pp. 100–13.
27. 'God's Grandeur', *Poems*, p. 66.
28. Jakobson, *Language in Literature*, p. 197.
29. Hopkins, *Poems*, p. 90.
30. Jakobson, *Language in Literature*, p. 211.
31. Saussure, *Course in General Linguistics*, p. 118.

CHAPTER SIX

Spirit: Wallace Stevens

Most of the ways in which poetic language is said to be poetic that are discussed in this book are more or less superficially or formally evident in the language, either in its metre, syntax, figurative constructions, phonological repetitions or elsewhere. This and the following chapter on Frank O'Hara focus on arguments suggesting that a force behind, and not immediately evident in, language is the source of its poeticalness. Such arguments beg the question: if the spirit (force, charge, drive) that manifests itself in poetic language is a poetic spirit, and is identifiable only in and through that language, can it truly be distinguished from the superficial or formal features of the language? Two characters in Friedrich Schlegel's *Dialogue on Poetry* set out the central problem succinctly:

> LOTHARIO. Every art and every discipline that functions through language, when exercised as an art for its own sake and when it achieves its highest summit, appears as poetry.
> LUDOVICO. And every art or discipline which does not manifest its nature through language possesses an invisible spirit: and that is poetry.[1]

How does one sense an invisible spirit? Or, to put it another way, if Roman Jakobson was right to insist with the poet John Crowe Ransom that 'poetry is a kind of language,' can there be a poetic spirit separable from particular linguistic manifestations that are in some way or another poetic?[2]

The supposition of a force that passes through the poet, or the language, without being part of the poet's intentional activity, nor being identifiable with some particular feature in the text, will be questioned in this chapter by examining various forms it takes between the mid-nineteenth and the early twentieth centuries. Such theories do not do enough to recognise the relation between the spirit of poetry and its material manifestation in language: poetic language is neither an unrestrained creative energy operating behind and making itself felt through language, nor is it the manipulation of linguistic structures according to certain formalisable rules. It is the inseparability of these two aspects of the act, understood in the historical uniqueness of particular poetic texts. A reading of Wallace Stevens' 'The Idea of Order at Key West' will demonstrate this inseparability in a genre of poem in which it is particularly evident, the romantic philosophical meditation on the nature and moment of artistic creation. The chapter will close with a description of Friedrich Hölderlin's writing on poetic spirit, as a means of demonstrating the existence of theoretical efforts to account for this inseparability in earlier nineteenth-century thought.

Critics in the later nineteenth and earlier twentieth centuries often attribute the disarming power of the romantic plain style to poetic spirit. Matthew Arnold's appraisal of the style-lessness of Wordsworth's most successful poems makes evident the degree to which inspiration, as the force behind poetry, is conceived of as extra-linguistic. Arnold describes the poetic urge:

> It is within no poet's command; here is the part of the Muse, the inspiration, the God, the 'not ourselves.' In Wordsworth's case, the accident, for so it may almost be called, of inspiration, is of peculiar importance. No poet, perhaps, is so evidently filled with a new and sacred energy when the inspiration is upon him; no poet, when it fails him, is so left 'weak as is a breaking wave.' . . . the right sort of verse to choose from Wordsworth, if we are to seize his true and most characteristic form of expression, is a line like this from *Michael* – 'And never lifted up a single stone.' There is nothing subtle in it, no heightening, no study of poetic style, strictly so called, at all; yet it is expression of the highest and most truly expressive kind.[3]

It is not possible to describe what it is that makes Wordsworth's most poetic language poetic: it has no determining formal features. Nor can Arnold really be searching for some as yet undefined super-segmental approach to the study of poetic language: he is not insisting on the narrative force of the poem; nor is he insisting on its qualities as a speech act (direct or indirect), nor on its flouting of conversational maxims, but on the expressiveness of the individual line. The spirit of the line, its inspiration, is felt as much as an absence as a presence. John Stuart Mill states a similar conclusion more bluntly: 'the genius of Wordsworth is essentially unlyrical'.[4]

A. E. Housman's 1933 Leslie Stephen lecture describes an intermittent and insecure spirit operating in poetry. Having said various unflattering things about eighteenth-century poetry, Housman notes, with what seems wilful refusal of any analytical impulse, that a line of poetry can be identified by its ability to make one's facial hair bristle whilst shaving. Housman finds an equivalent experience described in the Bible, an experience that makes the spiritual origins of the poetic moment evident: 'Then a spirit passed before my face: the haire of my flesh stood vp' (Job 4:15).[5] The tone and tenor of Housman's comparison suggests the claustration of poetic spirit, the banalisation of the sublime. Similarly, Housman is inclined to think that the periods after lunch, when he has drunk beer and gone for a walk, are the best times to write poetry: the Arnoldian presence of the inspiring other, even though Arnold himself is presented as an inspiring other in Housman's text, has been displaced by quotidian rhythms. The only interest Housman has in eighteenth-century poetry is in the work of the mad (he includes Collins, Smart, Cowper and Blake), and he approvingly cites Blake's 'My Spectre around me night and day', saying 'I am not equal to framing definite ideas which would match that magnificent versification and correspond to the strong tremor of unreasonable excitement which those words set up in some region deeper than the mind.' 'Meaning', as Housman says, 'is of the intellect, poetry is not.'[6] Poetry can be induced by trusting to one's pacifying quotidian routines, and can be recognised as a minor interruption of those routines.

Ezra Pound despised Housman's attitudes, which he early presented as a form of giving in to death in a 'Song in the Manner of Housman':

> O woe, woe,
> People are born and die,
> We also shall be dead pretty soon
> Therefore let us act as if we were
>   dead already.[7]

A considerable number of poems from Pound's earliest collections address or otherwise invoke the soul or spirit, calling for a renovation of poetical ambition. 'In Durance' has the poet's soul call after others who 'feel / And have some breath for beauty and the arts', and in 'Donzella Beata' the poet praises his own soul for having come to him, rather than modestly awaiting him in the next world. The soul is also given voice, addressing love in breathy terms in 'Speech for Psyche in the Golden Book of Apuleius'. Soul is called upon or spoken through in order to bring a new spirit to poetry. The spirit Pound seeks is ambitious to the point of being imperious. 'In the Old Age of the Soul' and 'Revolt Against the Crepuscular Spirit in Modern Poetry' express a preference for deeds before dreams, and accept dreams only of wild ambition – an ambition for poetry, expressed in militaristic, imperial terms, whereby poets are 'rulers though but dreams' ('Revolt').[8] Pound's rejection of Housman's banality involves calling on a further realm, that of soul or spirit. This realm speaks through Psyche, is evoked in descriptions of dream worlds and afterlives, but is present in the poetry only as nebulosity implying some other order without achieving it.

Later in Pound's career a scientific vocabulary displaces the poetic spirit, but the imperial concerns remain. Emerson Marks has noted that 'when

[Ezra] Pound speaks of poetry being highly *charged* with meaning he employs the adjective in two of its senses at once: both intellectually *laden*, and *imbued with electric potency*, or *galvanic*'.[9] Pound uses this vocabulary in an unabashed reference to his earlier work: 'What *is literature, what is language, etc??* // Literature is language charged with meaning. / "Great literature is simply language charged with meaning to the utmost possible degree" (E.P. in *How to Read*).'[10] Pound develops an organicist yet mechanistic view of the kind of meaning with which literary language is charged: 'Language is the main means of human communication. If an animal's nervous system does not transmit sensations and stimuli, the animal atrophies. / If a nation's literature declines, the nation atrophies and decays.' Pound argues that words have complex associations that develop over time: that language is inherited. But

> NEVERTHELESS you still charge words with meaning mainly in three ways, called phanopoeia, melopoeia, logopoeia. You use a word to throw a visual image on to the reader's imagination, or you charge it by sound, or you use groups of words to do this.

There is in Pound's galvanic language of poetry a view of social life and the language that it transmits as a business of strife, as a constant expenditure of energy in the battle against atrophy and desensitisation. As an example of this charged concentration Pound cites Yeats, 'The fire that stirs about her, when she stirs.' He says he is 'trying to indicate a difference between prose simplicity of statement, and an equal limpidity in poetry, where the perfectly simple verbal order is CHARGED with a much higher potential, an emotional potential'.[11] Pound shares with his antagonist Housman a sense that poetry is not rational, but emotional or spiritual, yet points to nothing that makes the lines he cites as charged as he claims them to be: to do so would in some sense be a distraction from their total linguistic subservience to an emotional reality, their most admirable feature; yet it thereby remains entirely unclear why one completely direct statement should be more charged than any other, unclear in what the special limpidity consists.

Pound is by no means the only theorist of poetic language in the first half of the twentieth century to be interested in charge, and the electro-chemical potential of words that can be released by a peculiar poetic care for their placement. A collection of essays from prominent critics of the early to mid twentieth century also emphasises charge. Philip Wheelwright says that the language of poetry is 'charged language, language of associative complexity' and not often available in contemporary cinema or drama.[12] Associative complexity is both the association of words with concepts (as well as those concepts with other concepts) and also the association of words with each other in the particular text. I.A. Richards reaches for the scientific metaphor, saying John Donne expands the meaning of phrases, 'making their implications explicit, increasing their interaction, as heat increases chemical interaction'.[13] Poetry is the exploitation of a reactive power inherent in language. Two decades later, after the Second World War, Winifred Nowottny, in a popular textbook, applies the idea of association explicitly to poetic diction: 'the question of the diction of poetry is a question of how words affect and are affected by the artistic contexts they enter'. The same text also retains a sense of mysterious infusion in poetry. Poetic structure lends some animating spirit to poetry that is inexplicable given the prose sense of the terms themselves: '"vastidity" of meaning in poems depends on the setting-up of tensions between the various meanings – the various patternings of experience – infused into its language by the power of the poem's structure'.[14] The vocabularies of charge, potency, electro-chemical energy and magnetism are all related to an earlier vocabulary of mysteriously infused spirits, describing a force that seems to emanate from poetic utterances and resists attribution to readily identifiable surface features of phonological, syntactic, or metrical construction.

Wallace Stevens contributed an essay to the volume on the language of poetry cited at the start of the previous paragraph, an essay that, in part, concerns poetry's escape from a reality conceived of as a painful degree of violence.[15] Stevens' poem 'The Idea of Order at Key West' enters directly into the discussion of the relationship between spirit and poetic language, at the same time as asking some fundamental questions of aesthetics in a transcendental philosophy: does a manner of perceiving a world make that world, and is such a manner of perceiving always more or less poetic?[16] Stevens' poem meditates on the relationship between song and world, beginning with the invocation of a female presence who is closely associated with creative impulses themselves related to the environment and its patterns.

The Idea of Order at Key West

She sang beyond the genius of the sea.
The water never formed to mind or voice,
Like a body wholly body, fluttering
Its empty sleeves; and yet its mimic motion
Made constant cry, caused constantly a cry,
That was not ours although we understood,
Inhuman, of the veritable ocean.

The sea was not a mask. No more was she.
The song and water were not medleyed sound
Even if what she sang was what she heard,
Since what she sang was uttered word by word.
It may be that in all her phrases stirred

The grinding water and the gasping wind;
But it was she and not the sea we heard.

For she was the maker of the song she sang.
The ever-hooded, tragic-gestured sea
Was merely a place by which she walked to sing.
Whose spirit is this? we said, because we knew
It was the spirit that we sought and knew
That we should ask this often as she sang.

If it was only the dark voice of the sea
That rose, or even coloured by many waves;
If it was only the outer voice of sky
And cloud, of the sunken coral water-walled,
However clear, it would have been deep air,
The heaving speech of air, a summer sound
Repeated in a summer without end
And sound alone. But it was more than that,
More even than her voice, and ours, among
The meaningless plungings of water and the wind,
Theatrical distances, bronze shadows heaped
On high horizons, mountainous atmospheres
Of sky and sea.
          It was her voice that made
The sky acutest at its vanishing.
She measured to the hour its solitude.
She was the single artificer of the world
In which she sang. And when she sang, the sea,
Whatever self it had, became the self
That was her song, for she was the maker. Then we,
As we beheld her striding there alone,
Knew that there never was a world for her
Except the one she sang and, singing, made.

Ramon Fernandez, tell me, if you know,
Why, when the singing ended and we turned
Toward the town, tell why the glassy lights,
The lights in the fishing boats at anchor there,
As the night descended, tilting in the air,
Mastered the night and portioned out the sea,
Fixing emblazoned zones and fiery poles,
Arranging, deepening, enchanting night.

Oh! Blessed rage for order, pale Ramon,
The maker's rage to order words of the sea,
Words of the fragrant portals, dimly-starred,

And of ourselves and of our origins,
In ghostlier demarcations, keener sounds.

The poem turns upon questions and distinctions. How is the spirit that sings
not, or not even like, the sea? How does the singing of the spirit make the
world in which she lives, and in what sense is only the world of her singing
'for' her? How is singing related to self-making? How does the rage for order
of the poet relate to the singing of the spirit? What will be the material manifestation of the 'ghostlier demarcations' and 'keener sounds' that characterise
the poet's song as it rages for order? The female who sings in this poem will
probably be taken to represent the idea of order, an idealisation of a certain
view of human cognitive or perceptive ability as creative and ordering. Her
singing is a figurative way of saying that the poet and his friend perceive some
immanent order in their environment. The sea is said to be 'merely a place
by which she walked to sing', she is seen 'striding there alone' (ll. 17, 41):
there is just enough insistence on scene for it to be imaginable that a woman
is singing as she walks by the sea, and it is hearing this song that produces the
meditation of the poet. The question of the poet and his friend 'Whose spirit
is this?' (l. 18), then, hovers between asking whether a woman is seen as a
spirit, or whether a spirit is seen as a woman.

'She' is immediately said to sing 'beyond the genius of the sea' (l. 1), initiating a series of disjunctive comparisons: the cry of the sea remains body,
and does not form 'to mind or voice' (ll. 2–5); the utterance of 'her' song
is made 'word by word', distinguishing it from the 'medleyed sound' of the
sea (ll. 9–11); she is the 'maker' of a song (l. 15) whereas the sea is 'merely
a place' (l. 18); upon her singing, 'the sea, / Whatever self it had, became
the self / That was her song, for she was the maker' (ll. 38–40). The spirit's
song is superior to and transformative of the sea, which is like 'a body wholly
body' (l. 3), something purely physical and without meaning, without an
animating spirit to transform its 'grinding' (l. 13) and 'meaningless plungings' (l. 30) into sense. The female spirit, then, is distinguished from the sea
by being more than body, more than meaningless sound, by being capable
of world-creating verbal acts. And yet the song, the production of the spirit,
must in many respects be like the sound of the sea in order for it to be distinguished in these precise respects. Simon Critchley takes it that 'the near
homophony and full rhyme of "sea" and "she" are not simply fortuitous', and
suggests that 'sea' represents the real, and 'she' represents the imagination.[17]
It is of course not fortuitous that these words can be regarded as coupled in
the ways Critchley mentions, and Stevens is careful to parcel them out, at
times in a chiastic arrangement (as in ll. 1, 8: 'She . . . sea', 'sea . . . she'), to
mark their coupling. But no such couplings are simply fortuitous: they are
the product of the simultaneous contingency (from an ahistorical point of

view) and necessity (from a historical point of view) of the organisation of a particular language. The suggestion that there could be fortuitous events of such a nature has a corollary in the presumption that expressive and structural ends of language are separable, and that meaning is their reunion. But such a separation and reunion is one of the superstitions against which I am arguing in this book, and one which Stevens' poem sets out, in its own way, to contest. This contest can be seen in the inseparability of elements in the poem that had previously appeared purely material or purely spiritual. The poet brings the brute material of natural sound closer to human speech: even if the sound were only the 'dark voice of the sea' (l. 21), 'it would have been deep air, / The heaving speech of air' (ll. 25–6). But this sound is said to be 'more than that, / More even than her voice, and ours, among / The meaningless plungings of water and the wind' (ll. 28–30). The material aspect of the environment here appears beyond the voices of the singer and the poet, as previously 'she' was 'beyond the genius of the sea' (l. 1). These elements, the material and the spiritual, are inseparable and mutually redefining: it is their interplay, not their separation, in the act of being distinguished, that makes them mean.

The manner in which singing creates worlds is complex and qualified:

She was the single artificer of the world
In which she sang. And when she sang, the sea,
Whatever self it had, became the self
That was her song, for she was the maker. Then we,
As we beheld her striding there alone,
Knew that there never was a world for her
Except the one she sang and, singing, made. (ll. 37–43)

In a strong reading of the first sentence quoted, the singing alone creates the world, though there may be a weak reading, exploiting the standing ambiguity between the objective genitive (the world is the thing she makes) and the possessive (she belongs to that world without necessarily being its maker). The world-making that poetry or song can be thought to perform might be restricted (for fear of suggesting there is no world unless someone is singing) to a subjective world, or a self.[18] Even in this kind of reading, large claims for the power of poetry to make realities can be made. One argument, working against Julia Kristeva (see 'Spirit: Frank O'Hara', 'Measure: Robert Creeley', and 'Equivalence: Thomas A. Clark'), has suggested that,

exceeding the release of drives and the rhythms of the body, a new level of significance comes into being when a work of art, in our case a poem, is composed. This creation, related to transcendence or transformation . . . indicates poetry's phenomenological and ontological relevance.[19]

Taken at its strongest, this is an assertion that certain realities do not exist until they are the subjects of poems, posing all kinds of ticklish questions concerning for whom these realities do or do not exist before or after the poem is made, whether these realities include basic conceptual or cognitive knowledge (of tables and chairs, for example) or comprise solely the complex realities of self-conscious reflection on the nature of human existence, and, indeed, where it might be appropriate to draw a line between these two descriptions of reality.

The poem is not expansive on selves, noting only that 'the sea, / Whatever self it had, became the self / That was her song, for she was the maker' (ll. 38–40), and that the poet's rage for order consists in finding words, including words 'of ourselves and of our origins' (l. 55). The singer appears to transform the material reality of the sea into her self, a self that is made through singing, so that one might take realities such as the sea as existent only in the poeticising consciousness of the individual subject.[20] But, as has just been noted, the sea, or the environment that is encountered in the poem, somehow exceeds the very singing of which it is now said to become part. The poem resists a reading from the perspective of a naïve subjective ideal-ism.[21] The words 'of ourselves and of our origins' that the maker (bringing together the male poet, who speaks in the first person plural of his feelings, and the female singer, who was the maker of the world) feels a 'rage to order' (l. 53) may proceed from the self, or speak about the self, again exploiting the scope of 'of', allowing the poem to suggest that the words which belong to the self will also reveal something about it, perhaps about its 'origins' in the kinds of poetical-aesthetic act of world creation for which the poem may be taken.

The poet's words here clearly share with the mysterious female singer the capacity to make, drawing on the traditional description of the poet as maker. Is it possible not to identify the world-making activity of the singer with the rage for an orderly making by which the poet characterises his own posi-tion? This making cannot be said, however, entirely to bring into being the material realities it describes through its spiritual exercise: those realities are already more than the song, their existence as participation in meaningful-ness is 'more than that' (l. 28). The scene itself seems to possess a tendency to order: as the poet and Ramon Fernandez turn back from their walk at nightfall, the lights on fishing boats 'Mastered the night and portioned out the sea, / Fixing emblazoned zones and fiery poles, / Arranging, deepening, enchanting night' (ll. 49–51). The lights give an astrological order to the sky, presumably by casting their image upon the reflection of the sky in the sea. This kind of orderliness is that sought by the poet, and with a self-evident circularity in this very poem, which orders words of the sea. The other kinds of words the poet seeks to order are of 'ourselves and of our origins', as noted above, but also 'of the fragrant portals, dimly starred' (l. 54), these dim stars recalling the fishing lights that appear as stars in the sea, suggesting that the portal is an entrance to another realm, another elementary aspect of the human environment (ocean, sky), and figuratively the liminal area between states of human subjectivity. The fragrancy of the portals, in this case, would have a beguiling incoherence. But the portals can also, more mundanely, be read as the porches of the houses that become visible as the poet and his friend return to town, fragrant because open to the air.[22] Are these words of the fragrant portals words that one speaks on the veranda of an evening, or words that figure sensuously a transition from one state of selfhood to another in a process of poetic becoming? Ordered poetic words in the poem are both of these things.

The final line of the poem suggests that all of the world-creating, subjectivity-defining activity described by the poem, and, by strong implication, performed by its ordering words of the sea, will take a specific form in 'ghostlier demarcations, keener sounds' (l. 56). To take the second of these terms first, the sounds of the poem represent an urge, a rage to order words in a manner that is keener, presumably, than some prior or ordinary order. Keenness is intensity or acuity of mind or body, a sharpness that is often associated with the wind or with blades, it is eagerness and cunning, mental and verbal incision. The sounds in which the order of the words will be made manifest will be keener in abstract and concrete terms: the mental acuity and incision of the words and their material intensity are not to be separated in this phrase, just as they cannot be in reading. Such keenness can be seen in any of the phonological equivalences the poem offers up: to offer the most crude of examples, in the alliteration of the sea that 'Made constant cry, caused constantly a cry' (l. 5), in the 'sky acutest at its vanishing' (l. 35), in the 'zone' echoed in 'emblazoned zones' (l. 50). The 'ghostlier demarcations' embody the same paradox in a keener form, delimiting something, marking it out, but somehow with the increased spiritual presence concurring with a less palpable material presence.[23] The demarcations might be taken as the orthographic form of words, the complement to their sounds, but they, as the sounds of the words, are also the shape and form of the utterance in general, its material form taken as producing meaning, as being an utterance and not just sound and shape. They could be any form of markedness. The way in which such demarcations manifest themselves in the poem could be found in any attention-bearing feature, as in the interaction between the markedness of the first letters of the alliterative line cited above ('Made constant cry, caused constantly a cry', l. 5) and their interference with the markedness of syllable stress, generally iambic and pentametric in the poem, that goes against this pattern to suggest five stresses on the first syllable of every alliterated word. Such demarcations might be thought particularly ghostly, particularly impalpable, as a reader's perception of patterns within what is real itself organises the attention and distribution of energy that makes patterns.

The argument of this poem, then, concerns the inseparability of the material and the spiritual in poetic acts that, as utterances, present form and meaning sometimes synthetically and sometimes analytically. It is self-instantiating because it says that what it is doing is what it describes (the making of ordered words about the sea), but also because it says that how it does what it does (employing ghostlier demarcations, keener sounds in the ordering of its words) is also a part of its explicit semantic content. It is a poem that, in asking what kind of spirit is involved in the making of poems, instantiates the materially integrated operation of that spirit. The distinction between an explicit content and a manner of delivering it is, of course, feeble, as is that between brute noise and human speech complicated by the poem when it suggests the environment is more than voice, and also when, playing with syntax, the constant cry of the sea is said to be 'not ours although we understood, / Inhuman, of the veritable ocean' (ll. 6–7). The adjective (inhuman) seeks the closest noun (we) to qualify, but the candidate is not suitable (speakers are normally human), and so the adjective reverts to the preceding noun (cry): the humanity that distinguishes the speaker from the sea is temporarily elided with the cry that the speaker understands although it is not his. Reading Stevens as a poet occupied by the mutual distinction of self and world that creates both self and world, and placing an emphasis on cognitive and linguistic aspects of that power to distinguish make Stevens sound close to earlier nineteenth-century German romantic philosophers.[24] To conclude this chapter I will suggest that a mutually illuminating comparison is possible between Stevens' poem and one text of German romantic poetology.

Friedrich Hölderlin presents many of the views that I have just attempted to read from Stevens' poem: he presents the opposition and reconciliation of self and other, sameness and difference, as a relation between possible perceptions of the self as chaotic, nature as organised, or, alternatively, the self as organised, nature as chaotic.[25] This reconciliation produces the highest human sentiments.[26] Nature begins as an aorgic principle opposed to human organisation, but then their polarities are reversed in a sense of the alternating interrelation of vital spirit and steady order in each sphere, the human and natural. Just as I was suggesting was the case in Stevens' poem, there is an alternation between identifying the human as the ordering principle beyond nature, and nature as the ordering principle beyond the human: both aspects of this alternation are vital (see also discussions of nature and artifice in 'Figure: Walter Ralegh' and 'Measure: William Wordsworth').

Hölderlin suggests that the poetic spirit is 'the communal soul which [is] common to everyone and proper to each'. There are in the poetic spirit 'harmonious alternation and progressive striving wherein the spirit tends to reproduce itself within itself and others'. Spirit aims at the 'communality and unified simultaneity of all parts'. There is a 'postulate which commands the spirit to move beyond itself and reproduce itself, within itself and others'.[27] The poetic state is a state in which a difference from the outer sphere is willingly entered into:

> the new state where man posits himself freely in harmonious opposition with an outer sphere that, precisely because he is *not* so intimately connected with it, he can abstract from it, and can abstract from himself insofar as he *is* posited in it, and [that he] can reflect upon himself insofar as he is not posited in it[.][28]

The environment presented in 'The Idea of Order at Key West' presents such an outer sphere. The complexity of the relationship between the sense of order and chaos, of the internal and external is immense, and difficult to present analytically. Connections and oppositions between all the elements of composition can be conceived as pertaining to the material or the formal aspects of the poetic life, alternately:

> Now, if what is directly opposed to the spirit, the organ by which the spirit is comprised and by means of which all opposition is made possible, could be looked at and understood not only as that by which the harmoniously con-nected is opposed in form, but also [as that] by which it is connected in form, if it could be looked at and understood not only as that by which the various unharmonious moods are materially opposed and connected in form, but also [as that] by which they are connected in material and opposed in form, if it could be looked at and understood not only as that which, as connecting merely formal life and as particular and material one not connecting but only opposing and separating, if it could be looked at as material, as connecting, if the organ of the spirit could be looked at as that which, in order to make possible the harmoniously opposed, must be *receptive* – for the one as well as for the other harmoniously opposed – so that, to the extent that it is a formal opposition for the pure poetic life, it must also be formal connection, that, insofar as it is mate-rially opposing for the fixed poetic life and its moods, it must also be materially connecting, that what defines and determines is not only negative, that it is also positive, that, if considered in isolation with what is harmoniously connected, it is opposed to the one as well as to the other, yet [is] the union of the two, if both are considered simultaneously, then that act of the spirit which, as regards the significance, entailed only a continuous conflict, will be as much a uniting one as it was an opposing one.[29]

The sequence of qualifications is virtually impossible to follow, but its purpose, to describe the state in which an act of the poetic spirit can be considered as uniting as much as opposing, is relatively clear. It is clear enough also in refusing any simple opposition in the material and formal aspects of acts of the poetic spirit: what connects materially and opposes formally must also be understood to oppose materially and connect formally.

I do not think Hölderlin is necessarily thinking of the features of poetic language in any simple sense when making this statement, but he might be understood on that level. When 'The grinding water and the gasping wind' (l. 13) are said maybe to stir in all the singer's phrases, the two noun phrases can be understood as formally opposed, contrasting the sea and the wind, but also formally connected, comparing their sounds; they are materially connected, in the serial alliteration of 'g', 'w', and the formation of the participial adjectives employed, yet opposed in the phonemes that follow the alliterating morphemes, and so on in innumerable ways. Conceiving of these oppositions and connections dialectically is an act of the poetic spirit, just as for Hölderlin conceiving of a world as composed of such connections and oppositions is an act of the poetic spirit, in both cases an act that cannot be conceived immaterially. Stevens' formally opposed and materially connected, materially opposed and formally connected language is adequate to an encounter with the world, the environment, the landscape of the poem that sees now the human self, now the natural world as ordered and hierarchical, now the human self, now the natural world as chaotic, aorgic and impulsive. This depiction of the standing of the sea, the wind, the singer, the poet in relation to one another, as beyond one another, or more than one another is an act of the poetic spirit, conceived of as a necessary striving with the material, as a necessity that emerges out of contingency.

With regard to necessity and contingency also, what Hölderlin has to say about the spirit runs parallel to the arguments concerning poetic language presented by this book. Hölderlin's editor notes that the unifying principle of reason is said to exist only through its interaction with contingent reality: 'rationality in general no longer unfolds as the mere transcendence of the empirical, but instead the implicit totality of the *ratio* is understood to be fundamentally contingent on its progressive integration with the realm of the sensible and particular'.[30] This view has consequences for Hölderlin's concepts of law and lawlessness, of free and restricted activity. The desiring imagination opposes itself to the moralising intellect, such that a congruence between them is possible, but merely contingent:

> In that anarchy of representations where the imagination is considered theoretically, a unity of the manifold, an ordering of perceptions was indeed possible yet accidental . . . In this natural state of fantasy where [the imagination] is considered in relation to the faculty of desire, moral lawfulness is indeed possible yet accidental.

There are only ever accidents of lawfulness or coherence, where what is desired turns out to be what is appropriate. There is a state of the desiring imagination that unites 'necessity and freedom, the restricted and the unrestricted', but 'It is [a] mere fortune to be thus attuned.'[31] There is nothing but luck in turning out to be one of those people whose desires correspond to the best choices, whose imagination acts, even before knowing it, in correspondence with the intellect. Such an interrelation between contingency and necessity is also evident in the attunement of poetic language, where the desiring imagination is united in a particular text with the law of the intellect, luckily.

Notes

1. Friedrich Schlegel, *Dialogue on Poetry and Literary Aphorisms*, trans., intro. and ed. Ernst Behler and Roman Struc (University Park and London: The Pennsylvania State University Press, 1968 [1799–1800]), pp. 75–6.
2. Roman Jakobson, *Language in Literature*, ed. Krystyna Pomorska and Stephen Rudy (London and Cambridge, MA: The Belknap Press of Harvard University Press, 1987), p. 93.
3. *Essays in Criticism: Second Series* (London: Macmillan, 1908 [1879]), pp. 155, 157–8.
4. John Stuart Mill, 'Thoughts on Poetry And Its Varieties' (1833), in *Autobiography and Literary Essays*, ed. John M. Robson and Jack Stillinger, *The Collected Edition of the Works of John Stuart Mill*, ed. J.M. Robson et al., I (Toronto: University of Toronto Press, 1981), 343–65 (p. 359).
5. A. E. Housman, *The Name and Nature of Poetry: The Leslie Stephen Lecture Delivered at Cambridge 9 May 1933* (Cambridge: Cambridge University Press, 1933), p. 47.
6. Ibid. pp. 16–21, 49–50, 44, 38.
7. Ezra Pound, *Collected Early Poems of Ezra Pound*, ed. Michael John King, intro. by Louis L. Martz (London: Faber and Faber, 1977 [1908–12]), p. 163. Martz notes, 'Introduction', p. xiv, that Pound believed 'the poetic power breaks through the crust of daily life and apprehends a transcendent flow of spirit, or energy, or divine power'.
8. Ibid. pp. 86, 26–7, 149, 91, 97.
9. Emerson R. Marks, *Taming the Chaos: English Poetic Diction Theory Since the Renaissance* (Detroit: Wayne State University Press, 1998), pp. 284–5.
10. Ezra Pound, *ABC of Reading* (New York: New Directions, 1960 [1934]), p. 28.
11. Ibid. pp. 32, 37, 96.
12. 'Poetry, Myth, Reality', in *The Language of Poetry*, ed. Allen Tate (Princeton: Princeton University Press; London: Humphrey Milford, Oxford University Press, 1942), pp. 3–33 (p. 3).

13. I. A. Richards, 'The Interactions of Words', in *The Language of Poetry*, pp. 65–87 (p. 83).

14. Winifred Nowottny, *The Language Poets Use* (London: Athlone, 1962), pp. 32, 97.

15. 'The Noble Rider and the Sound of Words', pp. 91–125 (p. 116).

16. Wallace Stevens, *Collected Poems* (London: Faber and Faber, 1955; repr. 2006), pp. 110–11.

17. Simon Critchley, *Very Little . . . Almost Nothing*, 2nd rev. edn (London: Routledge, 2004), p. 223. Critchley previously connects Stevens's sense of poetry replacing religion, and giving, through the violence of its language, a new turn to the plain sense of things, with Jena romanticism, including Hölderlin, pp. 118–19. He states that 'Stevens's conception of the task of poetry clearly situates him within the high tradition of early romanticism', p. 235. My argument about the inseparability of argumentative and formal features of the poem is directly opposed to Critchley's sense that there may be a 'problem with the prosodic or rhetorical dimension of the poem . . . that it is so luxurious that it risks obscuring the quite precise argument', p. 221.

18. Gerald L. Bruns, 'Stevens Without Epistemology', in *Wallace Stevens: The Poetics of Modernism*, ed. Albert Gelpi (Cambridge: Cambridge University Press, 1985), pp. 24–40 (p. 26), calls Stevens' 'poetry a poetry of world-making', but goes on to say why this should be regarded as a regrettable fact.

19. Jennifer Anna Gosetti-Ferrencei, *Heidegger, Hölderlin, and the Subject of Poetic Language: Toward a New Poetics of Dasein* (New York: Fordham University Press, 2004), p. 215.

20. The relationship between language, self and time has been stated in rather opaque terms by Kristine S. Santilli, *Poetic Gesture: Myth, Wallace Stevens, and the Motions of Poetic Language* (New York and London: Routledge, 2002), p. 95.

21. Critchley makes similar points, pp. 225, 231.

22. See OED, 'portal': 'In South America and the south-western United States: a veranda, a portico, an arcade.' Although Key West is in Florida, this seems a possible reading.

23. It is perhaps interesting to note that 'demarcation' comes into English from Spanish, having first been used, according to the OED, in a papal bull dividing the Spanish from the Portuguese New World in 1493. From Key West in Florida, a viewpoint onto Central and South America and the islands dotting the Atlantic, and in the presence (literal or metaphorical) of a Hispanic friend (whether or not the friend is ironically designated, and whether or not Ramon Fernandez is the Mexican-Parisian critic and essayist known for a sharp transition from socialism to collaborationism during the war), there is surely a sense that the demarcations of Stevens' world are geo-political realities, themselves also occupying the necessary border between fantasies of self creation and tough material practicality.

24. Charles Altieri, 'Why Stevens Must be Abstract, or What a Poet can Learn from Painting', in *Wallace Stevens: The Poetics of Modernism*, pp. 86–118 (p. 111) locates a similar negotiation of the ideal and material as is noted here.

25. In Gosetti-Ferrencei's Heideggerian reading, p. 5, the provisionality of the poetic subject is related to poetic language and its truths: 'poetic language, furthermore, is shown to be an access to truth neither as correctness nor as the correspondence between thought and actuality but as a process of partial, and therefore finite, disclosure'. Poetic language is considered as a means of rendering being, p. 99: 'If the meaning borne by poetic language seems elusive, that which it brings to words, when regarded ontologically, is the very elusiveness of Being – the impossibility of grasping Being as absolute presence ... Poetic language, through an array of formal strategies of indirection, expresses this play by evoking relations to the world which are other than a straightforward signification.'

26. 'The Ground for "Empedocles"' (c. 1799), in Friedrich Hölderlin, *Essays and Letters on Theory*, trans. and ed. Thomas Pfau (Albany, NY: State University of New York Press, 1988), pp. 50–61 (p. 53).

27. Hölderlin, 'On the Operations of the Poetic Spirit' (1800), in *Essays and Letters*, pp. 62–82 (p. 62).

28. Ibid. p. 75.

29. Ibid. p. 69.

30. Thomas Pfau, 'Introduction', in *Essays and Letters*, p. 3.

31. 'On the Law of Freedom' (1794), *Essays and Letters*, pp. 33–4 (p. 33); see also Pfau's introduction, pp. 15–16.

CHAPTER SEVEN

Spirit: Frank O'Hara

The tradition I sketched in the run-up to my discussion of 'The Idea of Order at Key West', that of identifying a spark or charge in poetic language, is sometimes manifested in psychologistic forms in the twentieth century: the energy expressing itself in poetic language is not that of a divine order-ing spirit, nor the character of a people, nor a latent 'chemical' power in the language itself, but in the psyche of the poet concerned. The surrealist and poet André Breton thought this way. Adopting the language of the poet-critic Pierre Reverdy, who said that one 'creates . . . a strong image, new for the mind/spirit [esprit], by bringing together without comparison two distant realities of which *the mind/spirit* [esprit] *only* has grasped the relations',[1] Breton writes in an explicitly Freudian context, intending to castigate 'certain ridiculous tendencies of spiritualism'.[2] The 'practice' of poetry is thought to bear revolutionary possibilities, possibilities created by the surrealist image:

> The value of the image depends upon the beauty of the spark obtained [from the interaction of two distant realities]; it is, consequently, a function of the differ-ence of potential between the two conductors. When the difference exists only slightly, as in a comparison, the spark is lacking . . . We are therefore obliged to admit that the two terms of the image are not deduced one from the other by the mind for the specific purpose of producing the spark, that they are simul-taneous products of the activity I call Surrealist, reason's role being limited to taking note of, and appreciating, the luminous phenomenon.[3]

Frank O'Hara, one of the subjects of this chapter, was familiar with this manner of addressing the spirit or spark or charge of poetic language, as he was with Pound's manner, discussed in the previous chapter. This chapter asks whether such psychic charges in poems may be attributed to the energy of an individual subject in opposition to language systems, or if psychic energy is fully linguistic and social. I will address a poem by O'Hara that is, as much of his work, egotistic and intensely sociable at once, the poem

'Mayakovsky'.[4] The two theoretical alternatives will be approached with reference to Julia Kristeva, who works with a concept of subjectivity constituted by drives known through their disruption of the symbolic order in language, and V. N. Voloshinov, who insists that psychic facts are only possible in language. O'Hara gave serious attention in his essay on Boris Pasternak's *Doctor Zhivago* to the mutual interrelation of individual and social energy, seeming to prioritise the individual:

> The human individual is the subject of historical events, not vice versa; he is the repository of life's force. And while he may suffer, may be rendered helpless, may be killed, if he has the perceptiveness to realize this he knows that events require his participation to occur ... This qualitative distinction between two kinds of significance is as foreign to our own society as it is to that of the U.S.S.R. (CP, pp. 506–7)

This characterisation retains a strong sense of the dialectical relationship between individual energy and historical events, particularly political violence. The life force cannot be separated from the broader historical event because its participation is always required for there to be historical events. This intertwining of the individual and the historical, which is thought of as alien to both post-war America and the USSR, has parallels in the linguistic sphere to be discussed shortly.[5] It also has parallels in O'Hara's interest in and writing about the visual arts. O'Hara describes Abstract Expressionism, a movement in American painting during the 1950s, as 'the art of serious men':

> They are serious because they are *not* isolated. So out of this populated cavern of self come brilliant, uncomfortable works, works that don't reflect you or your life, though you can know them. Art is not *your* life, it is someone else's. Something very difficult for the acquisitive spirit to understand, and for that matter the spirit of joinership that animates communism.[6]

O'Hara also cites the sculptor David Smith on the social mode of existence of the objects of art:

> no object he [the sculptor] has seen, no fantasy he envisions, no world he knows, is outside that of other men. No man has seen what another has not, or lacks the components and power to assemble. It is impossible to produce an imperceptible work[.][7]

The objects with which the artist's imagination works, and the objects it produces, are shared objects.

Vladimir Mayakovsky, the revolutionary era Russian poet who killed himself in 1930, gives his name to the title of one poem by O'Hara, appears in many others, is the dedicatee of 'Second Avenue', and the model for 'A True Account of Talking to the Sun at Fire Island'. The poem taking his name is a composition from four separate manuscripts, dating between February and July 1954. The poet James Schuyler wrote to O'Hara's editor with the following information about the poem:

> Two of these poems were 'found' by me at 326 East 49th – one in a book. Frank said he had forgotten about it when I produced it. I wanted him to include them in *Meditations in an Emergency*, but he didn't think them substantial enough to stand by themselves. I suggested he make one poem of them, and he dug out of his MSS pile the other two stanzas, which I don't think I'd seen before. He liked the result and said that since it was 'my' poem I had to think up a title – which I easily and instantly did – Frank had (again) been reading Mayakovsky and the book was on his desk. . . . The 'bricks' he was carrying were the supports of a John Ashbery bookcase[.] (*CP*, pp. 532–3)

Mayakovsky is known for his exuberance, his intense working of internal and terminal rhyme, his egotism, and all of these as they channel poetic personality. The book O'Hara was reading was presumably the compilation published in London in 1942, which contains Mayakovsky's poem on talking to the sun, 'A Most Extraordinary Adventure', and also the poems to which O'Hara has been said to allude in his 'Mayakovsky': 'Homeward' and 'A Cloud in Trousers'. The closest correspondences emerge in this passage from the latter poem:

> And I feel
> that 'I'
> is for me too shallow.
> Someone bursts out of me and won't be smothered.
>
> Hallo!
> Who's speaking?
> Mother?
> Mother!
> Your son is beautifully ill!
> Mother!
> His heart is on fire!
> . . .
> Mother! I can't sing.
> In the church of my heart the choir is on fire![8]

I will offer a brief characterisation of O'Hara's poem now, returning to some specific aspects later.

Mayakovsky

1
My heart's aflutter!
I am standing in the bath tub
crying. Mother, mother
who am I? If he
will just come back once
and kiss me on the face
his coarse hair brush
my temple, it's throbbing!

then I can put on my clothes
I guess, and walk the streets.

2
I love you. I love you,
but I'm turning to my verses
and my heart is closing
like a fist.

Words! be
sick as I am sick, swoon,
roll back your eyes, a pool,

and I'll stare down
at my wounded beauty
which at best is only a talent
for poetry.

Cannot please, cannot charm or win
what a poet!
and the clear water is thick

with bloody blows on its head.
I embraced a cloud,
but when I soared
it rained.

3
That's funny! there's blood on my chest
oh yes, I've been carrying bricks
what a funny place to rupture!
and now it is raining on the ailanthus
as I step out onto the window ledge
the tracks below me are smoky and
glistening with a passion for running
I leap into the leaves, green like the sea

4
Now I am quietly waiting for
the catastrophe of my personality
to seem beautiful again,
and interesting, and modern.

The country is grey and
brown and white in trees,
snows and skies of laughter
always diminishing, less funny
not just darker, not just grey.

It may be the coldest day of
the year, what does he think of
that? I mean, what do I? And if I do,
perhaps I am myself again.

The four sections of the poem move through various forms of more or less
narcissistic reflection on the feelings of abandonment, dejection, disillusion,
ecstasy, and abject yet camp self-pity that seem to make up the emotional
repertoire of the poet-speaker.[9] Each of these reflections, by being related in
a poem that takes a poet's name for its title, and by being associated with the
remarks on making poems in the second section, are reflections upon poetic
subjectivity, its impulses, rhythms and drives.[10] Taking a poet's name as its
title, even though the means by which it acquired that title are fortuitous,
the poem suggests it might be doing one or more of several things: addressing
the poet posthumously; speaking as if the poet, or in the poet's voice; speaking in some way so as to provide a picture or résumé of that poet's life and/
or works and/or attitudes. There are also various kinds of hybrid possibilities
here that seem rather plausible given the poem itself. Decisions, or, perhaps
more accurately, waverings between these possibilities are largely determined by the deployment of pronouns. Thus, to achieve continuity between
the 'I' of the first and second sections (as, with or without a knowledge of
the MS history of the poem, one is inclined to), a reader can posit a male,
homosexual speaker, who is a poet, who thinks about writing poems, who is
dejected by the idea of himself as a poet. O'Hara himself could fulfil most of
these positions, but then why agree to call the poem 'Mayakovsky'? Either the
poem addresses Mayakovsky, who is then the man whose return and kiss is
desired in the third person in the first section, becoming a directly addressed
second person of the second section; or what is known of Mayakovsky (his
heterosexuality, for example) needs to be forgotten in order to produce a consistent voice speaking from Mayakovsky's perspective, providing a selective
'Mayakovsky', with some features deleted, re-imagined, re-accented. This
complex process of poetic distinction, identification and absorption is the-

matised in the poem, as well as being played out at the level of its pronouns. The speaker begins by crying 'Mother, mother / who am I?' (ll. 3–4) and ends by suggesting that, in certain hazy conditions, 'perhaps I am myself again' (l. 49). One might also describe the 'leap into the leaves, green like the sea' (l. 36) that the poet makes, in his ecstatic phase, as a form of reabsorption, a dissolution of identity in poetic rapture. The poem concerns in large part the coincidence or non-coincidence of personalities with themselves and one another, the interplay of pronouns providing the location for the disclosures of poetic spirit that the poem makes.

The experience of reading 'Mayakovsky' is comparable to reading another poem by O'Hara ('For Grace, After a Party') and 'not yet knowing, or deciding to know, how to situate and flesh out its pronouns or how to specify the social meaning and detail of the desires that are summoned up in lyric to surround them'.[11] Disclosures of spirit often take the form of ambivalently hyperbolic or semi-ironised rhetorical gestures, such as the qualification of the reference to the speaker's temple, 'it's throbbing!' (l. 8), the command to the speaker's words to 'be / sick as I am sick, swoon, / roll back your eyes' (ll. 15–17), the description of the poet's beauty as 'wounded' (l. 19): the poet waits 'for the catastrophe of my personality / to seem beautiful again, / and interesting, and modern' (ll. 38–40). These gestures might be described as camp, but they also relate to those serious concerns of poetry: what can be said, to whom, with what personal consequences for both speaker and addressee.[12] The physicality of the poet is also tied to the poetic act. The throbbing temple (l. 8), the 'heart' 'closing / like a fist' (ll. 13–14), the 'rupture' leaving 'blood on my chest' (ll. 30, 29), the poet 'glistening with a passion for running' (l. 35) all figure the body as register or medium of the poetic act in one way or another.[13] In various ways, then, this poem rehearses the integration and disintegration of the poetic act within personal boundaries of identity, body, expressive gesture, and location.

This terrain of a poetic subjectivity at work in and against its socio-economic and linguistic environment is equally Kristeva's, who herself engages directly with Mayakovsky. For Mayakovsky, rhythm is the energetic charge of poetic language:

> Where this dull roar of a rhythm comes from is a mystery. In my case it's all kinds of repetitions in my mind of noises, rocking motions, or in fact any phenomenon with which I can associate a sound. . . . I don't know if the rhythm exists outside me or only inside me – more probably inside. But there must be a jolt to awaken it[.] . . . Rhythm is the fundamental force, the fundamental energy of verse. You can't explain it, you can only talk about it as you do about magnetism or electricity. Magnetism and electricity are manifestations of energy.[14]

This energy is probably more internal than external, but nonetheless corresponds to external rhythms. It requires a stimulus, a spark, but has an elemental energy.

Kristeva claims Mayakovsky's interest in rhythm as the feature that dominates poetic discourse is an example of the meeting of the semiotic and symbolic that, she contends, characterises poetic language. She suggests that the phonological patterning of Mayakovsky's verse, along with that of his contemporary Velimir Khlebnikov, should suffice to awaken scientific linguists to poetry. An interest in rhythm as a challenge to authority is said to be one reason for the poet being put to death, recalling the theme of an essay by Roman Jakobson on 'The Generation that Wasted its Poets':

> The poet is put to death because he wants to turn rhythm into a dominant element; because he wants to make language perceive what it doesn't want to say, provide it with its matter independently of the sign, and free it from denotation.[15]

Language here is conceived as something against which the rhythms of psychological drives, of quotidian life, and so on, strive: it is a force that can be made to perceive things, and that has preferences about what it does and does not do. In the next chapter I will describe the way in which rhythm, seen in particular in the repetition and semanticisation of phonological units, is taken to disrupt and dismay the symbolic order by Kristeva. I will show that rhythm, phonological concentration and other devices are not somehow separate from language, but part of its daily business. Here I will read Kristeva's work on pronouns and the relationships between utterances against O'Hara's poem.

Having noted that the Anglo-American tradition of philosophical linguistics has been attentive to the fact that language is used by subjects, and that pronouns, 'fixed points in a process, stases in a flux, momentary presences in the normative use of language,' carry the burden of placing this subjectivity within an utterance, Kristeva suggests that the opposition of 'I' to 'you' allows for the positing of a third person, a transcending 'I' outside the particular utterance, a third personal position that makes fiction possible. Dislocating play between these subject positions in an utterance is presented as an 'irruption of drives in the symbolic domain' which 'disrupt thetic positioning and, on account of this fact, all the tidy disposition of discursive instances [of the pronouns] commanded by it'.[16] Kristeva then analyses the 'Chants de Maldoror' of Lautréamont to show how a textual economy that engages in the perpetual shifting of subject positions differs from the normative use of language, suggesting that, 'put on trial/in process . . . by the introjected other, "I" is a rhythmic movement'.[17]

O'Hara's pronouns could be approached in this way. In various poems he employs 'you' in such a way that it hovers between an intimate second-person singular, and an impersonal pronoun ('one'), with the effect of bringing together the positions of speaker, (intra-diegetic) addressee and (extra-diegetic) audience. So in 'To You':

if the moon or a grasping candle
sheds a little light or even dark
you become a landscape in a landscape
with rocks and craggy mountains[.] (CP, p. 342, ll. 5–8)

The intimate address to a lover, the contours of whose body are exaggerated in this half-light, is legible as the speaker's imagined experience of his own body in such light, and remains open enough for readers to include themselves within the reference of that second-person/impersonal pronoun. In this poem O'Hara is not far from certain conventions of love lyric whereby the speaker and possible addressees are united: 'there's no need for vistas we are one / in the complicated foreground of space' (p. 343, ll.15–16). The addressee here, whatever combination of personality within the world of the poem and audience beyond the poem is taken to fill that role, joins with the speaker, either in the abstract (there's no need for a vista because you and I have combined, are one) or in becoming a vista (there's no need for a vista because we are a vista). Such transient coincidences of subject position take place in a poem that is concerned with what 'we love about art' (p. 342, l. 3), and in which the participants are compared to 'a couple of painters in neon' (p. 343, l. 23): the kind of thinking and speaking that art provokes is thinking and speaking that complicate the deictic function of pronouns. Again, in 'Having a Coke with You' (CP, p. 360), the specificity of the other person referred to as 'you' ('in your orange shirt', 'because of your love for yoghurt', ll. 3, 4) blends with the poet in the reflection on an exhibition of portraiture that 'you suddenly wonder why in the world anyone ever did them' (l. 12), only for the positions to be separated again: 'I look / at you and I would rather look at you than all the portraits in the world' (ll. 12–13). And again, this is a poem in which the apprehension of art objects is the occasion for the possible ambivalence in pronoun reference.

I have already suggested that in 'Mayakovsky' the poem's title creates a blend of possibilities for the subject-placing pronouns in the poem, somewhere between Mayakovsky and O'Hara, or one speaking as or through the other, and said that the poem is about the integration and disintegration of poetic subjectivity. The 'I' who begins the poem 'standing in the bath tub' (l. 2) is related to the 'he' whose return is desired; the 'I' of the second section is opposed to a 'you' who is loved by the 'I'; the 'I' of the third section is isolated from other pronouns; and finally the 'I' of the fourth section is related to a further, or the same, 'he'. The simplest solution to the pronouns of the poem is to maintain their consistency of reference, and have the poet address an absent lover in the first section, who is present in the second, absent and unreferred to in the third, absent and referred to in the fourth. But this solution is too neat, particularly in relation to the poem's final four lines:

> It may be the coldest day of
> the year, what does he think of
> that? I mean, what do I? And if I do,
> perhaps I am myself again.

The absent male is presented with a scene that perhaps figures the abject feelings of the poet, suffering in the cold, giving the question the tone of either an accusation or a rhetorical invitation to be impressed by the severity of the weather. As is frequently the case with O'Hara's poems, one has to find a highly specific phrasal intonation to prevent lines from being flat or absurd (what could anyone really think about it being the coldest day of the year?). But the flat or absurd senses linger on behind the often hyperbolic and exuberant intonations. Thus, 'I mean, what do I?' when richly intoned, switches the interrogation back towards the poet: how does he himself feel about this desolate, unfunny environment? But the flat intonation produces a corrective that suggests the poet has actually mistaken the persons of his poem: the 'he' is really 'I', the addresser and the addressee are the same person. This flat intonation produces an interpretation of the final line whereby the poet becomes himself again, uniting the 'I' and the 'he', in a narcissistic poetic act that has been the subject of the poem all along: the 'pool' the words formed and into which the poet 'stare[s] down / at my wounded beauty' (ll. 17–19) has the role of the pool into which Narcissus stares to admire his own reflection. All the pronoun positions are outlets for the poet.

Kristeva suggests that the continual shifts of pronoun reference in Lautréamont share the function of all poetic language – a challenge to the paternal, theological force of the symbolic order. The 'explosion of identity' is said to occur 'under the menace of an all-powerful, crushing father, depriving the "I" of its body, its skin, its scalp (displacement of castration)'. The disruption of pronoun position is, then, a symptom of the oppression enforced by the paternal, symbolic order, but also a means of combating it: 'the multiplication of each discursive shifter prevents any theologisation of the place of the "other"', thereby making a place for the semiotic in its contrapuntal relationship with the symbolic.[18] But O'Hara's pronouns do no such work. From an initial moment of crisis that sees the poet doubting his identity and calling upon his mother, the poem concludes with the possible identification of the poet and the powerful, adored, absent male figure of the first and fourth sections. This is a strongly homosocial poem that rejects the mother for an emergent poetic identity associated with absent and desired masculinity. Perhaps, then, O'Hara's pronouns do not follow Kristeva's model, or the socio-economic conditions in which his pronominal deictic shifts take place do not give them the same value as those of Lautréamont. (Kristeva works very hard to establish precise socio-economic conditions in which the poetic effects she describes take on their revolutionary character.) But to respond to the poem in this way is to ignore the tentativeness of its closure, and to give too much to the idea of the normative in discourse. The 'I' of the poem will be himself again only perhaps, and only 'if I do', where that 'doing' has no clear referent: is it that the speaker does think what he thinks about it perhaps being the coldest day of the year? Or that he does mean to ask what he himself thinks rather than what some other 'he' thinks of it being possibly the coldest day of the year? This is not a speaker who can be sure who he is, or even attribute mental contents to himself rather than to another. And therefore this speaker displays a strong sense of the inherently social nature of his utterance, through the very means of formally identifying his utterance as his, or another's: its pronouns.

I would like now to turn to V. N. Voloshinov, whose modelling of psychic life is more fully linguistic and social than Kristeva's. Voloshinov employs a vocabulary that has already been seen in Pound and Breton: 'Meaning is the *effect of interaction between speaker and listener produced via the material of a particular sound complex*. It is like an electric spark that occurs only when two different terminals are hooked together.'[19] But socio-linguistic interaction, rather than the energy inherent in language or released via a certain manner of disposing of it, is the focus of Voloshinov's text. Psychological realities are only to be understood as linguistic, and therefore material, realities. There cannot be any phenomena of the understanding, nor of the psychology that are pre-linguistic: people don't have understanding or psychology unless they have language. Language is inherently social:

> *consciousness itself can arise and become a viable fact only in the material embodiment of signs*. The understanding of a sign is, after all, an act of reference between the sign apprehended and other, already known signs; in other words, understanding is a response to signs with signs . . . Social psychology in fact is not located anywhere within (in the 'souls' of communicating subjects) but entirely and completely *without* – in the word, the gesture, the act.[20]

Voloshinov's insistence on the semiotic nature of human inner life goes deeper than even the understanding, arriving at experience itself: '*experience exists even for the person undergoing it only in the material of signs*'. This sense of the semiotic materiality of experience is in opposition to idealism, with its tendency 'to remove all sense, all meaning from the material world and to locate it in a-temporal, a-spatial Spirit'. Voloshinov states that any physiological process, such as the circulation of the blood or breathing, can be experienced semiotically, even though he is opposed to physiological explanations of language. Psychological introspection cannot take the observer behind language, because introspection is itself linguistic: 'in the process of introspection we engage our experience into a context of other signs we understand'.[21] To presume that one can identify a psychological level of meaning that is pre-linguistic, that posits a pre-social individual, is therefore to be regarded as an illusion of Freudianism.

Voloshinov's argument proceeds by a history of linguistic thought in which subjectivist and objectivist trends are opposed to one another, trends in which language is understood to be on the one hand the continual creative product of its users, the ever-changing material manifestation of the activities of the spirit, and on the other an abstraction behind the superficial phenomena of utterance that provides a normative identity for each particular instance: 'If, for the first trend, language is an ever-flowing stream of speech acts in which nothing remains fixed and identical to itself, then, for the second trend, language is the stationary rainbow arched over that stream.'[22] Voloshinov seeks a synthesis of the opposed elements of individual and society, utterance and language. The objectivist trend is mistaken because speakers do not experience their utterances in relation to an external norm, a static form towards which they orient themselves when speaking (such as a particular grammatical form, a declension of a noun, or a speech genre, such as the rhetorical question), but towards other sets of utterances. Understanding is understanding in relation to palpable socio-linguistic circumstances, and not abstract forms: 'orientation in the particular, given context and in the particular, given situation – orientation in the dynamic process of becoming and not "orientation" in some inert state'. Subjectivism is criticised for adhering to an illusion of a spiritual life distinct from language: 'Everything of real importance lies within; the outer element can take on real importance only by becoming a vessel for the inner, by becoming expression of spirit'. Voloshinov, on the other hand, consistently argues for the consubstantiality of spirit and social speech: 'the immediate social situation and the broader social milieu wholly determine – and determine from within, so to speak – the structure of an utterance'. Such an attitude has implications for the understanding of creativity in language, which must be re-described as the manipulation of particular ideological positions.[23] All such expressive utterances are ways of saying what is important, not at the crude level of identifying simple objects of appetite or desire, but in prioritising forms of utterance that are always oriented towards correlated social practices, modes of occupying the world, by using accent and evaluation to express the rank-ordering of various parts of a semiotic reality.

Kristeva insists that the fluid shifting of pronouns is beyond and against normative discourse. But Voloshinov's argument is that norms in discourse are always particular socialised norms rather than being idealised abstractions. That is, there would be no normative discourse that escaped entirely from potential shifts in pronoun reference, no completely unpoetic discourse, no discourse that failed somehow to reimagine who 'I' is. Even in very unpoetic discourse, the pronoun series is interrelated, and pronouns are no less open to thematisation, revaluation and re-accentuation than other nouns. 'We' or 'they', when used with non-specific referents ('we don't do that sort of thing round here', 'they would say that') contest and imply value, and imply values for the 'I', 'you' and other possible positions. O'Hara's poem concludes tentatively, redefining its 'I', the very poetic subjectivity that is its occasion, through, with and as other possible people.[24] The rapprochement of the two pronoun positions is not altogether unlike the spark created by the distance between two images grasped by the spirit, in Breton's development of Reverdy, with which this chapter began, only these two terms ('I', 'he') are not merely grasped by the spirit, but mediate the spirit in discourse.

Kristeva also presents allusions to other literary works as a means of disrupting the symbolic order in Lautréamont's text. She begins with a rigid reading of J. L. Austin's work on speech acts, arguing that if speaking can be an act, then 'certain utterances comprise in themselves a constraint upon the interlocutor'. Constraints upon the interlocutor are then divided into two kinds:

> the *juridical function* ('I impose conditions and a discourse-universe') and that which we will call the *possessive function*, which can either be of adherence or opposition ('I adhere to your speech or I refute it, but in any case I am possessed by it, and I possess it')[.]

The process of allusion is, according to Kristeva, marked by all predecessor texts having the character of law, imposing the juridical function, and by the new text seeking to appropriate the juridical role. Such modern texts as Lautréamont's do not satisfy themselves with producing an effect upon the person to whom they are addressed, as other illocutionary acts, but put in question and revitalise the very possibility of signification. The transformations Lautréamont's texts impose upon predecessor texts demonstrate that they are not content 'to comply with the jurisdiction of the presupposed'.[25] It is hard to see, however, how the possible relations between O'Hara's text and Mayakovsky's could be either juridical or possessive. Whatever conditions or discourse universe Mayakovsky might be taken to have imposed, O'Hara

takes liberties with it; and whilst there may be possession or at least ventrilo-
quy in the relationship, that possession takes place in the context of not being
sure whom one is, and so can hardly be a requisitioning of Mayakovsky's text.
So Mayakovsky might have imposed the presence of a mother and the sickly
beauty of the poet on the scene, but O'Hara blends the question asked on the
telephone ('who is it?') with the sense of fragmented identity in the direct
address to the mother ('who am I?').

By what law given in the predecessor text are the new elements determined? The imposition has no binding force. Likewise, can a speaker asking
'who am I?' be said to have possessed the words of a predecessor? The speech
acts and their interrelation cannot be codified so strictly. This issue of the
law given by the anterior speech act is connected to that of the reference
of pronouns: when the 'you' addressed by a poem might be someone who
has already spoken to the poet (an interlocutor in the world of the poem,
which may more or less coincide with the world beyond the poem; an earlier
poet), the poet's utterance may be taken as response to any number of preceding utterances, whether available to the reader or not. 'Trying to Figure
Out What You Feel' may be a poem on the difficulties of working out what
another person ('you' as second person) feels, or a poem of instruction on how
poets ('you' as impersonal pronoun) work out what they feel. One section of
the poem asks similar questions to those asked by the speaker of 'Mayakovsky'
('where are you where am I / where is the night', p. 362, 2.4–5). Three sections of the poem are written after other poets: Stefan George, René Char
and Tristan Corbière. Their being 'after' is an indication of their not being
translations, but still somehow responding to the work of those poets. But the
establishment of a law, derived from the utterances of the poets in question
(could suitable candidates amongst their works be identified – 'Bonsoir' by
Corbière, for example), and determining the form of O'Hara's utterance, is
impossible. Nothing Corbière says could make O'Hara say 'and as for the tire
I never / even liked the wheel' (5.9–10).

The analysis of the presuppositions required for there to be dialogue,
an economy of dialogue, into merely two kinds, the juridical and the possessive, is crude. It is consistent with a certain reading of J. L. Austin that
ascribes to him a very stern position: speaking in certain ways imposes
obligations or bonds upon other people. Certain followers of Austin, John
Searle, for example, may have taken him in this sense, and may themselves
have proposed an understanding of speech acts as binding in this repressive
sense, but it has been noted that there is also a more generous trend in the
interpretation of Austin, whereby a speech act is an offer, not an obligation.[26] Speech employs an endless multiplicity of genres, a typology of which
Voloshinov said was an urgent task of Marxist linguistics.[27] These genres are
porous. Some may presuppose no definite binds or commitments constrain-

ing the addressee to anything at all, but offering possibilities for response. All responses may well be constrained by the total social environment of the addressee, but these constraints are not produced by one utterance alone. To suggest that they are is to make an abstracted 'language' responsible for socio-political problems made by language users in various particular uses of language, and, concomitantly, to suggest that these political problems can be resolved by addressing an abstract linguistic issue. Correctives to the injustices of a discourse universe are not to be made in the abstract, by identifying and disrupting something oppressive in language; they are to be made by continuing to operate in language, adjusting norms that are always practical.

Kristeva's writing on poetic language poses an entity prior to the linguistic subject, the poetic subject, which agitates against the symbolic order in the production of text, of signifying practice, of the semiotic. Voloshinov, on the other hand, proposes a subject that is linguistic through and through, whose emancipation is not to be achieved by contesting language, as there is no emancipation from language. Voloshinov also writes about the presence of previous or presupposed words in a discourse, in his consideration of reported speech. He notes that reported speech and reporting speech can never be isolated from one another, and that the forms that particular languages employ for reporting speech are sociologically revealing: 'in the forms by which language registers the impressions of received speech and of the speaker the history of the changing types of socioideological communication stands out in particularly bold relief'. Distinguishing between referent-analysing and texture-analysing methods of reporting speech, whereby either the formal properties of the utterance are modified (as in the sequence of tenses) or the flavour or register of the utterance is modified, Voloshinov describes the phenomenon of speech interference:

> this phenomenon ... may take place to a certain extent in the texture-analyzing modification of indirect discourse, in those comparatively rare instances in which the reported clause contains not only some of the original words and expressions but also the expressive structure of the message reported.

The repeated exclamation or question 'mother!/?' brings the texture of Mayakovsky's text into O'Hara's, but the ways in which O'Hara varies the punctuation, and moves off in a different direction, suggest the interference is only partial. Voloshinov, then, provides a means of understanding the interrelation between texts and their predecessors that allows for the re-voicing, or re-accentuation of the reported speech without requiring a pre-linguistic subjectivity that disrupts the repressive order of language in such adoptions of others' speech: such relations inhere in all linguistic activity.

The interrelation between poets in this poem, then, can be understood as the interrelation of two linguistic personalities: 'the word is an expression of social intercourse, of the social interaction of material personalities, of producers'.[28] This kind of relation between two material personalities, two producers of language, is taking place in O'Hara's poem. It takes place in such a way that its means and methods, its evocation of the personalities by means of their words and the pronouns that stand for them, are thematised in the utterance itself, becoming its subject. This analysis follows a rationale different from the psychoanalytical basis of Kristeva's work, favouring a materialist account of the operations of poetic spirit in language (see 'Spirit: Wallace Stevens'). Readings of a poem and theoretical texts by Denise Riley in a later chapter ('Selection: Denise Riley') will suggest that such a materialist approach may also be sensitive to psychoanalytical traditions of thought.

Notes

1. Pierre Reverdy, 'L'image', in *Nord-sud, Self Defence et Autres Écrits sur l'Art et la Poésie (1917–1926)* (Paris: Flammarion, 1975), pp. 73–5 (p. 75). In 'A Step Away From Them', O'Hara writes 'My heart is in my / pocket, it is Poems by Pierre Reverdy', *The Collected Poems of Frank O'Hara*, ed. Donald Allen (Berkeley: University of California Press, 1995), p. 258. All further references are to this edition and will be given parenthetically as *CP*. Geoff Ward, *Statues of Liberty: The New York School of Poets* (London: Macmillan, 1993), pp. 73–4, discusses the surrealist theory of the image in relation to O'Hara, and mentions O'Hara's use of a line from Breton.
2. André Breton, *Manifestoes of Surrealism*, trans. Richard Seaver and Helen R. Lane (Ann Arbor: The University of Michigan Press, 1969 [1924]), p. 6.
3. Ibid. p. 37.
4. Louis Cabri of the University of Windsor, Canada has noted, in a recent abstract for a conference paper given at the University of Stirling, Scotland, that 'For O'Hara, the idea of the person is fully social, relational, and public.' Lytle Shaw, *Frank O'Hara: The Poetics of Coterie* (Iowa City: University of Iowa Press, 2006), p. 126, comments on this poem in a chapter (pp. 115–50) dedicated to Pasternak and Mayakovsky in O'Hara's work.
5. One might compare O'Hara's attitude to the individual and history to W. S. Graham's remarks on the relation between individual utterances and history. See the opening pages of 'Deviance: W. S. Graham'.
6. Frank O'Hara, *Art Chronicles 1954–66* (New York: George Braziller, 1975; rev. edn 1990), p. 6.
7. Ibid. p. 56. It should be noted that O'Hara can also talk of the 'spiritual reality of the artist' as revealed in action painting (p. 35).
8. *Mayakovsky and His Poetry*, ed. Herbert Marshall (London: Pilot Press, 1942;

rev. edn 1945), pp. 33–4. In a review of a recent selection of Mayakovsky's work, Marjorie Perloff notes the allusions. Available at <http://www.boston review.net/BR33.4/perloff.php> (last accessed 16 July 2010).

9. O'Hara came to have a difficult relationship with his mother, who became an alcoholic after her husband's death. His verbal altercations with her on the telephone were reported by guests at his apartment. See Brad Gooch, *City Poet: The Life and Times of Frank O'Hara* (New York: Alfred A. Knopf, 1993), pp. 210–11, 13.

10. Lytle Shaw has remarked on O'Hara's capacity to 'revel in the excessive, melodramatic qualities of a masculine subjectivity pushing the limits of its "freedom"' (p. 134).

11. Keston Sutherland, 'Close Writing', in *Frank O'Hara Now: New Essays on the New York Poet*, ed. Robert Hampson and Will Montgomery (Liverpool: Liverpool University Press, 2010), pp. 120–30 (p. 129, n.16). Sutherland also deals extensively with the relationship between O'Hara and Reverdy.

12. For a recent treatment of O'Hara's manner of performing himself in this poem see Drew Milne, 'Performance Over Being: Frank O'Hara's Artifice', *Textual Practice* 25: 2 (2011), 297–313 (pp. 307–11).

13. Although Schuyler's letter notes that the bricks were carried to help John Ashbery build a bookcase, the speaker appears like a real poet-worker. There is also the possibility of a terrible pun on the surname of Osip and Lilly Brik, the former a poetician who shares some of Mayakovsky's views on the social need for poetry, the latter the object of Mayakovsky's adoration. See Vladimir Mayakovsky, *How are Verses Made? With A Cloud in Trousers and To Sergey Esenin*, ed. and trans. G.M. Hyde (Bristol: Bristol Classical Press, 1990) and *Pro Eto – That's What*, trans. Larisa Gureyeva and George Hyde (Todmorden: Arc, 2009).

14. Mayakovsky, *How Are Verses Made*, p. 37.

15. Julia Kristeva, 'The Ethics of Linguistics', in *Desire in Language: A Semiotic Approach to Literature and Art*, ed. Leon S. Roudiez, trans. Thomas Gora, Alice Jardine, and Leon S. Roudiez (New York: Columbia University Press, 1980), pp. 23–35 (p. 31).

16. Julia Kristeva, *La révolution du langage poétique* (Paris: Seuil, 1974), pp. 315–16. All translations from this text are my own unless otherwise stated.

17. Ibid. pp. 317, 320.

18. Ibid. pp. 321, 331.

19. V. N. Voloshinov, *Marxism and the Philosophy of Language*, ed. and trans. Ladislav Matjeka and I. R. Titunik (Cambridge and London: Harvard University Press, 1986; first publ. Seminar Press, 1973 [1929]), pp. 102–3.

20. Ibid. pp. 11, 19.

21. Ibid. pp. 28–9, 36. Voloshinov bears comparison to the bio-semiotician Uexküll. See Alice Kliková, 'Lived Worlds and Systems of Signs: Uexküll's

Biosemiotics', in *Dynamic Structure: Language as an Open System*, ed. Johannes Fehr and Petr Kouba (Prague: Litteraria Pragensia, 2007), pp. 163–85.

22. Voloshinov, *Marxism and the Philosophy of Language*, p. 52.

23. Ibid. pp. 69, 84, 86 (but see also 57), 93.

24. David Herd, *Enthusiast! Essays on Modern American Literature* (Manchester: Manchester University Press, 2007), pp. 149–50 describes O'Hara's view of one's soul being what one is in other people. It is on account of O'Hara's sociability that Herd reckons him an enthusiastic poet.

25. *Révolution*, pp. 337–40, 347. For a discussion of the place of the term 'intertextuality' in Kristeva's early work see Mary Orr, *Intertextuality: Debates and Contexts* (Cambridge: Polity, 2003), pp. 20–32.

26. See James Loxley, *Performativity* (London: Routledge, 2007), pp. 40–2, 55. These arguments are discussed at slightly greater length in the 'Introduction'.

27. Voloshinov, *Marxism*, p. 20.

28. Ibid. pp. 119, 123, 130, 137, 153.

CHAPTER EIGHT

Measure: Robert Creeley

In the twentieth century, American poets, whether 'formalist' or 'experimental' are found relating poetic measure to the rhythmic structure of life. Howard Nemerov thinks that patterns in verse 'seem to represent the world itself in its either pious or stupid comings and goings, its regular recurrences and rhythmical repetitions, cosmic in the heavens, terrene in the tides, physiological in the beating of the heart'.[1] And William Carlos Williams urges poets to make experiments that 'will be directed toward the discovery of a new measure, I repeat, a new measure by which may be ordered our poems as well as our lives'.[2] Poetic measure, then, is believed to be related to the practical structures of daily life, and is a way in which humans can understand their relationship to larger structures of organisation that present themselves in the world. Thinking about measure in poetry therefore need not restrict itself to identifying the units in which lines of poetry are made, and cataloguing the rules for their combination.[3] This discussion of measure will move away from the understanding of metre that led Wimsatt and Beardsley in the late 1950s to attempt to refute new linguistic investigations into the nature of emphasis in English verse, noting disapprovingly that these new ways of describing metre encourage students to talk 'as if the meter itself could be the interaction between itself and something else'.[4] I hope also to avoid the tendency in thinking about metre that accords it a purely repressive function when seen in tension with other systems, such as speech intonation.[5] The chapter will instead move towards a conception of metre as one means by which poetic utterances mark themselves out, measure themselves in and against broader rhythmic patterns, and contrast these perhaps rather modest claims with the more dedicatedly political claims for poetic rhythm of Julia Kristeva.

Poetic measure is made up of relationships that are dynamic, and depends on sensitivity to other aspects of verse utterance in order to be described fully and convincingly. Formalist and structuralist poetics of the early twentieth century took a great interest in the question of rhythm understood in this dynamic fashion. In his essay 'Intonation as the Basic Factor of Poetic Rhythm', Jan Mukařovský, a member of the Linguistic Circle of Prague, argues against the idea that 'isochronism' (the repetition of identical units) should provide the basis for the study of poetic rhythm. He is not interested in breaking rhythm down into its smallest units, and using them to calculate the essential rhythmical character of any poem. He is interested instead in the inter-relation of different systems that make up the complex phenomenon of language use, and in this essay he focuses on the inter-relation of metre and syntax. Metre and syntax can at times suggest different intonations for a line of poetry. The effect that one system has on another gives the line its characteristic rhythm:

> the intonation of verse is always carried by a dual, virtual intonational scheme, and therefore it is always the resultant of the tension between two forces, the relation of which is characteristic for a given line, whether they agree or disagree.[6]

Intonation is neither static nor easily quantifiable, but results from the play between systems: even though metre is not the interaction between itself and something else, its role in the production of the rhythm of a poem cannot be ascertained without considering its interaction with other systems.[7] There might be extreme tensions between metrical and other systems where

> we have to fall back on the ear to tell us when the poet has overstepped the borders of metricality – or, rather, has begun to travel in the no-man's-land around its edges – by mismatching the rhythms generated by morphology and syntax with the rhythms created by the metre, or by making too free with the deviations allowed by the rules.[8]

But, on the whole, the interaction between metre, syntax and other aspects of the poetic utterance create the phenomenon experienced as poetic rhythm.

William Empson's poem 'Missing Dates',[9] from which I quote the first stanza, illustrates this kind of dual intonational pattern in verse:

> Slowly the poison the whole blood stream fills.
> It is not the effort nor the failure tires.
> The waste remains, the waste remains and kills. (ll. 1–3)

Here are three lines, of ten, eleven and ten syllables respectively, each of them suggesting at least one metrical scheme, with no two lines evidently presenting the same metrical scheme, and the first two appearing flexible depending on the intonational scheme according to which the line is produced. The third line is rigorously iambic and pentametric, and might well act retrospectively upon our reading (in the sense of an interpretation that might affect performance, and not just a single performance). One experiences double audition in reading the first and second lines, hearing two possible schemes at once.[10] The first line could be read as an anapaestic tetrameter (swwswwswwws, with 's' representing strong, 'w' weak) with the elision of two unstressed syllables at the end of the line. Such a reading produces an ironic relationship between the lilt of the metre and the sobriety of the thought. The second line might be heard as carrying only four stresses ('It is *not* the *effort* nor the *failure tires*'), but with a tendency to distribute emphasis quite evenly along the whole line, to give it a syntactical rather than a metrically regular intonation. This distribution is perhaps encouraged by the abstract, propositional form of the line. Does the regularity of the third line encourage the reader to look back at the preceding two lines and amend their shape, adding retrospectively the stress on 'blood' and 'nor' that were possible but not self-evident at first? If so, the lilt of the first line is lost, and there is a concentration of stress around 'whole blood stream', producing a heavier effect, whereby the circulation of the blood appears deadened by the weight of the intonation. And in the second line, the additional stress on 'nor' strengthens the sense of a contrast, isolating the two elements of the line, effort and failure, from any other possible element that might be added to the list of candidates for tiring (work, drink and so on): effort and failure are all there is; neither tires; and yet one is tired.

There is, then, no clear way to read the lines, and the tension between the one clear, regular metrical scheme offered by the third line, and the schemes of pronunciation that produce four-stress performances for lines one and two, modify one another. These modifications are slight, but they produce shifts in the tonality of the poem, affecting its ironies, its outlook: can one look with amused equanimity at the inevitability of death? Is life anything more than effort and failure? That these shifts in sense can be affected by shifts in relation between intonational and metrical schemes is understandable: these are questions of how the management of life's rhythms affects our attitudes. It seems to me to miss part of the interest of these lines to say that they could have come to Empson as a 'metre-making argument', as Emerson says poetry comes to its authors,[11] but that is neither to say that they lack argument, something of which Empson was very fond, nor metre. Rather, it is the possibility of reading the lines between schemes that makes the realisation of their scope of argument possible: the argument makes itself in the tension between metre and other features of the language of the poem, it is conceived rhythmically rather than metrically, as the confluence and contrast between systems, and not as the effect of one system alone.

Yuri Tynianov's investigation into the nature of verse language (to which Mukařovský refers in the essay cited above) considers poetry to be rhythmically conceived language. Tynianov identifies rhythm as the fundamental property of verse, and suggests that it can be recognised as dominant by the deformational effect it has on other aspects of language such as syntax. (Roman Jakobson has defined 'the dominant' in the structuralist lexicon as 'the focusing component of a work of art: it rules, determines, and transforms the remaining components. It is the dominant which guarantees the integrity of the structure.')[12] Tynianov, like Mukařovský, sees poetry as the struggle between different systems:

> metaphorically speaking, verse is revealed as a struggle of factors, rather than as a collaboration of factors. It becomes clear that the specific plus of poetry lies precisely in the area of this interaction, the foundation of which is the constructive significance of rhythm and its deforming role relative to factors of another order.

Tynianov thinks that rhythm always deforms other aspects of language and that verse is language that is already rhythmicalised – it is language conceived of rhythmically. He suggests ways in which verse rhythm can affect 'dead' metaphors, by encouraging them to take on both their live and dead meanings at once; he gives examples of the bleeding of sense from one clause to another as a result of the lexical openness caused by the rhythmical arrangement of the language.[13]

Another mode the deformation of language can take is by advancing words to unusual positions of prominence: 'The more insignificant and unobtrusive the advanced word, the more its advancement deforms speech'.[14] Tynianov gives the example of Mayakovsky, who advances words not normally emphasised by making whole lines of just one particle (see the preceding chapter). I would like here to introduce a short poem by Robert Creeley which deforms by advancing parts of words to unexpected positions.[15]

Song

The grit
of things,
a measure
resistant –

times walk-
ing, talk-
ing, telling
lies and

all the other
places, no
one ever
quite the same.

The present participles 'walking' and 'talking' are split across the lines, so that they appear as nominal roots with modifying participial suffixes. There is no evident pattern by which the lineation of this poem is arrived at: its lines have between two and four syllables and one or two stresses, which occupy various positions within the line; there are between zero and two unstressed positions separating stressed positions; the stanzas consist of ten, nine and thirteen syllables respectively, or four, five and seven stresses. Nonetheless, there are only two occasions on which the poem does not alternate stressed and unstressed positions: the two unstressed syllables that join lines three and four, and the two stressed syllables that make up line five. The poem is an iambic composition with no strong rule for lineation but a strong rule for stanza formation (that they must have four lines). It possesses a high degree of regularity in its alternation of stresses, but the lines present (after the comparative regularity of the first stanza, which forms two pairs of lines, with regular stress patterning within each pair) great irregularity in their form: in a poem of twelve short lines, six different arrangements of stress are used to make lines (ws; wsw; ss; sw; swsw; sws).

What is the poem about? The grit of things is their persistence, their toughness or their tendency to intrude and disrupt.[16] A resistant measure is made from things persisting, or from the abrasive presence of things: the quotidian has a stubborn rhythm. In what does this rhythm consist? In 'times' that perform such quotidian acts as walking and talking, acts which may themselves very easily be understood as resistant measures, forms of rhythmical activity that the human body engages in to persevere – but it is the abstract 'times' that are walking and talking, the periods themselves: time seems to have taken over the person experiencing or measuring it. In the same collection (*Words*) in which this 'Song' is found, a poem called 'The Measure' reports the speaker being caught 'in the time / as measure' (*CP*, p. 290). Is it the time that is the measure that catches the poet, or the poet as measure caught in time? The poetic act is one in which one cannot be sure if one measures oneself or is measured by something outside oneself. Telling lies is a different kind of activity from walking and talking, even if no less quotidian, but it suggests a tendency towards betrayal over time, a pointed changefulness.

Moving into the final stanza the poem transforms its temporal emphasis into a spatial emphasis, presenting the participial activities engaged in as places rather than times. It could be these places ('no one [place]') or some unspecified people ('no one') that are said to be never quite the same after the transformations undergone in the walking, talking and telling lies: the grit of things doesn't leave anyone or anything the same. Times and places move through us, as we move through them, with a persistent grittiness, that transforms us and them: to read this poem is to experience that movement, from one point of view predictable, from another resistant to recurrence, even provoking change. Creeley himself declared a great interest in measure, conceived neither as purely technical metrics nor the measurement of the world in relation to human values, but as a testimony to what one is by the very act of producing measured language:

> I want to give witness not to the thought of myself – that specious concept of identity – but, rather, to what I am as simple agency, a thing evidently alive by virtue of such activity. I want, as Charles Olson says, to come into the world. Measure, then, is my testament. What uses me is what I use, and in that complex measure is the issue.[17]

The poem is the measure of the language and its user taken in the act of its production. The advancement of the nominal and verbal parts of the present participle by splitting them across the line break is an example of the defor-mation that rhythmicalised speech (even when that rhythmicalised speech is so evidently a resistance to other possible forms of rhythmicalisation) forces on other aspects of language.

Similar themes are prominent throughout *Words*, though seldom achiev-ing the same concentration of expression. It is a collection of poems that immediately, in its opening poem 'The Rhythm', establishes parallels between the poet's thoughts and words, the time and space of the poem, and various forms of mundane rhythmical activity, such as walking, opening and closing doors, being born and dying. Brief, elliptical poems that attend to the transformations affected in and by the passage of time constitute one sequence within the collection. These poems all explore 'Measures – /ways of being in one's life' ('For Joel', CP, p. 370). Poems such as 'Walking', 'The Pattern', 'Going', 'A Method' all suggest the parallel between the time of the poem, time as measured by quotidian activity, and time in the more symbolic, epochal or existential sense of that in which our lives take place and by which they are limited. Such shifts in the poem are often made obvious by a shift in grammatical construction mid-way through a sentence (the trope known as 'anacoluthia'). Such a shift is seen in 'Song', affected by the conjunction 'and' that joins the second and third stanzas. 'The Measure' effects a similar transformation in its second half (it is a poem of three quatrains), shifting from a construction in which 'we think of' things, to one in which people think 'each for himself' (CP, p. 290). Such transitions often have an effect on the persons of the poem, in a formal grammatical sense: in the poem just cited there is a transition from the first person plural to the third person singular, as what we think of turns into what he thinks for himself. Such transitions of person can have the effect of challenging the massive egotism of the poems even as it is asserted, as the assertive and intrusive poetic persona becomes fragile and porous as well. I will return to the character of the poetic persona and his relations to others evoked by the poems in this collection shortly.

The topics just addressed (the measured nature of literary utterance, the deformation of other linguistic features in those utterances, the ethics and politics of the channelling of human poetic and rhythmic energy) are questions Julia Kristeva considers in her work on poetic language, in which the struggle of rhythm against the symbolic is presented as an analogue for, or even a mode of, the struggle for emancipation in society. Kristeva makes rhythm a highly political question. Poetic language occurs when a certain kind of encounter takes place between the semiotic and the symbolic: the semiotic is the expression of drives (basic human appetitive forces, shaped by the psychological history of the species and the individual) through the non-symbolic aspects of language, those aspects of language that do not attempt to place the speaking subject in relation to a world. Semiotic drives, however, can only express themselves through conflict with the symbolic aspects of language. Kristeva most consistently uses the word 'rhythm' to designate the manifestation of drives in, through and against the symbolic order of language. Linguistic science, she suggests, should recognise the rhythmic aspect of language because it is rhythm, the resistance to order, the enunciation of a subject within the constraints of an order, that brings the complexity of history and ethics into linguistics, precisely by offering a glimpse of the struggle of the individual subject within and against a system:

> Only by vying with the agency of limiting and structuring language does rhythm become a contestant – formulating and transforming . . . Poetic discourse measures rhythm against the meaning of language structure and is thus always eluded by meaning in the present while continually postponing it to an impossible time-to-come . . . Linguistic ethics, as it can be understood through Jakobson's practice, consists in following the resurgence of an 'I' coming back to rebuild an ephemeral structure in which the constituting struggle of language and society would be spelled out . . . [Generative linguists don't seem able to confront] language as a risky practice, allowing the speaking animal to sense the rhythm of the body as well as the upheavals of history[.][18]

At a general level, Kristeva's description of the articulation of the subject in and against the symbolic order of language seems to characterise the phenomena in Creeley that I have just been describing. But the specific claims Kristeva makes for rhythm do not snugly fit Creeley's practice. Kristeva claims that only a certain kind of linguistics (one recognising poetry as the articulation of rhythms continually deferring meaning and acting against a thetic and symbolic language) can be ethical. In her major work on revolution in poetic language, Kristeva is clear that rhythm in poetry is the manifestation of psychological impulses: 'Poetic rhythm does not constitute the acknowledgement of the unconscious but is instead its expenditure and implementation.'[19] Kristeva is thinking of rhythm as interruption rather than regularity, stimulation rather than security, and imagining that the great ethical and political imperative is to promote the irruptions that challenge fixed forms of social organisation that place the subject under restrictions. It is equally clear that Kristeva believes the poetic practice she comes to call 'text' is a socially revolutionary force, a practice producing real social consequences. It is in nineteenth-century avant-garde practices that Kristeva locates the revolutionary force of poetic rhythm, offering analyses of Stéphane Mallarmé and Lautréamont.[20]

I would like here to present one fundamental objection to Kristeva's account of the psychosocial efficacy of poetic rhythm. If poetic rhythm is the implementation and expenditure of the unconscious, how does that implementation and expenditure of disruptive energies register itself (for author, reader, or the world at large) in any shared, common world that might be understood as political, or intersubjective in any other way? What Kristeva suggests is that because language is related in its development to the structure of the psyche and of socio-economic relations, facts about language use have necessary consequences in the psychic and socio-economic realms. I think this belief is based on what one might call a 'microcosmic superstition', formed by deriving structural analogies from historical relations. Such derivation suggests that because the development of the capacity to use language is a condition of there being language, there must be a formal analogy between the process of language acquisition/development and the structure of language itself, and, indeed, between these two and any particular use of language. The fallacy here is that a causal relation implies structural similarity. Perhaps the objection can be made clearer by means of an analogy. Building is a necessary causal and historical condition for their being houses, but it does not follow that building (the activity) shares any element of its structure with houses. The activities of architects and labourers in designing and constructing the building need not have any structural relationship to the buildings themselves (neither do the people who built the front room, nor the activities they engaged in to build it, look like the room itself). Nor does any particular house summarise or re-enact the process of building houses in general. In fact, it is hard to see how there could be any kind of formal analogy at all between building and houses, even though the former is a necessary condition for the latter. Returning to language, if an infant experiences a stage in which she is placed, as a subject, by language, that experience is part of her historical entry into language. It does not follow that language as a system nor its particular utterances display moments of, or possesses devices for, subject placement: nor should it have to, because to be a language user is to have undergone that particular experience already.

It is especially clear that Kristeva believes particular uses of language can replicate the thetic moment in language acquisition/development, calling conservative poetry a 'surrogate for the thetic'.[21] The poetic act of subjecting oneself to highly conventionalised means of expression (if that is how poetic conservatism should be understood), no more replicates the placement of the subject in relation to the world in the process of language acquisition/development than a particular currency trade on the stock market replicates the historical evolution of commercial modernity: it may well be impossible without that history, but it does not recapitulate the features of that history (there is, for example, no process of industrialisation in a currency trade). Uses of language are a part of language, and not analogues for language. To believe that the parts of a system reproduce its total history and structure is, I suggest, a form of mysticism or superstition, in which a system, its history and components share an essence, and express it in various ways. If this objection stands, there is no clear way in which poetic rhythm, through its expenditure of energies, can effect analogous operations in the common, intersubjective psychological and political worlds. Revolutionary poetic language, that is, has to work in the same way as all language, by engaging all its resources of representation, reference, connection, implication and all the rest, including rhythm.[22] Poetic language may well draw on the knowledge that its speakers and hearers have of their total linguistic field, but there is no obvious reason for activity in one part of that field having more radical implications for any other part of the field than the slight adjustment that any new activity would contribute. The measure of a poem may be no more than this modest addition to the totality of language, a unique utterance that takes the measure of its own difference from what was already there. There need be no limit to the psychic or socio-economic consequences of composing or encountering such an utterance, but all these consequences are possible and not necessary: they depend upon the activity of people writing and reading, rather than being produced as necessary structural consequences.

One of the structures against which Kristeva believes the revolutionary poetic subject strives is the family. She suggests that homosexuality and anality are challenges to the family, and parallel to the challenge constituted by the irruptions of rhythm in poetic language.[23] Creeley's collection *Words* frequently returns to the rejection of the mother, one primary expression of the homosexual and anal drives. This impulse is closely connected to an intermittent, aggressive, phallic masculinity, one that associates penetration of the idealised female love object with detestation and punishment of the mother. In 'The Hole' these impulses are confronted directly, in combination with adulation of an elided phallic authority. The poem begins by acknowledging a silence to fill with 'A / foot, a fit', both units of song. The poem, then, is an attempt to fill the hole. It describes the speaker urinating in a lake, exploring his anus and wiping it after excreting, and the 'hero of the school' (who is said to have used a bottle to penetrate 'his girl'). The poem then progresses through a scene of marital rape, presents the speaker's mother and sister as analogues for the victim, notes the absence of the father and returns to the image of a male urinating in a body of water, this time 'the teacher' with a large penis, the naming of which is elided in a sublimated castration of the figure of authority: he 'took out his // to piss' (CP, p. 345). The poem continues, in a tonal reversal given the darkness of what has just been said, to claim pleasure is omnipresent. It closes with a demand:

>   Talk
>
> to me, fill
> emptiness with
> you, empty
> hole.

The hole, the generalised orifice, at once sexual and excretory, welcoming and rejecting, is empty, yet is asked to fill emptiness, and to do so by talking. The poem enacts a new violence in describing scenes of imagined or recalled sexual violence. It is a poem that recognises that the individual energies discharged in the measured speech of poems are not always kind, and the transformations they effect upon others are not always or necessarily desirable, for the speaker, or anyone else. But the fear of the void that Charles Altieri suggests characterises Creeley's work, should not be identified exclusively with women who are to be completed sexually and psychologically by authoritative men.[24] The masculine poetic voice may sometimes want to leave a mark on a woman, or in 'her mind' ('Going', CP, p. 330), but 'The Hole', for all its violence against others, is also a poem of violent self-disgust and recognition of the emptiness of the apparently aggressive, invasive male: it is as anal as it is phallic. The sexual politics and ethics of this poem are played out on a symbolic level, in Kristeva's terms. Its anality, its homosexuality (in heroising authoritative males), its rejection of family structure are evident at the propositional level of what the poem says. The poem's lineation, its promotion of unmarked parts of speech by means of their position in lines, the shifting of syntax within one phrase, the threat posed by the blank page to the short lines: these rhythmic features are not operating against the symbolic import of the poem, but in ensemble with it. Whether or not the ethics and politics of this poem are admirable, they are produced by the poem's language in its entirety.

I hope to have shown in looking at Mukařovský and Tynianov some ways in which structuralist poetics approaches the question of rhythm, and to have shown that tension between systems in a language and in the language of a particular poem are evident in measure. I also hope to have shown how poets themselves, by engaging with questions of measure and temporality in language, produce serious considerations of the role of measure in poetry and in life. Creeley and Empson, in their different ways, demonstrate that the measuring of language in poetry, the realisation of its equivalences and differences in relation to a more or less abstract metrical scheme, participates very fully in the reading of a poem, our (vocal or sub-vocal) performances of it, and our attribution of meanings to it (as paraphrases, convictions that the shape of those particular words is right, or however else we experience meaning). It is unsurprising that these poems should concern themselves with the passing of time, and the differences that are wrought upon people by the passing of time. It is, after all, in the language of particular poems that the negotiation between individual energies and external schemes must work themselves out in finding measures by which poems, and, if Williams can be credited, lives can be made. The production of these poems, instances of measured language, is a persuasive act, sometimes therapeutic, sometimes violent, an attempt to get us to see things in a particular way, to adopt particular feelings and attitudes towards duration and the passing of things: our understanding of the poems' construction, their subject and their mode of argument are furthered by thinking about the ways in which they measure the language. These functions can be called political in that they call for a critical attitude to how the energies of life are reigned in or expended, and they make that call by offering themselves as examples, not necessarily purely positive examples, of such an attitude. Such poems do not require a theory of language that attributes to their poetic activity necessary consequences for the language system, and any correlated political systems: particular utterances within languages have more limited but no less important consequences for language and language users. They cannot recapitulate or revolutionise in retrospect the history of language acquisition or development, but they can and must take their place in the recursive but unrepeatable sequence of speech that unfolds across human history, transforming that history by adding themselves to it.

Notes

1. 'On the Measure of Poetry', *Critical Inquiry* 6:2 (Winter 1979), 331–41 (p. 336).
2. *Selected Essays of William Carlos Williams* (New York: Random House, 1954), p. 340. I would like to thank Michael Kindellan for directing me to this essay.
3. See Simon Jarvis, 'Prosody as Cognition', *Critical Inquiry* 40:4 (December 1998), 3–15 (p. 6): 'prosody cannot be grounded on the model of the measurement of an object'.

4. W. K. Wimsatt, Jr and Monroe C. Beardsley, 'The Concept of Meter: An Exercise in Abstraction', *PMLA* 74 (1959), 585–98 (p. 596).

5. See for example Anthony Easthope, *Poetry as Discourse* (London and New York: Methuen, 1983), p. 68, where pentameter is the great enemy of spoken English.

6. *The Word and Verbal Art: Selected Essays by Jan Mukařovský*, trans. and ed. John Burbank and Peter Steiner, foreword by René Wellek (New Haven and London: Yale University Press, 1977 [1933]), p. 125.

7. For a more recent attempt at a detailed study of the relation of metrical and syntactical systems, see Donald Wesling, *The Scissors of Meter: Grammetrics and Reading* (Ann Arbor: The University of Michigan Press, 1996), who asks, p. 18, if 'metrists always recognize the way literary language must continually put into question its own rule-governed behaviour, its received ideas of intention, and its ontological status?'

8. See Derek Attridge, *The Rhythms of English Poetry* (London: Longman, 1982), p. 204.

9. William Empson, *The Collected Poems*, ed. John Haffenden (Harmondsworth: Penguin, 2000), p. 79.

10. See Martin J. Duffell, *A New History of English Metre* (Oxford: Legenda, 2008), p. 69.

11. Ralph Waldo Emerson, *Selected Essays*, ed. Larzer Ziff (Harmondsworth: Penguin, 1982 [1844]), p. 263.

12. 'The Dominant', in *Readings in Russian Poetics: Formalist and Structuralist Views*, ed. Ladislav Matejka and Krystyna Pomorska, intro. Gerald L. Bruns (Chicago and Normal, IL: Dalkey Archive Press, 2002; first publ. Cambridge, MA: MIT Press, 1971), pp. 82–7, p. 82.

13. Yuri Tynianov, *The Problem of Verse Language*, ed. and trans. Michael Sosa and Brent Harvey, afterword by Roman Jakobson (Ann Arbor: Ardis, 1981 [1924]), pp. 40–1, 59, 62.

14. Ibid. p. 82.

15. *The Collected Poems of Robert Creeley, 1945–75* (Berkeley and Los Angeles: University of California Press, 1982; repr. 2006), p. 274.

16. Ann Mandel, *Measures: Robert Creeley's Poetry* ([no location]: The Coach House Press, 1974), p. 11, quotes from this poem, and suggests it reveals 'the dance of objects' that is one way of expressing the measure of the individual in the world. Mandel notes the importance of measure to Creeley's enterprise, relating measure to care (*cura*), ritual and prayer.

17. Robert Creeley, 'Sense of Measure', in *Astronauts of Inner-Space: An International Collection of Avant-Garde Activity* (San Francisco: Stolen Paper Review Editions, 1966), p. 33. Confusingly, this essay is not listed in the contents page for the volume.

18. 'The Ethics of Linguistics', in *Desire in Language: A Semiotic Approach to Literature and Art*, ed. Leon S. Roudiez, trans. Thomas Gora, Alice Jardine,

and Leon S. Roudiez (New York: Columbia University Press, 1980), pp. 23–35 (pp. 29, 33, 34).

19. Julia Kristeva, *Revolution in Poetic Language*, trans. by Margaret Waller, intro. by Leon S. Roudiez (New York: Columbia University Press, 1984), p. 164.
20. Ibid. pp. 104, 148, 191.
21. Ibid. p. 83.
22. On this point see Calvin Bedient, 'Kristeva and Poetry as Shattered Signification', *Critical Inquiry* 16:4 (Summer 1990), 807–29 (p. 816).
23. Kristeva, *Revolution in Poetic Language*, pp. 104, 149, 176.
24. Charles Altieri, 'The Unsure Egoist: Robert Creeley and the Theme of Nothingness', *Contemporary Literature* 13:2 (Spring 1972), 162–85 (p. 177).

CHAPTER NINE

Deviance: W. S. Graham

Picking up on the discussion of identity and difference in 'Measure: William Wordsworth', this chapter focuses on deviance, a related topic. In order for a phrase to be deviant, it must be different from a more ordinary way of saying something similar or of employing the same construction. A similitude within dissimilitude is required here, as, if one were to see no resemblance between the ordinary and the deviant phrase, they would stand in no relation to each other at all, the one would not be recognised as a deviant form of the other (I shall go on to qualify this vocabulary of ordinariness and deviance somewhat). Perhaps the most obvious way of identifying such a difference and partial identity is at the formal or grammatical level: the deviant phrase relates to the ordinary phrase by sharing most of its constituents in more or less the same order, but with some variation (in word order, tense, substitution of parts of speech for one another and so on). But there may also be non-formal or super-segmental ways of identifying any deviance in a phrase. One of these, variation of the context, will be discussed later in this chapter.

One further informal way of identifying deviance, which might indeed be the most extreme form of the contextual method, is to claim that all utterance is necessarily deviant, because it is necessarily historically unique, deviating from all past utterances, even if only by context. Such is the view of W. S. Graham, the poet who provides the main focus for this chapter. Graham has a sense of history as the continual production of new human meanings, even when what is produced appears to be repetition:

> Let me be the poet writing in a disguise of the 1st person about the intricate marriage between those problems [of morality] and the poem and the searching reader ... History does not repeat itself. I am the bearer of that poetic outcome. History continually arrives as differently as our most recent minute on earth ... Each word is touched by and filled with the activity of every speaker. Each word changes every time it is brought to life. Each single word uttered twice becomes a new word each time. You cannot twice bring the same word into sound.[1]

The poem that will occupy much of this chapter is written in what one could call the 'disguise of the first person', in that the 'I' of the poem disguises as much as it reveals; it also addresses a searching reader, one who is said to come to the poem looking for something. Graham's poem employs the necessary historical variability of the utterance in the service of an investigation into the relationship between the persons created in and by the language of a poem: an investigation that is ethical in as much as it is interpersonal. One form in which to put the ethical realisation the poem makes is to say that it obliges a renunciation of mastery: if history is as much the determinant of what is said as is the individual speaker, then, as Robin Purves has said, 'the poetic text is constituted by social and historical aspects of a language system whose effects cannot be mastered by an individual designated as "author"'.[2] No matter to what extent repetition characterises the language that we use, the contexts in which it is used constitute an unfinished series, and so every new utterance will be, however filled with the past, uncannily new. In this sense, then, all usage is deviation, and Graham registers the appearance of ordinary-seeming phrases in all their difference in his poem.

The very imputation of a language system, however, is something that some readers of Graham have reacted against, finding in his work an alternative to structuralist and formalist accounts of language as a system, an alternative related to a Heideggerian sense of language as being in the world, and also a sense of the ever-evolving nature of language inadequately described by calling it a system or structure:

> Recognising from quite early on the special importance of the work on language in philosophical debate in our time, Graham's poetry presents language as the medium in which we move, dwell, and know the world. But unlike that tendency which seeks to explain literature and the world by means of the application of the language model and the methodology of linguistics (what we have come to call Formalism and Structuralism), Graham's work produces a living, animate, and mocking 'language' that resists codification, and seems at least as complex as what it has been made to represent.[3]

Language here is thought of as a human operation that is never fully describable, never behaving in quite the systematic way that the phrase 'structural linguistics' seems to suggest it will behave. One might reasonably, however, try to close some of this perceived gap between Graham and formalist and structuralist poetics, which also place great emphasis on difference and deviance. Jan Mukařovský notes that poetic language is to be thought of as a deviation from standard language:

> the violation of the norm of the standard, its systematic violation, is what makes possible the poetic utilization of language; without this possibility

there would be no poetry. The more the norm of the standard is stabilized in a given language, the more varied can be its violation, and therefore the more possibilities for poetry in that language.[4]

And again: 'it is precisely the *deviations* from standard literary usage which are evaluated in poetry as artistic devices'.[5] Deviation here requires a standard against which it is registered: it is not the constant, evolving deviance of Graham's thoughts on language.

Viktor Shklovsky also takes a great interest in deviance, but he concentrates his work around the term 'deautomatisation'. He suggests that habitual perception of objects automates the reactions of the perceiver, resulting in a qualitative loss in the human phenomenal world. Art is able to reverse this loss:

> art exists that one may recover the sensation of life; it exists to make one feel things, to make the stone *stony* . . . The technique of art is to make objects 'unfamiliar,' to make forms difficult, to increase the difficulty and length of perception because the process of perception is an aesthetic end in itself and must be prolonged.

From this Aristotelian understanding of the value of the activity of perception, an emphasis on the disorderly nature of poetic utterance is reached: 'we can define poetry as *attenuated, tortuous* speech. Poetic speech is *formed speech* . . . poetic rhythm is similarly disordered rhythm'.[6] Poetry can be imagined as the definitively deformed type of utterance at the same time as it is imagined as the definitively formed utterance: deformation is hyper-formation rather than non-formation. When poetic language is described as deformed language, one should not necessarily imagine an unformed phrase, a 'natural' or 'ordinary' phrase, which is then subjected to a process of deformation by a poetic principle. All language is formed in some way; all language is behaviour shaped by some loose principles. A reader of a poem can often identify a deformation of a particular phrase or expression, or manner of producing phrases or expressions, in the language of a poem (I shall mention several of these shortly). But this kind of comparison between what has been said and what might have been said is something undertaken whenever an attempt is made to work out the implications of an utterance, and not just to work out the form of a deviant utterance. Alternatively, when poetry is said to render ordinary language deviant, it should not be imagined that a particular poetic usage has necessary consequences for the whole language (see also on this point the remarks on Kristeva in 'Measure: Robert Creeley').

In Keats's lines 'But when the melancholy fit shall fall / Sudden from heaven like a weeping cloud' one finds one of two deviations: either the substitution of an adjective for an adverb, or the variation in word order that separates 'Sudden' from 'fit'.[7] It is evidently not the case that all adverbs must after this moment in 1820 be substituted for adjectives, nor that adjectives may always be placed two words distant from the noun they qualify, nor that the implied transfer of properties from the subject of the sentence to the verb go on to achieve a corresponding reorganisation of collective habits of perception. It is just a local variant of language. I will suggest that this presumption of the consequentiality of linguistic deviance is a significant problem for one of the prominent avant-garde theories of poetry from North America. No matter how violent deviations appear, the medium in which they occur remains the same medium. The advent of cinema, for example, may, as Mukařovský suggests, affect the life of human gesture, but it does not make it anything other than gesture.[8] The same is true, I suggest, of deformations within language: however much the linguistic domain is altered and extended by deviation, it remains the linguistic domain, and does not become non-linguistic cognition.[9] Stylistic originality in the arts more generally 'means that the style of the artist(s) has expanded the scope of the medium in a very small way by opening up a new mode of sensibly interpreting the world'.[10] Deviations are part of the continual process of extending language, whether poetic or ordinary.

Graham's poem 'The Secret Name' stages an encounter between its speaker and its addressee (who may, at least some of the time, also be the speaker) in a landscape that is highly specified yet highly abstract.[11] That encounter is an encounter with and within language – with the language used in the poem, and the language the poem is about (the secret name). In these respects the poem is comparable to others by Graham. Language is often the addressee of Graham's poems, addressed in a manner that recalls love lyrics in which the addressee is cruelly playful; and yet the language addressed is also the poet's language, even the poet himself: 'This morning I am ready if you are, / To hear you speaking in your new language . . . You enunciate very clearly / Terrible words always just beyond me' ('A Note to the Difficult One', NCP, p. 206). Encounters with language occur in landscapes that travesty the specific geographic locations to which they are tied: 'How pleased I am / To meet you reading and writing on damp paper / In the rain forest beside Madron River' ('Language Ah Now You Have Me', NCP, p. 208). These travesties of place can be playful, as in the poem just cited, or more severe, as when the poet's relationship to language is imagined through a composite image of fishing at night, welding by the river Clyde, and being burnt in a burial boat ('Seven Letters', NCP, pp. 120–40). The attempts these poems make to picture relations between people and their language and other people necessarily have an ethical aspect. This reading of 'The Secret Name' will be broken into stages that relate to the various ways of conceiving deviance under discussion.

The Secret Name

1

Whatever you've come here to get
You've come to the wrong place. It
(I mean your name.) hurries away
Before you in the trees to escape.

I am against you looking in
At what you think is me speaking.
Yet we know I am not against
You looking at me and hearing.

If I had met you earlier walking
With the poetry light better
We might we could have spoken and said
Our names to each other. Under

Neath the boughs of the last black
Bird fluttered frightened in the shade
I think you might be listening. I
Listen in this listening wood.

To tell you the truth I hear almost
Only the sounds I have made myself.
Up over the wood's roof I imagine
The long sigh of Outside goes.

2

I leave them there for a moment knowing
I make them act you and me.
Under the poem's branches two people
Walk and even the words are shy.

It is only an ordinary wood.
It is the wood out of my window.
Look, the words are going away
Into it now like a black hole.

Five fields away Madron Wood
Is holding words and putting them.
I can hear them there. They move
As a darkness of my family.

3

The terrible, lightest wind in the world
Blows from word to word, from ear
To ear, from name to name, from secret
Name to secret name. You maybe

Did not know you had another
Sound and sign signifying you.

How does linguistic hyper-formation in the phrases of the poem extend the process of perceiving the things in the poem? Prepositions and nouns play an important role. In the first stanza of the first section the addressee's name hurries away 'Before you in the trees to escape.' The prepositions here are ordinary, but their ambiguity contributes to the abstraction of the represented space of the poem, and also to the confusion of the addressee and his or her name. Is the name 'before' the addressee in time or in space? One might have expected the name to hurry away 'into' the trees, but the choice of 'in' produces a stasis. It is also applicable, grammatically, to the addressee as much as the name, and both the addressee and the name could be in the trees. It proves difficult to separate out the addressee, her or his name, and the landscape in which this name that will not be found is sought.

Some nominal forms in the poem also demand extended attention. The third stanza of the first section talks of a 'poetry light', a phrase that follows the normal rules for compound nouns of this kind (fridge light, for example, and, from Graham, 'poetry arm', meaning the ability to make poems), but unites elements that require some effort to reconcile.[12] The poetry light is outside, the light in the landscape that encourages poetry, the light of poetry imagined as something that inhabits the landscape. The landscape belongs to the poem as a space the poem makes, yet the poem also seems to inhere in the landscape. The phrase allows the poetry light to be either interior or exterior. There is a similar construction in the fourth stanza of the first section, 'I listen in this listening wood.' If the woodland is listening, as the speaker is listening whilst in it, then the phrase is a noun qualified by a participle, and describes the eerie experience of feeling as though one is being listened to by woodland when in it. Or it may be that the phrase follows the rule for compound nouns such as 'drinking den', where it is not the den that does the drinking, but its occupants. In this case the woodland is where one goes to listen. The process of perception is extended and attenuated by this difficulty; furthermore, the difficulty may be given a purpose: the speaker, the addressee and the wood are all, potentially, listening. Here the purpose changes the nature of the thing perceived, rather than merely extenuating the process of perception. The poem is a product of that listening, in the dual sense of existing in talking about it, and of being the result of the listening described. The listening may be listening in, hearing what someone, even oneself, has to say, without being the primary intended addressee; or it may be a listening out, a particular attentiveness to one's surroundings and circumstances. The phrase allows both possibilities at once.

The same stanza contains one of the few tropes of the poem, the metaphor by which the feathers of a bird are compared to the boughs of a tree. It is a metaphor that is difficult to take in its metaphorical sense: it is much easier to be under the boughs of a tree than to be under a bird's wing. The metaphor, that is, compares the primary object (the bird's wing) to a secondary object (a tree or trees) which is much more readily integrated into the context of the poem so far. Who is under these boughs is also a question. The speaker thinks the addressee might be listening, but they are both candidates for being underneath the boughs. The word order brings speaker, addressee and environment together. Whoever it is that is under the boughs is grammatically qualified as 'fluttered frightened', with these qualities evidently applying most readily to the bird that figures in the metaphor. Similar effects are found in the second stanza of the second section, where the speaker invites the addressee to look at the words 'going away / Into' the wood 'like a black hole'. Prepositions again produce effects by redundancy here: if the words go into the woodland, observed from a fixed point at a distance, they must go away into it. The 'away' duplicates sense already made, thereby suggesting that the words' going away is terminal or permanent, as indeed suggested by the woodland being like a black hole. But, grammatically, the 'like' might be thought most obviously to qualify the going away of the words, not the wood. The words themselves can be a dark place. Ambiguities created by ordinary features of word order, rules for compound noun formation, the variety of concrete and abstract senses that prepositions have, deautomatise the language of this poem. It is deviant by being perfectly ordinary, by making perfectly normal features of a language system uniquely attention-seeking in an unrepeatable utterance.

Graham's poem represents one way in which both the systematic and the unrepeatable aspects of language are evident in an utterance. In feeling the peculiarity of certain phrases in the poem, a linguistic system is evoked by the reader, who reads what is said against other things that can be said, things that are like but unlike. Graham's utterance is historically unique but only possible because of the historical variation in duration of the language as a system. Language as system is continually being displaced by language as historical utterance, which is to admit that neither conception of language is in itself sufficient: poems help us to realise this fact, and its large conceptual consequences. The boldest way of describing these consequences would be to say that they determine the nature of the social reality we make and inhabit, as the transformative potential of any utterance is a social fact, something relevant to any language user. The North American movement known as L=A=N=G=U=A=G=E writing, which pursues in its theoretical work (roughly contemporaneous with Graham's poem, first published in 1973), a highly explicit political model of the interrelation of system and unique, deviant utterance.[13] It is a model that mistakes both what kind of system a language is, and how utterances are related to systems.

Some writers attempt to apply and even to embody a defamiliarisation not just of objects perceived, but also of the process of perception itself. Bruce Andrews, a practitioner-critic and political scientist who formerly applied structuralist methods to the analysis of developments in international relations, gives an aspirational description of the reading process demanded by avant-garde and new media poetry: 'If readership is the software, then the writing isn't "laying bare the device" of literature, so much as laying bare *ourselves* as the device.' Andrews provides a basic description of L=A=N=G=U=A=G=E writing that makes clear its debt to structuralist thinking: 'So-called Language Writing distinguishes itself: / First, / by challenging the transitive ideal of communicating . . . Second, / by foregrounding in a pretty drastic way the materiality (and social materiality) of the reading surface'. The object of this reading practice is to alter the social practice of the reader by altering her relation to language and the kinds of social reality constructed by it. Andrews frequently adverts to the strangeness of such writing, but insists that its strangeness is not a distance from daily life: 'But this writing, mostly, is too strange. / Strangeness puts things right in your face, right up to our ears. / Strangeness doesn't endistance.'[14]

The pleasure that texts give is regarded as central to this work of practical defamiliarisation: 'deviance would be so much sweeter', Andrews says, if representations could be loosened off from words.[15] He is interested in the way that certain kinds of writing can make of language an 'Other' in which the injustices of late capitalism are righted, making it a 'non-imperial state: without need for the expansion or externalization that comes from the refusal to redistribute the surplus at home'.[16] Within this generally communitarian ethos, however, Andrews maintains an emphasis on the individual creative act that is the disrupting and deviant force in writing, and which attempts to alter the possible world of socio-economic relations, or praxis:

> MAIN OPPOSITION: between acceptance of rules (in this case, of composition, of positivist inquiry, of discourse) OR stress on individual choices & disruptions & deviations (flows) & perspectives to the point where signs appear recognizably conventional . . . Deviations, by breaking out, do more than charge & discharge energy, however voluptuously – scramble codes, DISORIENT language. (Constant rupture constant improvisation for readers, producing flows rather than a determinate picture of 'a whole'). They stretch the boundaries of that whole, of human use, of what can be written / felt – are praxis.[17]

In this American post-structuralist poetics certain kinds of individual deviant operations within language make of it a utopia in which the beginnings of a practical justice can be found, language being the medium of practical consciousness. Marx does write that language is practical consciousness, but the emphasis of his text is on the reality of that consciousness always being of a social order:

> Language is as old as consciousness, language *is* practical consciousness that exists also for other men, and for that reason alone it really exists for me personally as well; language, like consciousness, only arises from the need, the necessity of intercourse with other men.[18]

Andrews, when quoting this passage, makes little of Marx's insistence on the reality of consciousness being its reality to others, and places more emphasis on the individual psyche than its interaction with social norms.[19] He imagines a poet gloriously picking a way through the mines of ideologically saturated language, rather than being fruitfully overdetermined by that language, to pre-empt a distinction made by Denise Riley (see 'Selection: Denise Riley').

Andrews thinks of social life as a structure: 'only a dramatic change in the structure of capitalist society is likely to disorganize the fetish, the narrowness of readership (& therefore the capabilities of writing) the dominance of ideological restrictive notions of what poetry & language can be'.[20] But there remains the question of how the force of deviant operations within a structure might have consequences for other parts of the structure or other related structures, and these are political and ethical questions.[21] There are difficulties with writing from a position beyond any such structure, as Andrews seems to want to: however such an imaginative structure is attacked, it preserves its structural coherence.[22]

Language may be described as a structure, but there are problems with taking certain properties of certain kinds of structure and imagining that, because language is a structure, language too must have those properties. If we imagine that language is the kind of structure that we find in architecture, or in anatomy, for example, we are likely to think that an operation performed within one part of the structure will affect the rest of that structure, and any related structure. Andrews talks about language as if it were this kind of structure, a fully integrated system in which interventions have necessary, immediate and predictable consequences for all parts of the system. But language may be thought of as a more open structure, and this is indeed the focus of some recent work on the legacy of Saussure that investigates the transformative effect of the individual moment of linguistic creativity (the utterance, the gesture, the event) upon the linguistic structure (the sign system, the state, the language):

> Despite the fact that language and thought are inextricably linked, it is always possible to transgress the ready-made meanings that are inscribed in the given system of signs and find new ones. If nothing else, then literature and poetry

clearly demonstrate this fact ... It is this creative deformation that makes language move and reveal a new set of meanings.[23]

Saussure's own hints at the kind of structure and system unique to a language, support this view of the openness of the language system. Language is structured to an approximate degree that makes it susceptible to study, and that degree of structure is produced socially by its users:

> The structure of a language is a social product of our language faculty ... All individuals linguistically linked in this manner [through the speech circuit] will establish among themselves a kind of mean; all of them will reproduce – doubtless not exactly, but approximately – the same signs linked to the same concepts ... If we could collect the totality of word patterns stored in all those individuals, we should have the social bond which constitutes their language. It is a fund accumulated by the members of the community through the practice of speech, a grammatical system existing potentially in every brain, or more exactly in the brains of a group of individuals; for the language is never complete in any single individual, but exists perfectly only in the collectivity.[24]

In this kind of socially produced linguistic collective there can be no predicted effect of one's performances within the system or structure as it is available to or used by any other individual or group.

Estrangements of ordinary language in poetic utterances can only have a political value if they are taken to be political by a readership. There is no reason to think that poetry in general just is political on account of its deviance: to think in this way is to think that language exists somewhere beyond people as a structure that can be modified without reference to the historical series of utterances. The structure language has might only ever be found in a condition of instability that, it has been claimed by the strand in American poetics I'm discussing, is uniquely the product of estranging poetic interventions.[25] Even a strictly hierarchical approach to the systematic nature of language and literature recognises that there will be feedback in the relationship between systems that will produce oscillation in a reactor: that is, to be a system at all, language must be open to receiving feedback from the other systems that constitute its environment.[26] L=A=N=G=U=A=G=E poetics posits an individual psychic energy within language that, by poeticising, deviates, and thereby alters the fabric of the language system (conceived of as discrete from use and users) for other users. But language is always intersubjective: it never exists for me first and others only later. It is fully and always, in its deviance as much as its orderliness, a common property.

Graham's poem makes the intersubjectivity of language palpable for his readers as an inter-personal, and therefore ethical fact. The peculiarity of the poem's scene and its language conspire to produce unusual implications from ordinary phrases. The final stanza of the first section begins with a colloquial-sounding idiom, but soon moves towards a complex statement encouraging revision of the opening phrase. The speaker hears 'almost / Only the sounds I have made myself.' There are other sounds, but it is not clear what they are. The sounds that a speaker makes are normally the sounds of words, but describing them here as sounds and not as words makes the sounds seem closer to involuntarily expressed, physically immediate noises, as words themselves sometimes are. There is also a temporal peculiarity here, as a speaker's sounds are normally words that have a temporally very limited existence. The speaker might be thought more easily to hear the sounds he makes than those he has made. Perhaps certain qualities of the poetic moment are caught by this temporal complexity? Poems are not, on the whole, momentaneous things, but develop over time, in conception, drafting, revision, reading, publication and so on. The author of a poem would encounter sounds that she had made in almost all of these acts, in reading, revising, publishing, and even, in those cases where the words seem to come to the poet as a memory of other words already spoken, in conceiving the poem. The speaker hears almost only the sounds he has made himself in this act of poetic making. And if we turn back to the opening phrase of the stanza we might ask if the colloquial phrase 'To tell you the truth' carries the weight of 'in order to tell you the truth'. The speaker listens to the words he has made himself in order to tell the truth.

The section closes with further blending of the represented space of the poem, the qualities of the speaker and the poem itself. The word order that produces a straightforward sense for the lines ('I imagine the long sigh of Outside goes up over the wood's roof') has been derailed in such a way as to suggest it might be the speaker who is up over the wood's roof (just as it was unclear if the addressee was in the trees in l. 4), and to remove the verb ('goes') quite a distance from the preposition that one expects to accompany it. The going of the sigh can therefore seem directionless and abstract. The position of the speaker is merged with that of the sigh. This latter effect relates to the projection of poetic activity onto the space represented in the poem, a characteristic feature of Graham's work, in which the representational work of language is undermined by the poet's allusions to his own activity in making the world represented. In 'About the Stuff' the fire of the poem or poetic inspiration (the poet calls language a 'lens') is presented as capable of setting fire to the rural landscape presented in the poem, blending the mental space of the poet's activity, and the represented space of the poem (*NCP*, p. 314). In 'The Secret Name', the space ('Outside') is sighing, has breath and voice. In some sense this is just a description of the noise the wind makes as it passes over the tops of trees, a noise typical of the outside. But of course the word 'Outside', here given an initial capital to mark it out as a word as much as a proper name for a place, contains a 'sigh' in the first phoneme of its second syllable. The speaker imagines that when he speaks the word 'outside', as he does here, the word sighs, and that sigh goes up over the wood's roof. This plain language, demonstrating deviance from syntactical norms by an obtrusive yet ordinary word order, describes the tendency of feelings to come to us mutually from our own interiority, from other people, from the landscape we inhabit, and from the words that go along with them all.

Graham's poem engages in a direct interrogation of the relationship between its speaker and addressee. The second section begins with the speaker operating at the extradiegetic level, commenting upon the situation in the abstract represented space he has been describing in the first section, referring to himself and the addressee as 'them', separating the 'I' and 'me'. The poem itself occupies the position that the bird (l. 14) and the trees (l. 4) had occupied, with two people sheltering under its branches, and walking, as they had already done (l. 9), but walking in a landscape populated with words, which here are 'shy', perhaps hinting at the embarrassment of the covert encounter. The second stanza of this section insists that 'It is only an ordinary wood', 'the wood out of my window', but the second half of the stanza confirms what most of the poem has been demonstrating, that this landscape is inhabited by words. The woodland, now identified as Madron Wood, continues to have an unsettling relationship to the words: it holds them and puts them. Is the holding embrace or detention? And what is it to 'put' a word? It is possible to use a verb that normally takes a preposition (put in, out, away, up etc.), without one (as in 'get' uttered as an imperative meaning 'go', OED V.31.d). Here the putting seems a description of the placing of words by one another called, in certain circumstances, poetry. The strangeness of the act of poetry itself is made evident in these expressions. The speaker hears the words, which 'move / As a darkness of my family', recalling the darkness of the black hole, and also suggesting either (or both) a darkness that belongs to the speaker's family, one of the obscure, covert things in family relations that shift and shape the patterns those relations take, or a darkness with which the speaker feels kinship.

The final section of the poem consists of just two sentences. The first identifies the light yet terrible wind that blows from word to word, the wind that makes connected speech, communicative action and human community possible. This wind recalls the sigh of Outside, and again the active power of speech, including poetic speech, is found in the landscape. It is a spirit that moves from term to term, animating them. The poem closes with another direct address from the speaker, who, in a moment of summation, presents what has gone before in the poem as 'another / Sound and sign signifying you' (ll. 37–8). As has been seen with 'and' in l. 11, the sound and sign could here be two separate things added together, or two ways of describing the same item: the conjunction prizes the sound of the word away from its being a sign, prizes its performance on one occasion away from its imbrication in a structure; and yet at the same time identifies these divided aspects of sound and sign. The speaker tells the addressee that she or he was probably unaware that what has now been said does indeed signify him or her, although the name that has been spoken is not the name to find which the addressee came to the poem. With subtle exploitation of the standing potential for ambiguity in English, this poem produces deviant utterances that explore the conditions of their own possibility. Graham's poem and his thoughts on poetry do not permit him to claim for the strangeness of his utterance any transformative effect beyond the poem itself, on a secreted, underlying structure; but he does not need such a claim to engage in a revaluation of the relationships between people and their language; for that, only attention to the peculiarity of his ordinary language is required. Language creates and answers the needs people have, with slight yet adequate movement, a movement of the language between accommodation and deformation: 'This night moves and this language / Moves over slightly / To meet another's need / Or make another's need' ('Seven Letters', 'Letter III', *NCP*, p. 127).

Notes

1. W. S. Graham, 'Notes on a Poetry of Release', in *The Nightfisherman: Selected Letters of W. S. Graham*, ed. Michael and Margaret Snow (Manchester: Carcanet, 1999), pp. 379–83 (pp. 379–80). Compare Henri Lefebvre, who insists that the first and second '1' in the sequence '1, 1' are different in as much as one is the first, the other the second, *Rhythmanalysis: Space, Time and Everyday Life*, trans. Stuart Elden and Gerald Moore, intro. by Stuart Elden (London and New York: Continuum, 2004), p. 7.
2. 'W. S. Graham and the Heidegger Question', in *Complicities: British Poetry 1945–2007*, ed. Robin Purves and Sam Ladkin (Prague: Litteraria Pragensia, 2007), pp. 4–29 (p. 20).
3. Tony Lopez, *The Poetry of W. S. Graham* (Edinburgh: Edinburgh University Press, 1989), p. 24. Lopez suggests that Heidegger's thinking might provide a more suitable context for Graham's work. For Heidegger in Graham see also Adam Piette, '"Roaring between the lines": W. S. Graham and the White Threshold of Line Breaks', in *W. S. Graham: Speaking Towards You*, ed. Ralph Pite and Hester Jones (Liverpool: Liverpool University Press, 2004), pp. 44–62 and Robin Purves, 'W. S. Graham and the Heidegger Question', *passim*.
4. 'Standard Language and Poetic Language' (1932), in *A Prague School Reader on Esthetics, Literary Structure, and Style*, ed. Paul L. Garvin (Washington, DC: Georgetown University Press, 1964), pp. 17–30 (p. 18).

5. Jan Mukařovský, 'On Poetic Language' (1940), in *The Word and Verbal Art: Selected Essays by Jan Mukařovský*, trans. and ed. John Burbank and Peter Steiner, foreword by René Wellek (New Haven and London: Yale University Press, 1977), pp. 1–64 (p. 8).

6. Viktor Shklovsky, 'Art as Technique' (1917), in *Russian Formalist Criticism: Four Essays*, trans. and intro. by Lee T. Lemon and Marion J. Reis (Lincoln, NE and London: University of Nebraska Press, 1965), pp. 3–24 (pp. 12, 23–4).

7. John Keats, *Complete Poems*, ed. Jack Stillinger (Cambridge, MA: Harvard University Press, 1978), p. 283.

8. Jan Mukařovský, *Aesthetic Function, Norm and Value As Social Facts*, trans. Mark E. Suino (Ann Arbor: Department of Slavic Languages and Literature, The University of Michigan, 1979 [1936]), p. 40.

9. N. Fabb, 'Is Literary Language a Development of Ordinary Language?', *Lingua* (2009), doi: 10.1016/j.lingua.2009.07.007, suggests that there are certain kinds of avant-garde literary practice that employ 'non-linguistic cognitive principles', p. 3, and therefore do not qualify as literary uses of language. I disagree with Fabb, and, for different reasons, with Simon Jarvis, 'For a Poetics of Verse', *PMLA* 125:4 (October 2010), 931–6.

10. Paul Crowther, *Defining Art, Creating the Canon: Artistic Value in an Era of Doubt* (Oxford: Clarendon Press, 2007), p. 39.

11. W. S. Graham, *New Collected Poems*, ed. Matthew Francis (London: Faber, 2004), pp. 237–8.

12. 'Seven Letters', 'Letter II', *NCP*, p. 123. For this phrase and some other remarks on this sequence of poems, see Dennis O'Driscoll, 'W. S. Graham: Professor of Silence', in *The Constructed Space: A Celebration of W. S. Graham*, ed. Ronnie Duncan and Jonathan Davidson (Lincoln: Jackson's Arm, 1994), pp. 51–65 (p. 55).

13. Geoff Ward, 'Language Poetry and the American Avant-garde', *British Association for American Studies Pamphlet Series* 25, notes the novelty of one Language theorist's 'internalization of political struggle within a macrocosmic linguistic model' and yet also the weakness of any such claim to political influence beyond the audience for a particular poem, pp. 16, 18. L=A=N=G=U=A=G=E writing has in some sense seized upon and reversed the values of Donald Davie's paranoid judgement that 'it is impossible not to trace a connection between the laws of syntax and the laws of society, between bodies of usage in speech and in social life, between tearing a word from its context and choosing a leader from out of the ruck. One could almost say, on this showing, that to dislocate syntax in poetry is to threaten the rule of law in the civilized community.' *Purity of Diction in English Verse and Articulate Energy* (Manchester: Carcanet, 2006), p. 86.

14. Bruce Andrews, 'The Poetics of L=A=N=G=U=A=G=E'. Available at <http://www.ubu.com/papers/andrews.html> (last accessed 10 June 2006).

For the political writings, see <http://www.arras.net/andrews_poli_sci.htm> (last accessed on 10 June 2006). Charles Bernstein, 'Artifice of Absorption', in *A Poetics* (Cambridge, MA: Harvard University Press, 1992), pp. 9–89 deals extensively with the ways in which language can become or refuse to become an immersive medium for a reader.

15. Bruce Andrews, 'Text and Context', in *The L=A=N=G=U=A=G=E Book*, ed. Bruce Andrews and Charles Bernstein (Carbondale and Edwardsville: Southern Illinois University Press, 1984), pp. 31–8 (p. 33).

16. Ibid. p. 36.

17. 'Encyclopedia / *the world we will know*', in *The L=A=N=G=U=A=G=E Book*, pp. 244–7 (pp. 246, 247).

18. Karl Marx and Frederick Engels, *The German Ideology*, ed. and trans. S. Ryazanskaya (London: Lawrence and Wishart, 1965/Moscow: Progress, 1964 [1845–6/1932]), pp. 41–2.

19. 'Writing Social Work and Political Practice', in *The L=A=N=G=U=A=G=E Book*, pp. 133–6 (p. 133).

20. Ibid. p. 136.

21. An exchange on this theme, but in relation to the writing of Ron Silliman, is recorded in Jerome J. McGann, 'Contemporary Poetry, Alternate Routes', in *Politics and Poetic Value*, ed. Robert von Hallberg (Chicago and London: The University of Chicago Press, 1987), pp. 253–76; Charles Altieri, 'Without Consequences Is No Politics: A Response to Jerome McGann', in *Politics and Poetic Value*, pp. 301–7; Jerome McGann, 'Response to Charles Altieri', in *Politics and Poetic Value*, pp. 309–13. I would like to thank Sam Ladkin for directing me towards this exchange.

22. Bob Perelman, 'Building a More Powerful Vocabulary: Bruce Andrews and the World (Trade Center)', in *The Marginalization of Poetry: Language Writing and Literary History* (Princeton: Princeton University Press, 1996), pp. 96–108, makes a comparison between Andrews' attempts to break the structure of language and the difficulty of bringing down the World Trade Centre, which had recently been attacked.

23. Petr Kouba, 'Beyond Phenomenology of Language', in *Dynamic Structure*, pp. 104–29 (pp. 106–7). See also in the same volume Yong-Ho Choi, 'Saussure and Ricoeur at Odds with the Question of Meaning', pp. 130–59 (p. 140), where the pragmatic moment is presented as the moment at which the closed world of signs becomes the open system of signification.

24. F. de Saussure, *Course in General Linguistics*, ed. Charles Bally and Albert Sechehaye, with Albert Riedlinger, trans. Roy Harris (London: Duckworth, 1983 [1915]), pp. 9, 13.

25. Louis Armand, 'Language and Interactivity', in *Dynamic Structure*, pp. 247–60 (p. 259) talks of language systematicity as an '*event state*' or 'programmatic *structural ambivalence*', identifying the creative moment with the very openness of the system itself.

26. Piotr Sadowski, *Systems Theory as an Approach to the Study of Literature: Origins and Functions of Literature* (Lewiston; Queenston, Ontario; Lampeter, Wales: Edwin Mellen Press, 1999), pp. 24–6.

CHAPTER TEN

Figure: Tom Raworth

Metaphor, as will already be evident from 'Figure: Walter Ralegh', has been thought characteristic of poetic language. A recent book on the subject states that 'metaphor has always been, and still is, the main device of poetry'.[1] Several important accounts of metaphor have been offered from diverse quarters in recent decades, and I want to engage with three of them in this chapter: the cognitive account of metaphor as conceptual mapping; Donald Davidson's insistence that the meaning of a metaphor is just its literal meaning; Paul de Man's argument that knowledge about the operations of the mind has the structure of metaphor, of substitution. All of these accounts are, to one degree or another, oriented by cognition rather than language, by the idea that cognition might be an operation distinct from and underlying language. They all also depart from a tradition that metaphors report the perception of a new likeness between two objects. The poem with which this chapter engages is figurative in many highly complex ways: it employs metaphors announced and unannounced by predication; it provides images of poetry itself; it provides images of the mind making poems which are themselves made (in part) of images; it presents various terms and scenes that cannot be taken in any simple sense as figurative or literal, as being themselves or pointing to something else. Reading the poem, one might even say one is not sure when one is or is not encountering a metaphor. Furthermore, the poem playfully complicates its metaphorical organisation by the very fact that the metaphors it employs are in a poem, in a certain kind of utterance with its own sequence, moment, history of being (pre-composition, composition, performance). Indeed, one of the discursive subjects of the poem is the kind of historical moment that the writing of a poem represents. In this sense the poem, without ceasing to be highly poetical, conducts a critical investigation into how minds and language work just as philosophical and serious as the theoretical writings also addressed in this chapter.

Gaslight

a line of faces borders the strangler's work
heavy european women
mist blows over dusty tropical plants
lit from beneath the leaves by a spotlight
mist in my mind a riffled deck

of cards or eccentrics
was i
a waterton animal my head
is not my own

poetry is neither swan nor owl
but worker, miner
digging each generation deeper
through the shit of its eaters
to the root – then up to the giant tomato

someone else's song is always behind us
as we wake from a dream trying to remember
step onto a thumbtack

two worlds – we write the skin
the surface tension that holds
                                    you
                                    in
what we write is ever   the past

curtain pulled back
a portrait behind it
is a room suddenly lit

looking out through the eyes
at a t.v. programme
of a monk sealed into a coffin

we close their eyes and ours
and still here the tune

moves on[2]

The poem can be considered as tripartite, with a central section explicitly
discussing the nature of poetry and poetic creation, and two outer sections
that offer more or less legible contexts for the central discussion. It is vital
to my analysis of the poem that these outer sections may, but need not, be
taken as figuring the mental and linguistic processes described explicitly
(and yet figuratively) in the middle section. This seriously playful poem has
fun with the idea that we might not know the status of our own cognitions;

its self-referentiality and tendency to focus attention on its own modes of making meaning provokes a sense of uncertain ground, precisely because one is unsure what is ground and what is figure. Such a feeling of uncertainty and yet voluptuous rightness is one of the characteristics of poetic language at the explication of which I am aiming in this book.

In some poems Raworth offers tentative (or provocative) descriptions of his practice: 'sometimes a fragment of language / illuminates a world not consistently round / breathing its air'.[3] Likewise, the central section of 'Gaslight' refuses and then offers metaphors for poetry. Poetry 'is neither swan nor owl / but worker, miner': poetry should not be thought of in terms of grace, flight, wisdom or other avian attributes, least of all the virility of Zeus or the wisdom of Athena, embodied in those two birds in certain mythical narratives. The poem prefers to identify with worker and miner, in a gesture that perhaps embarrassingly affiliates the traditionally leisured pursuits of the language arts with labour (though Raworth in a later poem, 'The West', is evidently conscious of the embarrassment the association should cause: 'inhuman luxury / writing this / hidden labour / around the world').[4] There are other reasons for the association with the miner: there is a miner bird (aptly known as a noisy miner), and miners would in the later nineteenth century have worn gaslights, acetylene torches, for their work. But the poem refuses graceful, traditional figures for the poetic act and prefers an association with labour. Poetry digs 'each generation deeper / through the shit of its eaters': the consumers of poetry themselves produce waste (memories of lines, new poems, or even critical thinking) through which poetry itself then digs, both consumed and working in the waste of its own having been consumed. The circularity of this image is further complicated by syntactical ambiguity: is 'each generation' the object of 'digging', or a temporal clause qualifying 'digging'? Perhaps poetry submerges each generation deeper and deeper into the shit of its eaters? But would that be the eaters of poetry or the eaters of the generation, its over-consumers? These two syntactical ambiguities present a more socially oriented reading of the nature of the work poetry does. The circularity of the image train continues in the following line when poetry arrives at 'the root – then up to the giant tomato', this succulently absurd image of the fruits of poetic labour suggesting that poetry nourishes its own roots and becomes its own fruit, being transformed from a shit-shovelling miner to a life-giving moisture.

The following section confirms more plainly that poets are always working with other people's poetry in their heads, which may also be the realisation of the earlier poem, 'Sing', whose title is what the poet is impelled to do, and is impelled to do so by 'the pressure of air i / don't remember'.[5] The other songs in 'Gaslight' are 'behind us', a haunting as the poet moves from the dreamlike state of conception to the act of composition, which is more a remembering;

those songs are then figured as a thumbtack on which one steps, the nasty shock on getting out of bed: other poems are both the haunting behind and the nasty shock in front of the poet. The final part of this middle section proposes that there are 'two worlds', which, from what has just been said concerning poetic memory and the creative act, and from what is to follow, are the worlds of past and future, the worlds of poems made and poems to be made. Writing is 'the skin' between these two worlds, something integral to them, organic, porous, and yet marking them out from the rest of the world, it is 'surface tension'. The line-grouping here offers (at least) two ways of being read, the lineation and alignment of final words or phrases in the lines suggesting that 'the past' be read both as a continuation of the phrase that runs down the right hand side of the page ('holds you in the past') and at the same time together with the longer line ('what we write is ever the past'). This *mis en page* shares in some of the possibilities of Raworth's poems in two columns, such as *Ace*, in which two relatively distinct series can provoke or solicit their being read in parallel (as when the left column reads 'he sees / a / cross / connection').[6] The writing itself, then, is as circumscribed by the past as is the 'you' addressed in the lines, it consigns others and itself to the past, it is an act of historicising a moment, an act that marks this particular time as distinct from all others, the time that is produced by that verbal past, expressed by this verbal present, inviting and excluding various verbal futures.[7] So in this central section of the poem, poetry is not a swan nor an owl, but a worker, miner, comestible, waste product, plant, fruit, song, dream, thumbtack, world, skin and surface tension, but perhaps above all it is writing, a peculiar mark-making that makes moments.

The concluding section of the poem plays with pictures of the mind and its operation. One source for the poem's title, and some of its imagery, is the film (or rather two films based on a play by Patrick Hamilton) *Gaslight*, in which the principal action revolves around a husband's psychological assault on his wife, tormenting her by making her doubt her senses and memory. The flickering of the gaslights in their home is one of her perceptions upon which he casts doubt. Attacking someone's sense of the reliability of their senses as a form of psychological torture is now known as 'gaslighting'. Other features of the poem can be traced to this text. In the 1944 American film version directed by George Cukor, the husband has previously murdered his wife's aunt, by strangulation. His current marriage is part of a scheme to obtain a particularly magnificent set of jewels. When the husband and his new wife take up home in the murdered aunt's London townhouse, a portrait of the aunt (a singer) is revealed from behind a drapery. Several settings of the film are misty, including the opening sequence in which the history of the strangling is mostly revealed. Ingrid Bergman, who plays the niece and victim of the gaslighting, may correspond to the heavy European women.[8] The poem draws on scenic and narrative features of the film, and thematises the uncertainty of sense data, but treating *Gaslight* as an intertext by no means resolves the issues of 'Gaslight'.

The transition from the second section of the poem is not made in clear terms, so that the two main objects of the first line-grouping, the portrait behind a curtain and the 'room suddenly lit' both present themselves as candidates for continuations of the preceding subject, the act of writing itself. The bald predication ('portrait . . . is a room') is also of course a figure, but there are no sufficient grounds here to determine which item, the portrait or the room, figures the other, and both already seem candidates for figuring mental interiority, the getting, having and revealing of ideas. Raworth's writing often reflects on the processes by which its own stock of images becomes available to it, persisting in the memory ('thought, memories, dreams continue in the clamped skull'), with characters in these narratives having their own consciousnesses, in which archetypal filmic images ('breakfast / at the savoy : the intruder', for example) are also stored.[9] In 'Gaslight' the revelation of the portrait is a peeling back of an exterior to reveal a likeness, true likenesses of people being often thought of as a matter of interiority mysteriously making itself visible externally (the idea of the consciousness as a room furnished by ideas is found in John Locke, and criticised by Paul de Man, as I shall go on to note more fully below). The next line-grouping continues to present images of mental interiority. It is not clear who is 'looking out through the eye', either the subject of the portrait, or the consciousness figured by the lit room, yet the second preposition ('through') argues that the origin and goal of the looking is behind the eyes, that there is something behind the eyes that looks.[10] The TV programme is an image, in the most straightforward sense. The 'monk sealed into a coffin' again suggests the corporeal limitations placed upon a spirituality that is characterised by retreat. The poem closes with a closure of the eyes, 'their eyes and ours', where 'their eyes' may be understood as the eyes of the subject of the portrait, or the subject whose consciousness is presented as a room, or the subject whose consciousness is looking out. This closure is a retreat into interiority, but even there ('here', encourages the misprision 'hear', even in silent reading) the tune (the songs of other people behind the poet) 'moves on': even in the attempt to retreat within, there is a constant motion. Even when the various pictures of the interiority that one might think it is the job of poetry to reveal become the sole focus of the poet's attention, there is a movement, even if only a movement through those very images, that is the poem itself as a tune, a mark or gesture in time.

The opening of the poem remains to be discussed. One encouragement to read the portrait, the room, the monk in the coffin and so on as images of mental interiority is the more direct figuration of the mind in the opening section. The mind is pictured as 'a riffled deck / / of cards or eccentrics'. The contents of the mind (ideas, concepts, images) are pictured as cards, shuffled and placed in no particular order, but, importantly, ready to play and perhaps to gamble. One doesn't normally have a deck of eccentrics, nor does one shuffle them, so this is itself an eccentric image of the poet's mind, and one that prepares the ground for future eccentricity in imagery. The poet then asks 'was i / a waterton animal', Charles Waterton being an early nineteenth-century traveller, naturalist and taxidermist, one of whose practices was to make uncanny composite figures from parts of various animals, including one called 'The Nondescript', made from (the rear end of) a howler monkey.[11] The poet wonders if he is dead, if his body has been filled up with something else, if his mind, his 'head', does not simply belong to someone else. This is a poem in which mental contents are pictured as not being private property, as not being arranged in a particular order, but as being eccentric, kitsch and uncanny (the stuffed animal).

It is not particularly clear, however, that these figures figure mind, or figure only mind. A syntactical ambiguity ('mist in my mind a riffled deck') allows either the mist or the mind to be figured in the riffled deck. The mist itself is another possible picture of the mind, the diffusion, obscurity, existence between states that will feature later in the poem. But the way in which the mist comes to figure is problematic, and the aspect of the poem that is most resistant to this reading of it as a series of critical reflections upon the images of mind and poetry that are belied by the processual-historical nature of poetic composition. The mist comes into the poem as part of a series of images that will not cohere with such a reading, nor with each other: there is no palpable relation between the 'strangler's work', the 'line of faces', the 'heavy european women', the mist, the 'dusty tropical plants' and the spot-light, nor necessarily between them and the poem's title, 'Gaslight'. Some of these features can be traced to the film to which the poem is related, but not all of them, the tropical plants, for example. 'Gaslight' suggests a particular historical moment from the mid nineteenth and the early twentieth century, an industrial heritage, whether at work or play, and also suggest the atmos-pherics of a criminal scene. The 'spotlight' on the dusty tropical plants echoes the gaslight, but suggests a mid to late twentieth-century civic or theatrical environment. So there is dissonance in the scene-setting of the poem, just as there is dissonance between the titles and the contents of many of Raworth's shorter poems. There is also dissonance in the very collocation of mist and dust, furthered by the spotlighting. All I can say about this series of images that opens the poem is that they are there, that they are the means by which a more legible train of images commences, and in this way they are a rather convenient demonstration of the eccentricity, the contingency of the contents of the mind and utterances of the poet.[12]

I would like to turn now to the accounts of metaphor offered by certain cognitive poeticians in order to demonstrate the recalcitrance of a poem such as Raworth's to their methods. I will mention three approaches: those of George Lakoff and Mark Turner, Reuven Tsur and Peter Stockwell. In each case, I will suggest that emphasis on the schematic correspondence of one concept or set of concepts to another risks eliding the particularity of the poetic utterance, such as I have just tried to describe. In cognitive poetics, cognition is conceived of as an embodied human act, which, whilst it may have determinate linguistic forms, is prior to and independent of those forms. Language is presented as a distraction from the cognitive processes that underlie and drive it. Lakoff and Turner concern themselves with the organisation of concepts into schemes and domains, schemes being a specific ordering of concepts within a particular domain.[13] Conceptual metaphors map one domain onto another: 'Metaphors are conceptual mappings. They are a matter of thought, not merely language.'[14] For the metaphor to be rich and appropriate there must be a structure for the different related elements in each domain, a variety of slots in that structure that can be filled differently, and similarities in causal structure across the two domains mapped: in short, the two domains mapped onto one another must have generic level equivalences. (A sceptic might ask whether much more is being said here than that the things compared in a metaphor are similar.) Concepts compared in metaphors may themselves be metaphorical or non-metaphorical: 'to the extent that a concept is understood and structured on its own terms – without making use of structure imported from a completely different conceptual domain – we will say that it is not metaphorical'.[15] The example of a dog is given, in which the physical form of the dog is non-metaphorical, its loyalty metaphorical, demonstrating the tendency of cognitive poetics to prioritise spatial manifestations and relations.

Conceptual metaphors are not the work of individual poets, but of an entire culture, a common way of perceiving the world:

> The basic metaphors are not creations of poets; rather, it is the masterful way in which poets extend, compose, and compress them that we find poetic. . . . On various traditional views, metaphor is a matter of unusual language, typically novel and poetic language, that strikes us as deviant, imaginative, and fanciful. We and other researchers have argued instead that metaphor is a conceptual matter, often unconscious, and that conceptual metaphors underlie everyday language as well as poetic language.[16]

The poetic, artful use of common metaphors defamiliarises: 'What makes poetic metaphor noticeable and memorable is thus the special, nonautomatic use to which ordinary, automatic modes of thought are put.'[17] Poetic metaphor may criticise the very metaphorical mappings that we use to understand reality:

> through the masterful use of metaphoric processes on which our conceptual systems are based, poets address the most vital issues in our lives and help us illuminate those issues, through the extension, composition, and criticism of the basic metaphoric tools through which we comprehend much of reality.

Avant-garde literary practice is particularly interested in this form of criticism of conceptual metaphors, attempting

> to step outside the ordinary ways we think metaphorically and either to offer new modes of metaphorical thought or to make the use of our conventional basic metaphors less automatic by employing them in unusual ways, or otherwise to destabilize them and thus reveal their inadequacies for making sense of reality.[18]

But there is a problem here: if basic conceptual mappings are realities, because of certain generic level similarities between the domains to which the mapped concepts belong, how can those realities be undone by particular uses of the metaphor?

Lakoff and Turner identify the metaphor of the great chain of being as vital for various mappings, but also an ideological imposition upon people who find themselves subjugated in part by the prevalence of this metaphor in conceptions of social life. If there are generic level structural and causal similarities between the concepts, then they just can be mapped, whether or not they should be. Lakoff and Turner here throw into doubt the neutrality of their own preferred models of conceptual mappings such as 'LIFE IS A JOURNEY' and 'STAYING ALIVE IS A CONTEST'.[19] If one starts to question whether or not life is structurally and causally like a journey, one has to have a certain concept of life, and not all people in one culture share one picture of life. Mechanisms have been introduced into cognitive poetics to limit the damage of conceptual differences of this sort, such as the tendency towards 'good examples' or 'prototypes' of particular concepts, versions of the concept that fit best.[20] But are there really prototypes or good examples of the concept of 'life' that can be said naturally to exclude outlying concepts, and would those good examples or prototypes all suggest that life is a journey? A suicide, for example, might not feel it is. In some sense, the avant-garde poet Lakoff and Turner depict is simply loosening the rigidity and normativity that they themselves have insisted upon in their account of metaphor. In Raworth's poem, one might recognise an avant-garde attitude in the mapping of the 'mind' as 'a riffled deck / / of cards or eccentrics'. The underlying conceptual mapping might be identified as the mind as a collection,[21] but that general conceptual mapping cannot provide any fine account of the expression: cards are designed exclusively for play, mental contents are not; mental contents are ordered, a riffled deck is deliberately disordered. And this is before one takes account of the apparent equivalence of cards and eccentrics.

Tsur however offers an alternative understanding of conceptual metaphor as the cancellation of attributes: having identified the metaphor by a literal impossibility or incongruity, the reader cancels out features of the objects that do not correspond to arrive at what does, thereby making a new meaning. Tsur is critical of Lakoff's later work because it displays a desire to resolve all conceptual difference too quickly and easily into conventional scheme relations: he has a limited capacity, Tsur argues, for 'exposure to uncertainty'. Tsur says that he is trying to distinguish between two approaches to metaphor:

> One of them works with pre-established meanings; the other one with an indefinite range of potential meanings, changing subsets of which may be realized in changing contexts. These are two alternative interpretative strategies. The respective cognitive attitudes are rapid and delayed conceptualization. They have different advantages and disadvantages. The former is advantageous when speed of response is required, while accuracy and subtlety are less important; the latter is advantageous when the obverse is the case.[22]

Certainly the delayed conceptualising attitude is required when attempting to work out in what respects cards and eccentrics are unlike: decks of cards contain suits, that is, genres of things, as well as series; they also have picture cards representing types of social function or personality; eccentrics do not share a centre, and so might be thought not to follow series, to be beyond genres, to stand to one side of normative social functions and personality types. But here one sees that the unlikeness that has led to cancellation stems from the very concept of unlikeness: eccentrics are not like the others. How can their properties have been metaphorically foregrounded by restating in various ways one basic sense of the word 'eccentric'? If the theory of cancellation is redundant here, neither it nor the theory of conceptual mapping has much success with the series of statements, or images, that concentrate themselves in the metaphor in the first half of the line just cited: 'mist in my mind'. This mist is the one that blows over dusty tropical plants, and may or may not have something to do with the 'line of faces', 'the strangler's work' and 'heavy european women'. These items present incongruities that require interpretation through their semantic disjunction, but very little by way of features that can be mapped or cancelled in order to produce an interpretation: it is not clear if they are to be understood in relation to one another metaphorically or not. These opening lines seem to me to play with the idea that minds map or cancel features of items presented to cognition in order to arrive at harmonious or normative interpretations; rather, these lines show how haphazard the process of getting to where one finds oneself is.

Peter Stockwell has a slightly different solution to the question of how avant-garde writing criticises standard conceptual mappings, suggesting that the unconventional mappings of a surrealist poem (he takes Keith Douglas where Lakoff and Turner had taken André Breton) require one to proceed as if the mappings were conventional in a different discourse universe, where, for example, geraniums really did explode. Stockwell suggests that 'instead of mapping between cognitive models, my reading accounts for the discomfort of surrealism by understanding it as an enforced restructuring of existing familiar source domains'.[23] The unconventional mappings, conventional in their own discourse world, must here be mapped back onto the conventional discourse world in order to enact this forced restructuring. But does this set of operations have any purchase on the opening lines of 'Gaslight'? There is no discourse world in which a mind being like a riffled deck of eccentrics makes more or less sense, nor, on the contrary is it necessary to invent a discourse world in which there are 'heavy european women': there are doubtless some in the conventional discourse world. It is the uncertain relation of these elements one to another, uncertain in everything but their appearance in this particular poem, that makes them resistant to this, as to any other, conceptual-cognitivist reading.

Towards the end of their text on metaphor, Lakoff and Turner criticise the philosopher Donald Davidson for his refusal to acknowledge the role of concepts in metaphor.[24] Davidson has an unusual view of metaphor, that 'metaphors mean what the words, in their most literal interpretation, mean, and nothing more'.[25] Whilst he makes some reference to the theories of inventive construction and inventive construal, of passing interpretations (see 'Introduction'), the main purpose of Davidson's essay is to maintain a rigid distinction between meaning and sense, whereby meaning is the property of the words in the sentence, whilst sense is that which can be made of them by a speaker or hearer. Davidson thinks 'metaphor belongs exclusively to the domain of use', that is, the meanings of metaphors are plain assertions, but the likeness claim made by them is a matter of use only.[26] It has been noted that Davidson does not here deny that literal meanings can require contexts, as for example, when a temporal specification requires contextual knowledge to understand its meaning. 'Davidson is not saying that meaning and truth are independent of context, but rather, that meaning and truth are independent of the context of *use*.'[27] What a sentence is used to do (to convince its hearer, for example) is of no relevance to its meaning. The tendency of previous schools of thought on metaphor has been to 'fasten on the contents of the thoughts a metaphor provokes and to read these contents into the metaphor itself', thereby confusing the meaning of the metaphor with the interpretation or sense that it may bear for particular users.[28] Thus, when Raworth says that 'poetry is neither swan nor owl / but worker, miner' he means just that. But the sense of the phrase is an interpretation, and involves the strategies of imputation, glossing, invention and so on involved whenever one person tries to understand what another person says: 'all communication by speech', after all, 'assumes the interplay of inventive construction and inventive construal'. Metaphors, Davidson maintains, are just one amongst 'endless devices that serve to alert us to aspects of the world by inviting us to make comparisons'.[29] Similarities, in this understanding, are simply patent, and yet we need to be invited to notice them. Poetry just is like a miner, working in the dark to explore and exploit subterranean regions. The metaphor invites us to compare what is similar in the ideas that we have of poetry and of miners; that it compares the two terms is self-evident; that they might share features is to do with our ideas of the two objects in question and not the metaphor.

Davidson would say, then, that the meaning of the words 'poetry is . . . miner' is that poetry is a miner, and he confines any talk of what one might mean by saying poetry is a miner to the realm of paraphrase or interpretation. But to say that the meaning of the phrase is patent is very different from saying that the similarity the phrase invites us to see is patent. Davidson has a peculiar and extensive idea of similarity whereby anything can be like anything else because, in the model of linguistic meaning and truth Davidson has developed, any two things can be said to share a disjunctive property: neither a cactus nor a banana is a sheep, therefore they share the property of not being a sheep.[30] In the case of Raworth's metaphor there is no particular patency in the comparison, especially as the metaphor digs through the 'shit' of poetry's 'eaters / to the root – then up to the giant tomato': because the object of the comparison (poetry) has also taken up a role in the set of ideas and concepts that are used to figure it.[31] It is an interpretation of the words, a sense to them, that points to the rather remote similarities between poetry and other things discussed earlier in this chapter, and not simply their meaning. Yet the reader can find non-trivial ways in which poetry and miner are alike, ways that don't simply rest on disjunction (such as neither of them being fizzy-pop).[32]

Furthermore, the meanings of words in a poem, and other places, for that matter, are not as patent as all that. There is the syntactic ambiguity in the run of Raworth's metaphor that presents at least the possibility that 'each generation' could be taken nominally instead of temporally: one needs to ask what is meant by the words before one has the meanings of the words. Critics of Davidson's essay have pointed to its overdependence on a distinction between meaning and sense: 'The meaning/use distinction will not work, because meaning is always a product of both semantics and pragmatics, of language and use.' The criticism extends to the patency of the conceptual world Davidson presents, one of absolute legibility, as opposed to the world of partial, passing, and intermittent interpretations: 'literal meaning must remain open and incomplete . . . for it contains, within itself, some irreducible quantum of metaphor, induced by the unfinished state of the world itself'.[33] The meaning of a metaphor is always something that is meant by that metaphor because the ideational schemes people have of their worlds are not perfectly clear and patent, but require more work. The phrase 'what we write is ever the past' does not have distinguished literal and metaphorical meanings before a reader attempts to construe how the predication is working here, whether writing is an action that creates a past, or whether it is an action that is always in the past. When the poem says that 'someone else's song is always behind us', there are several meanings of 'behind' from which to choose: is the case that with this song behind us we need fear nothing; that the song is, like a pantomime villain, behind us; that the song is behind the things we say, as plotters are behind plots? These are real meanings, impossible to attribute in any order without some sense to the phrase. There is a necessarily processual quality to the metaphors of this and any poem because they take place in a particular utterance, because they need to be construed contextually, in relation to the poem, the authorship, the wider textual world, in order to have anything like what Davidson conceives of as a literal meaning: it is such a process that invites a reader to compare writing poems to having 'someone else's song' behind one, and to stepping on a 'thumbtack'.

Far from being non-conceptual, then, Davidson's account of metaphor requires us to have good concepts of things named by words, concepts we can adapt, but which are not reciprocally tied to the literal meanings of words, which apparently remain untouched by the comparisons made between them and similar items. In making the work of metaphor non-linguistic, his approach resembles that of the cognitive poeticians. Paul de Man, on the contrary, attempts to demonstrate that all knowledge has the form of metaphor, of rhetorical substitution of one term for another. Metaphor, he says, has long been a difficulty for philosophy, to such an extent that it seems 'philosophy either has to give up its own constitutive claim to rigour in order to come to terms with the figurality of its language or that it has to free itself from figuration altogether'. De Man suggests that even when philosophers attempt to banish figurative language, they employ it so fully and constantly that 'such far-reaching assumptions are then made about the structure of the mind that one may wonder whether the metaphors illustrate a cognition or if the cognition is not perhaps shaped by the metaphors'. The antagonistic attitude philosophers have taken to metaphor is illustrated by reference to a series of attempts to distinguish philosophy's work of literal and systematic definition in non-metaphorical language, but 'in each case [those of Locke, Condillac, Kant], it turns out to be impossible to maintain a clear line of distinction between rhetoric, abstraction, symbol, and all other forms of language'. The closing section of Raworth's poem is unclear as to whether it provides a figurative expansion of the preceding section, just as the opening section of the poem may or may not offer a rich background for the metaphors of mist in the mind and the mind as a deck of cards: it is not clear that this language is being used symbolically or figuratively. Yet the portrait behind the curtain, the lit room, the eyes can all be read as relating to the writing mind that features prominently in the poem. Poems don't necessarily make claims to rigour of any kind, but, de Man says, literature is the place where 'the possible convergence of rigor and pleasure is shown to be a delusion', as the pleasure of wit (substitution, figure) is always non-rigorous. Raworth's poem supplies pictures that might be pictures of the writing mind, obscuring the language of epistemology by allowing its words to hover between figural potentials, but the force of the poem is not necessarily 'proliferating and disruptive', as de Man characterises the power of figurative language.[34] As John Barrell has noted, of Raworth's work in general, this poem presents 'the coherence of the self and the release from the constraints of coherence as the equally impossible alternatives which define the limits of utterance'.[35] The poem is about the complex moment of writing, relating to the past, and the songs of other people heard there, and the future, towards which the 'tune / / moves on'. It is not just an instance of certain pictures of the writing mind, it is also an organisation of those pictures into a complex sequence, that makes, in the slightly paradoxical sense of the phrase, a historical moment. It is the fact that all figures are in particular utterances, in particular forms of words as made and shared, and not in conceptual mappings, cancelled attributes, blended discourse worlds, a meaning of words distinct from any use, and so on, that prevents the idea of their being nothing but figurative meanings from being bleak: when there is a path through the substitutions, when they can or even must be activated in some specific order, and when that order is unrepeatable and yet completely related to the other utterances through which it becomes possible and which it makes possible, there is the potential of poetry. The resistance of this poem's opening and closing sections, and the exuberant plumness of its central figures, testify to the idiosyncrasy of poetic performance.

Notes

1. Simon Brittan, *Poetry, Symbol, and Allegory: Interpreting Metaphorical Language from Plato to the Present* (Charlottesville and London: University of Virginia Press, 2003), p. x.

2. *Collected Poems* (Manchester: Carcanet, 2003), pp. 101–2. Peter Middleton, 'Silent Critique: Tom Raworth's Early Books of Poetry', in *Removed for Further Study: The Poetry of Tom Raworth*, ed. Nate Dorward (Toronto: The Gig, 2003), pp. 7–29 (pp. 24–6), offers a reading of the poem that touches on issues of intertextuality, interiority and the insufficiency of the poem as a criterion for its own interpretation.

3. Tom Raworth, *Windmills in Flames: Old and New Poems* (Manchester: Carcanet, 2010), 'Baggage Claim (a slugging welterweight natural)', pp. 53–4 (p. 54).

4. *Collected Poems*, p. 348. See 'Selection: William Cowper' for more on this topic.

5. Ibid. p. 3.

6. Ibid. pp. 200–25, citation from p. 209.

7. Peter Robinson, *Twentieth-Century Poetry: Selves and Situations* (Oxford: Oxford University Press, 2005), pp. 225–7, quotes 'Gaslight' on the fact that other people's songs are always behind us when discussing an exchange of letters between Raworth and his father, and, more broadly, Raworth's relationship to pop art and the new.

8. *Gaslight*. Dir George Cukor. Metro-Goldwyn-Mayer. 1944. Private correspondence between the author and Tom Raworth, 8 August 2011.

9. 'The Corpse in my Head', *Collected Poems*, p. 68; see also 'End Again', p. 115.

10. Ludwig Wittgenstein, *Tractatus Logico-Philosophicus*, trans. D. F. Pears and B. F. McGuiness (London: Routledge, 1961), p. 57, No. 5.6331, notes that 'the form of the visual field is surely not like this' and produces a diagram in which the visual field begins behind the eye.

11. See Yolanda Foote, 'Waterton, Charles (1782–1865)', *Oxford Dictionary of National Biography* (Oxford: Oxford University Press, 2004) online edn, 2008. Available at <http://www.oxforddnb.com/view/article/28817> (last accessed 3 July 2010); Brian W. Edginton, *Charles Waterton: A Biography* (Cambridge: Lutterworth Press, 1996), pp. 103–7. Tom Raworth noted in private correspondence with the author, 8 August 2011, that he was thinking of 'The Nondescript' when writing this poem. For a photograph of this figure see <http://www.wakefield.gov.uk/CultureAndLeisure/HistoricWakefield/People/CharlesWaterton/charles3.htm> (last accessed on 15 January 2012).

12. Robert Sheppard, *The Poetry of Saying: British Poetry and its Discontents, 1950–2000* (Liverpool: Liverpool University Press, 2005), pp. 173–4 treats the tendency in Raworth's work of the 1970s towards disconnected filmic images, projected at too great a speed to enable their complete processing. Robin Purves has noted the dangers of reading coherent visual image trains into Raworth's poems, suggesting that Raworth's work (at least at certain points) 'frees itself from poetry's conventional relation to explicatory discourses *and* from the trappings of the visual represented in language'. 'Aspect

Shifts: On Tom Raworth's *The Big Green Day*', *Journal of British and Irish Innovative Poetry* 2:2 (2010), 171–87, pp. 176–8, 182.

13. George Lakoff and Mark Turner, *More than Cool Reason: A Field Guide to Poetic Metaphor* (Chicago: The University of Chicago Press, 1989), p. 51; see also Peter Stockwell, *Cognitive Poetics: An Introduction* (London: Routledge, 2002), p. 16.

14. Lakoff and Turner, *More than Cool Reason*, p. 107; see also Stockwell, *Cognitive Poetics*, pp. 106–7.

15. Lakoff and Turner, *More than Cool Reason*, pp. 51, 61, 65, 77–8, 83, 57.

16. Ibid. pp. 54, 136.

17. Ibid. p. 72; see also Stockwell, *Cognitive Poetics*, p. 14.

18. Lakoff and Turner, *More than Cool Reason*, pp. 215, 51–2, see also 203–4.

19. Ibid. pp. 166–7, 212–13, 3, 16.

20. Reuven Tsur, *Toward a Theory of Cognitive Poetics*, 2nd edn (Brighton: Sussex Academic Press, 2008), pp. 258–9; Stockwell, *Cognitive Poetics*, p. 29.

21. Compare David Hume, who asserts that notions of personal identity 'are nothing but a bundle or collection of different perceptions' in flux, *A Treatise of Human Nature*, ed. L.A. Selby-Bigge, 2nd rev. edn, ed. P.H. Nidditch (Oxford: Clarendon Press, 1973 [1739–40]), p. 252, I.iv.6.

22. Tsur, *Toward a Theory of Cognitive Poetics*, pp. 257, 585, 590–91.

23. Stockwell, *Cognitive Poetics*, p. 114.

24. Lakoff and Turner, *More than Cool Reason*, p. 218.

25. Donald Davidson, 'What Metaphors Mean', in *The Essential Davidson*, intro. by Ernie Lepore and Kirk Ludwig (Oxford: Clarendon Press, 2006), pp. 209–24 (p. 209).

26. Ibid. p. 210.

27. Richard J. Fogelin, *Figuratively Speaking* (New Haven and London: Yale University Press, 1988), p. 53.

28. Davidson, 'What Metaphors Mean', p. 222.

29. Ibid. pp. 209, 217.

30. Fogelin, *Figuratively Speaking*, pp. 59–61.

31. Compare William Shakespeare's simile in *Henry V*, 'Then should the warlike Harry, like himself / Assume the port of Mars', I.Prologue.5.

32. For a reading of Davidson's theory of metaphor that regards it as having more than trivial consequences, in particular for the way in which distinctions between use and meaning are drawn up, see Marga Reimer, 'Davidson on Metaphor', in *Figurative Language*, ed. Peter A. French and Howard K. Wettstein (Oxford: Blackwell, 2001), pp. 142–55, esp. p. 154.

33. Mark Gaipa and Robert Scholes, 'On the Very Idea of a Literal Meaning', in *Literary Theory After Davidson*, ed. Reed Way Dasenbrock (University Park, PA: The Pennsylvania State University Press, 1993), pp. 160–79 (pp. 168, 178). See also the remarks on competence and performance in 'Selection: Denise Riley'.

34. Paul de Man, 'The Epistemology of Metaphor', *Critical Inquiry* 5:1 (Autumn 1978), 13–30 (pp. 13, 16, 28, 30).
35. John Barrell, *The Flight of Syntax: Percy Bysshe Shelley and Tom Raworth: The William Matthews Lectures 1990 Delivered at Birkbeck College, London* (London: Birkbeck College, [1990]), p. 24.

CHAPTER ELEVEN

Selection: Denise Riley

My main concerns in this chapter are the restrictions placed upon the selection of words that make up poems, whether these restrictions are more personal or social (if that distinction makes sense), and how selection for poems relates to selectional procedures in language more generally. In relation to this last topic I consider selection in the work of the generative linguist Noam Chomsky. Whilst generative grammar and modern logic understand selection as an operation pertaining to particular terms in an individual's lexicon, following, or refusing to follow, certain rules, other theorists of literary language have focused on the selection of registers of speech and the interaction of those registers within one utterance, even within one word. This second strand in thinking about poetic selection retains close connections with the socio-political commitments of authors interested in poetic diction (see 'Selection: William Cowper'). Mikhail Bakhtin's work on speech genre and dialogue is the main contribution to such thinking considered here. The chapter will conclude with a reading of a poem by Denise Riley that makes deliberate selection errors (self-evidently a problematic category) and incorporates various sociolinguistic registers in its utterance.

In the 1950s and 1960s Noam Chomsky developed a theory of syntax that puts selection almost entirely to one side, as a matter of stylistic interest only.[1] Chomsky defines syntax as

> the study of the principles and processes by which sentences are constructed in particular languages. Syntactic investigation of a given language has as its goal the construction of a grammar that can be viewed as a device of some sort for producing the sentences of the language under analysis.[2]

He notes that 'grammar is autonomous and independent of meaning', illustrating this assertion with his famous exemplary phrase, evidently regarded as both grammatical and meaningless, 'colourless green ideas sleep furiously'. Chomsky proposes a transformational grammar: 'A grammatical transformation T operates on a given string . . . with a given constituent structure and converts it into a new string with a new derived constituent structure.' (A string here is a selection of noun phrases, verbs and so on, schematically representing a sentence.) Chomsky thinks transformational grammar has a greater descriptive power than earlier models and can, from a 'kernel' of a few simple active sentences, produce a complex grammar.[3]

This analysis makes meaningless sentences a matter of semantics rather than grammar, noting, nonetheless, that there are selectional rules, semantic rules violated for particular stylistic effects:

> strings such as [colorless green ideas sleep furiously] that break selectional rules are deviant. It is necessary to impose an interpretation on them somehow . . . Sentences that break selectional rules can often be interpreted metaphorically (particularly, as personification . . .) or allusively in one way or another, if an appropriate context of greater or less complexity is supplied. That is, these sentences are apparently interpreted by a direct analogy to well-formed sentences that observe the selectional rules in question.[4]

Selectionally deviant sentences, then, are compared to related well-formed sentences and supplied with a context in order to produce an interpretation of them (something that is rather different from a meaning for them: see the remarks on Davidson in the previous chapter). The relevance of this description of selection error to poetic or literary uses of language has been noted in a popular textbook of logic:

> The kind of mistake which occurs in sentences like . . . [the pianist then played a red hat topped with geraniums and wisdom] is called a *selection mistake*. (The term is based on a grammatical theory of Noam Chomsky.) Selection mistakes are easy to recognize by their bizarre and poetic feel. In fact they play an important role in poetic or metaphorical writing. By committing a selection mistake deliberately, a writer can force his prosaic readers to forget the literal sense of what he says; since they can make nothing of his words if they take them literally, they have to notice the colours and overtones.[5]

Here the selection error is poetic because it renders language opaque. Colours and overtones have been excluded from the logical use of language to be readmitted only when the selection error indicates a poetic statement is being made. But what these colours or overtones might be, how anyone becomes aware of them, and why they are not just as present in logical or ordinary language receive no consideration. It is only from the logical point of view that such selections are mistakes, and that colours and overtones are not attended to always.

The distinction between poetic and non-poetic utterances is not as clear as it is made to seem above. One critic and theorist suggests that a sentence in poetry containing selection errors should deviate for some particular reason, relating purposefully to non-deviant sentences. The inane exemplary sentences of grammatical and logical textbooks do not relate purposefully to non-deviant sentences (other than in their role as examples in a particular kind of argument, and so in one very specific context).[6] It is not in poetic language understood abstractly that the artistic principles of poetic selection should be sought, but in particular poems, where the bizarre, poetic or deviant selection errors can be understood as having a purpose. Reading poems closely demonstrates how particular deviant selections take their place within language, rather than sitting outside or alongside it. Poems themselves (or poetic careers, epochs, schools) are the contexts in which or with reference to which the selectional errors of poetically deviant sentences are most obviously to be understood. Poems are made by selections of words that are constantly critical of their own grounds for selection. One generative poetician who believes poetry to be 'the most linguistic of all language manifestations', something not to be 'seen as an imposition on natural language', argues that poetry breaks down traditional distinctions in generative grammar between competence and performance, between the ability to say something and actually saying it, a distinction that can only ever have an analytical value, as without utterances there is no structure.[7]

Selection is not, however, just a matter of idiolect, of a relation between competence and performance in individuals, but also of sociolect, of the relationship between different groups of speakers of the same language. It is perhaps striking, given the prominence of questions of social register in the British poetic tradition of the eighteenth and early nineteenth centuries, that the work of Mikhail Bakhtin identifies the novel as the genre that engages most fully with these concerns, suggesting, indeed, that poetic language excludes the competing registers that the novel welcomes. Bakhtin argues that there has never been an adequate theory of artistic prose, and elaborates such a theory in contradistinction to theories of poetic language. Bakhtin insists on the necessary presence of other people in the linguistic world of any one speaker, who is always also a respondent:

> any speaker is himself a respondent to a greater or lesser degree. He is not, after all, the first speaker, the one who disturbs the eternal silence of the universe. And he presupposes not only the existence of the language system he is using, but also the existence of preceding utterances – his own and others' – with which his given utterance enters into one kind of relation or another (builds on them, polemicizes with them, or simply presumes that they are already known to the listener). Any utterance is a link in a very complexly organized chain of other utterances.[8]

All utterances select some feature or features of previous utterances to which they respond. Every linguistic act is undertaken in relation to other linguistic acts, and it is in certain forms of the relationship between such acts that Bakhtin finds literary value. Those literary genres that realise most completely this co-presence of others' speech in the individual utterance are the most valuable, because they realise the genuine conditions of inhabiting a world formed through ideologically saturated and socially concrete language:

> We are taking language not as a system of abstract grammatical categories, but rather language conceived as ideologically saturated, language as a world view, even as a concrete opinion, insuring a *maximum* of mutual understanding in all spheres of ideological life . . . The authentic environment of an utterance, the environment in which it lives and takes shape, is dialogized heteroglossia, anonymous and social as language, but simultaneously concrete, filled with specific content and accented as an individual utterance.[9]

Dialogized heteroglossia is the relationship between two or more different languages, in a sense of 'languages' incorporating natural languages, registers, idiolects and any other mode of providing a view of the world, that allows them to relate to one another, and 'reaccentuate' one another by transposing and criticizing the valuations of reality inherent in those languages.[10]

The most straightforward way in which Bakhtin identifies other languages at work within the unitary language of the novel's text is through modes of speech and narration, the interrelationship of which define the novel: 'The novel can be defined as a diversity of social speech types (sometimes even diversity of languages) and a diversity of individual voices, artistically organized.' Yet the fact of dialogized heteroglossia can be seen even at the level of the single word:

> the word, breaking through to its own meaning and its own expression across an environment full of alien words and variously evaluating accents, harmonizing with some of the elements in this environment and striking a dissonance with others, is able, in this dialogized process, to shape its own stylistic profile and tone.

One environment in which these alien words and accents strike upon one another is the market place, a scene in which the private is made public.[11] The novel in English provides plenty of examples of encounters between different languages (here understood as idiolects) in the market place. Frances Burney's Evelina notes with amusement that her hostess in London, Mrs Mirvan, has a word for visiting shops – going '*a shopping*'.[12] And Charles Dickens very often presents the vocabulary and speech habits of different social strata in counterpoint with one another at markets, and inns, as when poor Jo responds to Allan Woodcourt's attempts to feed him: 'I don't care for eating wittles nor yet for drinking on 'em.'[13] In these two examples different social groups encounter one another's vocabularies in the forum. Bakhtin represents this kind of encounter with the alien world as central to the literary value of the novel, to its art.

One of the great values of these encounters between languages is the critical reflection upon one's own language, and therefore one's entire socio-historical position, they encourage. Critical reflection of this sort, Bakhtin says, is absent in poetic style:

> a critical qualified relationship to one's own language (as merely one of many languages in a heteroglot world) is foreign to poetic style – as is a related phenomenon, the incomplete commitment of oneself, of one's full meaning, to a given language.[14]

With this comment Bakhtin begins his attack on the monological quality of poetic style in the narrow sense, an attack which has prevented the value of Bakhtin's work to the close study of poetics being fully realised.[15] For Bakhtin, poetic language is centralizing and monologic, orderly without disordering, formal without deforming. I will cite passages from *Dialogic Imagination* at length, to give a flavour of the sustained nature of its antagonism towards poetic language:

> The world of poetry, no matter how many contradictions and insoluble conflicts the poet develops within it, is always illumined by one unitary and indisputable discourse . . . The idea of a special unitary and singular language of poetry is a typical utopian philosopheme of poetic discourse: it is grounded in the actual conditions and demands of poetic style, which is always a style adequately serviced by one directly intentional language from whose point of view other languages (conversational, business and prose languages, among others) are perceived as objects that are in no way its equal . . . Poetry also comes upon language as stratified, language in the process of uninterrupted ideological evolution, already fragmented into 'languages.' And poetry also sees its own language surrounded by other languages, surrounded by literary and extra-literary heteroglossia. But poetry, striving for maximal purity, works in its own language *as if* that language were unitary, the only language, as if there were no heteroglossia outside it. . . . If, during an epoch of language crisis, the language of poetry *does* change, poetry immediately canonizes the new language as one that is unitary and singular, as if no other language existed.

Bakhtin is not denying dialogicity to poetic language altogether, he is rather noting its resistance to dialogue. The social contexts of language in poetry are 'accented in the abstract', being subordinated to the hegemony of the poet's voice.[16] The monologism of poetry is, then, a question of its attempt to delimit the ideological range of its vocabulary.

An example might help to illustrate what Bakhtin means by the resistance of poetry to dialogised heteroglossia, as he provides none himself. Thomas Campion is one of a number of late sixteenth- and early seventeenth-century poets and composers to realise the musical value of the street vendors' cries heard in London, and to incorporate them into a work:[17]

There is a Garden in her face,
Where Roses and white Lillies grow;
   A heav'nly paradice is that place,
Wherein all pleasant fruits doe flow.
   There Cherries grow, which none may buy
   Till Cherry ripe themselves doe cry.

Those Cherries fayrely doe enclose
Of Orient Pearle a double row,
   Which when her lovely laughter showes,
They looke like Rose-buds fill'd with snow.
   Yet them nor Peere nor Prince can buy,
   Till Cherry ripe themselves doe cry.

Her Eyes like Angels watch them still;
Her Browes like bended bowes doe stand,
   Threatening with piercing frownes to kill
All that attempt with eye or hand
   Those sacred Cherries to come nigh,
   Till Cherry ripe themselves doe cry.

This strategy of incorporating the voice of the street vendor into a work of art might seem closely related to the incorporation of other alien words into the discourse of the novel as found in Burney and Dickens, and Campion's editor notes that the street cry (imitated in Campion's musical setting) 'undercuts, with its earthy commercialism, the high Petrarchan style of the rest of the song'.[18] But Bakhtin's characterisation of the abstract way in which the poetic phrase is re-accented, brought into a new context, and so brought into dialogue, catches an important feature of the poem: the street cry in one sense is not incorporated into the poem, or incorporated only so as to indicate a difference between the world of the poem and the world of the street market, not their proximity.

Poetic language looks down upon the language of business, the cry. Its placement as a refrain in a series of stanzas contributes to this limited incorporation. The lips are significantly unlike cherries in that they are not for sale (l. 5). The street cry only applies to them ironically, or provocatively, because they resist the public exposure the street cry indicates. Despite their appearance as a delicious form of produce that one is normally able to purchase in the public context of the market, the lips resist being bought, even by a 'Peere' or 'Prince' (l. 11) until they themselves cry 'Cherry ripe' (ll. 6, 12, 18). The desired object excludes itself from the market, from exposure in front of others. The woman's lips will cry 'cherry ripe' at some point, as the refrain of the poem indicates a temporal limit to the woman's unavailability. They are to be understood as advertising themselves, and, metonymically, the woman herself, to be ready for participation in the game of courtship only when they do make this cry, a cry that can be understood either as the simple physical appearance of the woman's lips, or as the kinds of courtship utterance the woman might make at this future point. 'Cherry ripe', however, is not a phrase these lips will ever actually pronounce: the street cry is not used to bring the common life of the marketplace into the refined world of the courtly seduction, but to show how subtle and poetic that courtly world is in appropriating the street cry to its own ends. Or, if this is not a poem that wittily re-imagines the perceived sexual display of a courtly lady's lips by means of a street cry, but a poem that celebrates the perceived sexual availability of female street vendors, the exclusivity of the two worlds is even more strongly marked. The kind of re-accentuation taking place is monologic, imposing upon the phrase a very specific function within the social and linguistic context of the poem. The selected feature that this poem re-accentuates is treated poetically, rather than admitting a conflicting view of the world into the poem.

Some forms of lyric poetry, then, provide supporting evidence for Bakhtin's claim that poetry re-accents other languages in a very abstract fashion, and resists dialogization.[19] Bakhtin does, however, acknowledge that poetry engages with social processes: 'even the poetic word is social, but poetic forms reflect lengthier social processes, i.e., those tendencies in social life requiring centuries to unfold'.[20] What kinds of tendency does Bakhtin think poetic forms attend to? One obvious candidate is love and the forms of speech and behaviour associated with it. As Bakhtin points out,

> our speech, that is, all our utterances (including creative works), is filled with others' words, varying degrees of otherness or varying degrees of 'our-own-ness,' varying degrees of awareness and detachment. These words of others carry with them their own expression, their own evaluative tone, which we assimilate, rework, and re-accentuate.[21]

All poems are selections of the words of other people, re-accented in various ways. The ways in which others' words are used to present and interrogate the emotional introspection of the lyric poet can be seen to change, as the love feelings that the lyric poet participates in have also changed, between the early seventeenth century and 1993, the year the poem by Denise Riley on which I will focus to exemplify such change was first published. Riley is interested in the issues raised in Bakhtin's thinking about speech genre and re-accentuation. She describes a feeling of 'linguistic guilt', caused amongst other things by her words' 'echoing of others' speech, which I can never adequately acknowledge, within my own speech', a situation she recognises as being still more extreme than Bakhtin's description of the word that is always half another's word: 'poetry in its composing is an inrush of others' voices'.[22] Such anxiety is evident in this poem.

A misremembered lyric

A misremembered lyric: a soft catch of its song
whirrs in my throat. 'Something's gotta hold of my heart
tearing my' soul and my conscience apart, long after
presence is clean gone and leaves unfurnished no
shadow. Rain lyrics. Yes, then the rain lyrics fall.
I don't want absence to be this beautiful.
It shouldn't be; in fact I know it wasn't, while
'everything that consoles is false' is off the point –
you get no consolation anyway until your memory's
dead: or something never had gotten hold of
your heart in the first place, and that's the fear thought.
Do shrimps make good mothers? Yes they do.
There is no beauty out of loss; can't do it –
and once the falling rain starts on the upturned
leaves, and I listen to the rhythm of unhappy pleasure
what I hear is bossy death telling me which way to
go, what I see is a pool with an eye in it. Still let
me know. Looking for a brand-new start. Oh and never
notice yourself ever. As in life you don't.[23]

This poem may concern Riley's 'best subject: the unease of continual, and politically alert, self-analysis'.[24] An agonised poet is excluded from nature and is threatened by the impossibility of love, and, concomitantly, the impossibility of poetic speech. The poet experiences absence, either existentially or by having been left by someone. The poet does not want absence to be beautiful, as it now appears, and knows that it was not so in the past (ll. 6–7), but the alternatives to feeling abandoned are being falsely consoled by forgetting what has happened, or not being gripped by serious emotional attachments in the first place, 'and that's the fear thought' (l. 11). The rain falls in this poem, with a 'rhythm of unhappy pleasure' (l. 15), associating the rhythm of the poem with that of the rain, an association that becomes clearer in the phrase 'rain lyrics' (l. 5). Lyrics, the words of the song the poet remembers and the words of her own song, come along naturally like rain, they fall, rather than being summoned. So Riley hints at the uninvited presence of the other lyric in her imagination, and its sudden capacity to describe, and travesty, a state of mind. The poem ends with desperate phrases indicating the poet's dependence on others ('Still let / me know', ll.17–18) and a naive hope ('Looking for a brand new start' l. 18). The final injunction is not to notice oneself, to avoid the very kind of lyric introspection that the poem holds up as a possibility, and from which its speaker fears being excluded.

In the acknowledgements to the collection in which it appears, Riley provides the following references:

> 'A misremembered lyric' uses a phrase from 'Rhythm of the Rain' written by Gummoe, sung by The Cascades, and from 'Something's Gotta Hold Of My Heart' by R. Cook and R. Greenaway, recorded by Gene Pitney; the poem also quotes a line from Graham Greene's version of a 1930s song.[25]

In calling up the remembered words of songs which come to the poet as words neither entirely her own, nor entirely another's, this poem re-accents the texts from which it selects in order to perform the anxiety felt at the poet's possible exclusion, through the impossibility of participating in the rituals and behaviour of love, from a world that appears adversarial. Robert Sheppard identifies Riley's 'weaving of song lyrics into the text (so that what is quotation and what is not, what is expressive and what is ironic, is unclear)' and notes that the poem thereby 'enacts the remembering and misremembering of a nostalgic and narcissistic content that the poems themselves appear to offer'. But this introspection might seem to be at odds with a view of 'a social dimension for poetry *embedded in* its artifice', rather than in imitating a social world, a central feature of post-war British poetry, in Sheppard's view.[26] Is this not to say that these lyrics within lyrics are at the service of monological introspection?

The song performed by Gene Pitney, but also by many others, talks about keeping the soul and senses apart, and so is slightly misremembered or at least misquoted. The line from 'Rhythm of the Rain' ('Looking for a brand new start') is remembered precisely, as is also the peculiar question and answer 'Do shrimps make good mothers? Yes they do' (l. 12), the last of Riley's citations. The line feels like a deliberate mistake, a selection error. One might try to integrate it into a run of images of abandonment and the external world, but the abandonment the poet experiences is more likely to be amorous than filial, and the world of falling rain and upturned leaves is neither easily nor simply that of shrimp behaviour. The context that is most immediately provided for the line does not explain its deviance simply: it retains a bizarre feel, leaping in from a different register, presenting a challenge to the reader's capacity to make the poem a coherent utterance. The line reproduces the title, and refrain, from a 1924 song by The Two Gilberts, a comic number about setting up a shrimp farm near Bognor and planting monkey glands in the sand to encourage their procreation.[27] Knowing its context, the line adds a troubling suggestion of the industrialisation of maternal feeling to the poem. But the line is already re-accented when Riley encounters it in Greene, already given a new situation.

This remembered lyric, it seems to me, is re-accented in a less abstract manner than Campion's citation of the street cry: less is done to integrate it into a poeticised understanding of the place of the individual speaking subject. The older lyric appears in the poem without being as fully integrated into a monological utterance, the expression of a unique poetic point of view, as the more recent lyrics, and it has an alienating effect, causing the reader to ask, even without knowing that a citation is being made, whence it is these words have come. The inner consciousness divulged seems to be made up of things from outside. As Riley puts it in other poems, the speaking 'I' of the poem stands 'outwardly silent but vibrantly / loud inside with others' gossip about itself, like "the unconscious"'; or again 'I'm not outside anything: I'm not inside it either'; or again, in a poem that closes with a citation of a Neil Sedaka song, 'Perhaps the passions that we feel don't quite belong to anyone / but hang outside us in the light like hoverflies.'[28] In a recent theoretical work Riley echoes that last formulation closely: 'Perhaps the unconscious hangs out there, between people, as the speech that they produce between them and are produced by.'[29]

Riley's concern with the categories of psychoanalysis adds a further dimension to the resignation of sovereignty one might see at work in her work of selection, but psychology in her view 'cannot be cleanly isolated and extracted from the language, syntax, and grammar of self-description'. With the incorporation of these lines, then, Riley comes closer to Bakhtin's sense of dialogized heteroglossia, and demonstrates how, over the course of centuries, the traditions of lyric poetry change, finding new resources to point to their very frailty, and their proximity to misfire. The selections that this poet makes open up the poem to registers regarded as popular, familiar, common, such as those of popular song, at the same time as working into its texture the arcane and haunting refrain of a song that is no longer an object of common knowledge. The citation is an example of the 'transformative reiteration' Riley identifies as operating in echoes.[30]

Riley's poem presents readers with phrases that seem at the same time to be self-selecting, to impose themselves from without, but which also constitute the peculiar intersection of the poet's vocabulary with the total vocabulary of her language and culture. In this sense, the poem goes well beyond the nostalgic and narcissistic, as it makes 'the unconscious' or an inner voice out of social realities and external voices. It is a poem that manages an extremely difficult artistic feat, that of placing outside of oneself the language that one is made of, so that it both renders an intense moment of interior life and also engages critically with the modes by which language makes people into what they are. Riley manages this without valorising the poem as 'some solitary and glorious resistance by a discerning subject skirting her way through a minefield of words', being more interested in the poet's '*over-determination* by so very many words that the determining cover of any single one of them gets blown'.[31] The language of this poem, to use a formulation Riley applies to language in general, is 'an ordinary ekstasis', an ordinary ecstasy, or being outside of oneself. Riley's poem works through the agonies of selecting and being selected by a language that always comes to its speakers both as the language of other people, and as the medium of the most pressing inner expressive necessities. Her re-accentuation of that language, her shaping it into the argument of this poem, is poetic in as much as it presents and criticises and renovates the ways in which language makes sense. In this way the poem becomes part of the therapeutic realisation that the potential violence of ideologically hateful inner speech can be neutralised by a recognition of its entirely contingent nature, a contingency that is at once threatening and beautiful: 'There is an unholy coincidence between beauty and cruelty in their [inner speeches'] verbal mannerisms; citation, reiteration, echo, quotation may work benignly, or as a poetics of violent diction.'[32] I hope to have shown in this reading of Riley's poem how the social resonance of diction, always an act of selection from the speech of other people, retains a critical efficacy for poets throughout the history of the discussion of choices of word, vocabulary and register. The argument of the poem is found in large part in its selections.

Notes

1. Manfred Jahn, '"Colourless Green Ideas Sleep Furiously": A Linguistic Test Case and its Appropriations', in *Literature and Linguistics: Approaches, Models, and Applications: Studies in Honour of Jon Erickson*, ed. Marion Gymich, Ansgar Nünning and Vera Nünning (Trier: Wissenschaftlicher Verlag, 2002), pp. 47–60 (p. 51). Jahn also lists the large number of poetic appropriations of Chomsky's selectionally faulty sentence, demonstrating, of course, that selection errors are only errors in certain circumstances, and require a text pragmatics to account for possible contexts for utterance, including contexts that might be considered poetic.
2. Noam Chomsky, *Syntactic Structures* (The Hague; Paris: Mouton, 1957), 'Introduction', p. 11.
3. Ibid. pp. 17, 44, 80.
4. Noam Chomsky, *Aspects of the Theory of Syntax* (Cambridge, MA: The MIT Press, 1965), p. 149.
5. Wilfred Hodges, *Logic* (Harmondsworth: Penguin, 1977), p. 21. The second, revised edition of this text was published in 2001.
6. Gerald L. Bruns, *Modern Poetry and the Idea of Language: A Critical and Historical Study* (New Haven and London: Yale University Press, 1974), p.

249. Bruns uses 'colorless green ideas sleep furiously' as an example. I noted in 'Measure: Robert Creeley' Julia Kristeva's feeling that generative grammar does not allow the acknowledgement of language as a risky practice, *Desire in Language: A Semiotic Approach to Literature and Art*, ed. Leon S. Roudiez, trans. Thomas Gora, Alice Jardine and Leon S. Roudiez (New York: Columbia University Press, 1980), p. 34.

7. Nina Nowakowska, *Language of Poetry and Generative Grammar: Toward Generative Poetics? (With Sample Analysis of T. S. Eliot's Poems)* (Poznan: Uniwersytet im. Adama Mickiewicza w Poznaniu, 1977), pp. 6, 72, 51. Other linguists claim that every utterance requiring contextual interpretation is a challenge to the opposition of language to speech: 'the distinction between linguistic praxis and language as the system that informs it collapses at precisely those points where the meaning of a sentence cannot be calculated . . . from the meaning of its lexical components'. Peter Auer, Elizabeth Couper-Kuhlen and Frank Müller, *Language in Time: The Rhythm and Tempo of Spoken Interaction* (Oxford: Oxford University Press, 1999), p. 5.

8. M. M. Bakhtin, 'The Problem of Speech Genres' (1952–3), in *Speech Genres and Other late Essays*, trans. Vern W. McGee, ed. Caryl Emerson and Michael Holquist (Austin: University of Texas Press, 1986), pp. 60–102 (p. 69). Compare the openness of Bakhtin's account of utterance as a response here to Julia Kristeva's writing on intertextuality, discussed in 'Spirit: Frank O'Hara'.

9. M. M. Bakhtin, *The Dialogic Imagination: Four Essays*, ed. Michael Holquist, trans. Caryl Emerson and Michael Holquist (Austin: University of Texas Press, 1981 [1975]), pp. 271–2.

10. Bakhtin, *Speech Genres*, pp. 61, 80; Bakhtin, *Dialogic Imagination*, pp. 291, 419.

11. Bakhtin, *Dialogic Imagination*, pp. 262, 277, and, for example, p. 131.

12. Frances Burney, *Evelina*, ed. Edward A. Bloom and Lillian D. Bloom (Oxford: Oxford University Press, 1982 [1778]), p. 27.

13. *Bleak House*, ed. Norman Page, intro. by J. Hillis Miller (Harmondsworth: Penguin, 1971 [1852-3]), chapter XLVII, p. 692.

14. Bakhtin, *Dialogic Imagination*, p. 285.

15. Michael Eskin, *Ethics and Dialogue in the Works of Levinas, Bakhtin, Mandel'shtam, and Celan* (Oxford: Oxford University Press, 2000), p. 114. See also Donald Wesling, *Bakhtin and the Social Moorings of Poetry* (Lewisburg: Bucknell University Press; London: Associated University Presses, 2003), p. 19: 'Bakhtin openly and several times disrespected poetry as an art form. How can his writings be taken against his expressed opinions, as contributions to poetics and the reading of poetry?' Alastair Renfrew, *Towards a New Material Aesthetics: Bakhtin, Genre and the Fates of Literary Theory* (Oxford: Legenda, 2006), p. 151 suggests that Bakhtin's antagonistic view of poetry and novelistic prose is a retrograde response to older (and dead) debates concerning the formal distinction of poetic from ordinary language.

16. Bakhtin, *Dialogic Imagination*, pp. 286–8, 399, 297.

17. Thomas Weelkes, 'The Cries of London', *Music in Early Seventeenth-Century England: Anthems, Madrigals and Consort Music* (Arles: Harmonia Mundi, 1970–72; released as a CD 1992) is an example of a single voice rendition of several traditional cries above a viol consort. The cries are studded with bawdy and obscene suggestions.

18. *The Works of Thomas Campion*, ed. Walter R. Davis (New York: Norton, 1967 [1617]), p. 178.

19. Yury Lotman, *Analysis of the Poetic Text*, ed. and trans. D. Barton Johnson (Ann Arbor: Ardis, 1976), pp. 108–11, argues that all poetic language, even that of monological poets, is dialogically related to other languages.

20. Bakhtin, *Dialogic Imagination*, p. 300.

21. Bakhtin, *Speech Genres*, p. 89.

22. Denise Riley, *The Words of Selves: Identification, Solidarity, Irony* (Stanford: Stanford University Press, 2000), pp. 2, 63, 65.

23. Denise Riley, *Mop Mop Georgette: New and Selected Poems, 1986–1993* (Saxmundham and London: Reality Street, 1993), p. 31. Riley has written on Voloshinov's *Marxism and the Philosophy of Language*, a book many take to be written by or at least substantially indebted to Bakhtin, see Jean-Jacques Lecercle and Denise Riley, *The Force of Language* (Houndmills: Palgrave Macmillan, 2004), pp. 26–36, 59. See Renfrew, xi, for a recent refusal of Bakhtin's authorship of that text.

24. Stephen Burt, 'To be sheer air, or mousseline! The Song of Theory in the Poems of Denise Riley', *TLS*, 23 April 2004, 11–12 (p. 11).

25. Riley, *Mop Mop Georgette*, p. 72.

26. *The Poetry of Saying: British Poetry and its Discontents, 1950–2000* (Liverpool: Liverpool University Press, 2005), pp. 164, 7. Riley's use of lyrics is frequently noted, as in Peter Riley, 'Quotation: It Don't Mean a Thing', *Jacket Magazine*, 32 (2007). Available at <http://jacketmagazine.com/32/k-riley.shtml> (last accessed 17 July 2008). Her allusions and re-accentuations are not limited to popular song. Lines 16–17 of 'A Misremembered Lyric' recall W. H. Auden, 'To Limestone', ll. 93–5: 'when I try to imagine a faultless love / Or the life to come, what I hear is the murmur / Of underground streams, what I see is a limestone landscape.' *Collected Poems* (London: Faber, 1994), p. 542. My thanks to Jim Stewart for pointing out this echo.

27. The song was Regal release G1866 in March 1924.

28. Denise Riley, 'Laibach Lyrik: Slovenia, 1991', 'Knowing in the Real World', 'Rayon', in Riley, *Mop Mop Georgette*, pp. 8, 33, 41.

29. Riley, *The Words of Selves*, p. 15.

30. Ibid. pp. 35, 20.

31. Riley, *Force of Language*, p. 25.

32. Ibid. pp. 33, 49–50.

CHAPTER TWELVE

Equivalence: Thomas A. Clark

Thomas A. Clark's *The Path to the Sea* contains several poems, or sequences of poems, most of which were published separately as pamphlets. Clark's poems reflect on and are also made by perceptions of an environment, one that is given scale and significance by the quotidian yet metaphysically rich act of walking. This interest in walking, in measuring the environment by human and poetic modes of perception, places Clark close to other poets who figure in this book, such as Wordsworth and Creeley. These are long-standing concerns for Clark: earlier sequences such as 'Through White Villages' and 'From Sea to Sea' relate to walks in designated landscapes.[1] Producing a poetry of calm observation and reflection, on the broadest features of a landscape – its prevailing weather, its flora and fauna, its shapes – Clark nonetheless produces moments of intensity in these measured sequences of observation and reflection.

In this chapter I will be focusing on one kind of intensity produced in *The Path to the Sea*, a seeming surplus of meaning accruing around a particular phoneme. This effect is surprising in writing that seems so keen to avoid 'effects' understood in any superficial or showy sense: the reader is unsure how the writing has produced such an intensity of effect in such a seemingly neutral fact as a phoneme; but a set of perceptions and reflections in no sense radically out of the ordinary have undoubtedly been marked out as exemplary, emphasised, load-bearing. Such an experience is probably familiar to most readers of poetry, and it is partly because of the familiarity of the experience of uncertainty as to how a phoneme has come to be so important that I want to concentrate on it here, suggesting that Clark encourages readers to take what might be called an 'environmental' approach to feelings of significance that accrue around particular phonemes, just as the poetry also encourages readers to take such an attitude to the formation of meanings in the human occupation of the landscape. The experience is slightly different to that produced by Clark's work with repetition and variation, as, for example, in 'Coire Fhionn Lochan', a poem made of five quatrains, each line of which has the form 'x of the little waves', where x is a gerundive such as 'leaping' or 'splashing'; or 'By Kilbrannan Sound', a poem of eight lines, each taking the form 'the y of a black stone', where y is a noun describing the stone's appearance, and beginning 'gl', such as 'glint'.[2] The build of those poems from delimited linguistic materials is prominent. In *The Path to the Sea* there is a less programmatic distribution of the same phonetic material, the equivalences readers perceive are the product of an attention that searches out its objects, whether intuitively or self-consciously.

'Creag Liath' is the fifth sequence of the book and was published separately in 2003.[3] Creag Liath is a plausible Gaelic place name, translating as 'grey rock'. There is an island, commonly known as Craigleith, in the Firth of Forth, East Central Scotland, but the title of the poem refers to no place in particular, but a composite, abstract or desired place. The poem is partly modelled on the twelfth-century Irish poem known as 'Arran', which celebrates the environment of that West-Coast Scottish island, combining and recombining references to its rich plant and animal life, both wild and cultivated.[4] My discussion will focus on this sequence, and those that surround it, but draws examples from the entire volume.

'Creag Liath' runs over four pages, each page containing four quatrains each of whose lines comprise around five to ten syllables, three or four of which carry a beat, and which inconsistently employ feminine rhymes (aspen/bracken, p. 39), and half- or consonantal rhymes (drop/shape, p. 39) either in couplets or as cross rhymes. The sequence sets out details of the physical appearance of the landscape with occasional remarks on its relation to time, to human physical habitation, and to the feelings produced by inhabiting that landscape. The island is 'a few strides east to west' (p. 37), yet has a resilience: it is an 'island persisting in itself / drawing the mist about it / firm ground to stand on' (p. 38). The sedimentary deposit, which has been eroded by rain, is interrupted by 'coarse-grained granite / with crystals of amethyst, topaz' (p. 39). There are wild flowers to be found on 'wet rocks / strewn across meadows' (p. 39). There is 'a wind to lean against / a wind that can drop / to make you doubt your shape' (p. 39). The poem remarks what is 'east' and 'west', that there is couch grass 'to stabilise / peat', that there is a 'sandpiper piping from a stone / lifting and settling on a stone', that there are primroses in a 'nest of rock' (p. 40). The final stanza is the most abstract, remarking, perhaps on the location of the nest of rock, perhaps on the island as a whole, that it is

> where strict limits engage
> particulars, set at a distance
> from distraction and noise
> balanced on the crest of a wave (p. 40)

And so this sequence concludes, with four occurrences of the phoneme 'st' in four lines, a sizeable fraction of its eighteen occurrences across sixty-four lines.

Reading this final stanza, I find myself inclined to say that there is something precise, crisp, clear and detached about the phoneme. Its sound seems to unite the values carried by the words in which it happens to occur: its precision comes from 'strict', its detachment from 'distance', 'distraction' and 'crest', its clarity from being distant precisely from 'distraction'. I experience a certain amount of semantic bleeding, seeing 'distance' here *as* 'strict', seeing a peculiar distance and detachment *in* 'crest', associations I do not think I would necessarily be inclined to make if I encountered these terms in different circumstances. No doubt the previous occurrences of this phoneme in the text so far have added to the cumulative effect that I experienced when first reading this passage, and which has brought me back to it to study it more closely.[5] I feel when reading and rereading this passage that something significant is happening in the measuring out of this phoneme along the poem, and the book as a whole, and that this significant thing is closely connected to the poem's more evidently semantic and illocutionary aspects: the phoneme seems to be encouraging attentiveness to an environment at the same time as making an environment that the reader can inhabit. The equivalence perceived between different occurrences of this phoneme across a variety of contexts enables such a response. I will try to refine this intuition about the operation of the phoneme in the poem by comparing it to methods for understanding the meaning of (sound) patterns in poetry from various cognitive and linguistic points of view.[6]

Reuven Tsur has worked intensively on the question of the significance of sound patterning in poetry from the perspective of cognitive linguistics and poetics. His account of the means by which sound patterns are perceived as expressive rests on a model of normative cognitive processing: there are normal ways in which phenomena (speech sounds, visual phenomena) are processed, and ways in which this process can be disrupted. Poetry, and here the way in which sound patterns work in poetry, is to be understood as a disruption to ordinary modes of perception: 'poetic effects arise from a disruption of the smooth functioning of cognitive processes'.[7] Tsur describes two modes for perceiving the sonic information that is one of the transmitters of language, and suggests a third. The non-speech mode of acoustic perception is that in which sound is heard purely, without reference to the speech sounds that a speaker might be producing. In this mode, the overtones that produce a particular tone colour (sound, disregarding properties of volume, pitch and attack) may carry value even if they are not consciously perceived. The speech mode of acoustic perception is much more intentional, working from the same unattended overtones, towards tones that are interpreted in relation to the intentional articulatory gestures producing them, and as meaningful linguistic elements. Non-speech perception perceives sound, but speech perception works away from sound towards meaning: 'speech perception is based on the fact that we attend away from the acoustic information that reaches our ear to the articulatory gesture that produced it; and from the articulatory gesture to the intended abstract phonetic category'. The poetic mode of perception is a hybrid: 'Some perceptual quality of the acoustic signal sometimes intrudes into the speech mode, creating the poetic mode.'[8] On this basis, Tsur suggests that there may be more than a metaphorical or haphazard association between the darkness of back vowels and the darkness with which they may come to be associated in particular poems, with one aim of his book being the establishment of a set of phonological universals that are mapped onto other relevant areas of cognitive life in an intersubjective and transcultural fashion (although he acknowledges the last of these assertions can only be made with appeal to intuition).

Part of Tsur's reason for thinking that particular sounds can have concrete relations to certain emotional tones, or physical qualities, is that, as infants acquire language, some sounds from the wide range that are employed for expressive purposes are rejected for referential purposes more immediately, and do not return to the repertoire until much later than others. The sounds that are so rejected tend to be regarded as more beautiful than others. Tsur believes that the two purposes of infant language are co-present in poetic language:

> in child language there are two distinct uses of sound: *referential*, which is non-emotional, and *expressive*, making use of sounds that are not yet used for 'arbitrary linguistic signs.' In poetic language we have both mounted one on top of the other.[9]

There is a clear parallel here to the interference of non-speech acoustic perception in the speech mode that Tsur posits. The phonological universals that Tsur suggests deriving from this attention to the interference of one mode of speech perception on another are used to describe the phonological character of particular poets and periods. Tsur refers to a study by the Hungarian linguist Ivan Fonagy that divides poems by the same author into 'tender' and 'angry' categories.[10] For his own part, Tsur states that the dense semantic texture of certain lines of a Hungarian poem is matched by perceiving 'some dense texture of diffuse energy and rich precategorical sensory information by way of perceiving the phonetic categories dominant'. He also uses his phonological universals to make broader judgements about the nature of the poetry of a particular poet, epoch or style: Boileau and Pope, neoclassicists, are 'clear-cut, polarized, symmetrical'; Baudelaire and Verlaine, symbolists, prefer 'chaotic overdifferentiation'.[11] Just as it seems crude to the point of being trivial to divide the poems of an author into the groups 'aggressive' and 'tender', so too the characterisation of the phonology of lines as 'dense' or 'symmetrical', with the predictable corollary that their semantic content too is polarized or dense, can seem crude, and also self-instantiating: if one is looking for a way to characterise the sound of a line of poetry, the qualities to which it refers semantically will probably propose themselves as candidates.

The French linguist, poet and poetician Henri Meschonnic has criticised the approach taken by Fonagy for being binary, and therefore simplistic, as well as circular (separating the sound and sense only to reunite them later), in his attack upon the positivistic attitude to phonosymbolism. He also believes the statistics provided by Fonagy provide no significant evidence of differentiation between categories.[12] Meschonnic identifies a feature of this account of phonosymbolism that it shares with other theories of mimesis: it posits the interference of different levels of linguistic perception, thereby at the same time separating two aspects of a phenomenon, and yet allowing them to interact. The symbolic or referential business of language is presumed to operate discretely, at least at the analytical level, from its expressive or rhythmic qualities. The interference of the two is where poetry occurs. Yet the experience of reading Clark's sequence is not one of disturbance, interference or disruption, rather one of concentration. When reading about the granite containing 'crystals of amethyst, topaz / blue-beryl, smoky quartz', the reader attends to the referential business of language, finding the concepts that go along with these signifiers, but also apprehends the phonemic echo I have pointed out above, along with various others, attributing value to it without losing sight of reference. There is no palpable interference in the referential process, or in the speech mode of acoustic processing: there is no obvious danger of perceiving the lines as not-speech, no matter how richly one perceives their sound. Tsur wants to discriminate between those associations that link cognitively related domains (the darkness of a vowel, and the darkness of an environment) and those which are only haphazardly connected by the material fact of the language. How is it to be decided which levels of perception are related, which are the cognitively related domains, and which are haphazardly related, in any particular reading? Such mappings of cognitive domains always require arbitrary policing (see 'Figure: Tom Raworth').

A further objection to Tsur's scheme can be built up from the nature of the phonological or phonemic information that is deemed relevant. Tsur's approach requires that either sound, or the muscular-articulatory remnant of sound if a silent reading is concerned, provide the basis for phonological expressivism. But these are features of a poem that do not require sounding to participate in an expressive pattern, even if that expressive pattern is predominantly sounded. The very first occurrence of 'st' in *The Path to the Sea* is in 'unfasten' (p. 7), where the 't' is not sounded. There are further occurrences of this sort ('listen', p. 76; 'rustling', p. 83). The occurrence adds itself to the visual pattern that is evidently in part coextensive with the acoustic

pattern. And this pattern too is correlated with related acoustico-visual patterns that might not possess the same imperceptible pre-cognitive information upon the processing of which Tsur's argument is based: if, despite the
fact that they do not occur in an uninterrupted chiastic sequence, I relate
'topaz' and 'quartz' through the reversal of 't' and 'z', and also relate this
pattern to 'st' and further to 'ts' in the book as a whole, I am doing more
than allowing an expressive function to subconsciously perceived information: I am allowing visual and acoustic patterns to interrelate over time in
a reading process that is not conceived of as a single, linear performance,
but as a set of relations built up over various complete or partial readings,
re-readings, misreadings, rememberings and misrememberings. The fact
that I respond to the visual trigger 'st' as much as to the acoustic trigger 'st'
is supported by my regarding solely acoustic occurrences such as the 'st' in
'extends' (p. 73) as marginal or partial instances in the pattern. Cognitive
processing, I would suggest on this experience of reading, is not normative
with disruptions or interferences; it is constantly adaptive. It does not discriminate between referential and expressive material, between non-speech,
speech and poetic modes of acoustic perception, only to reintegrate them at
a later stage: it works continually and, in a positive sense, indiscriminately
with the information processed.

Tsur's scheme of phonological universals, then, does not offer a perfect or
complete explanation of how 'st' comes to be invested with the significance
it acquires over the course of Clark's book. I have already noted some facts
about the way in which this acoustico-visual pattern comes to be significant
that are not purely a matter of its sound. Nor do these patterns seem to be
de-semanticised before being reunited with their semantic content in an
expressive gesture: the words remain whole. The two parts of the phoneme
can be found at some distance from one another, and yet still register to
the reader as part of the pattern: 'st' develops a kind of gravity that attracts
nearby phenomena. So the two letters split across two words are heard
together ('comes to', p. 15) as they are when occurring in one word, yet
not in uninterrupted sequence or across more than one word ('settlement',
'sit', p. 15; 'sweeten', p. 17; 'swift sortie', p. 21; 'same tone', p. 23). In such
cases, the attention the reader lends to these phrases across multiple readings furthers the semantic bleeding mentioned above, and may also pick out
frequent 'full' occurrences of 'st', making 'stone' (which, along with its plural
and compounds, occurs eighteen times in the book) audible and visible
through 'same tone'.

Such acoustico-visual patterns are not without semantic content.
Languages are systematic, and the material form of words in languages
is not unrelated to their semantic properties. This simple fact has poetic
consequences, as in the following description of a seal:

the seal in the cold water
rises to a clarity
or curiosity, a lapping
of silver, a lapping of grey (p. 17)

The relationship between 'clarity' and 'curiosity' is picked out by their alliteration and an internal feminine rhyme, but also by their sharing a nominal
form: they are both abstract nouns formed from adjectives. The lines present
alternative ways of understanding an alternative: the seal's appearance is
either to be understood as a moment of clarity that is curiosity, or as either
clarity or curiosity. The parallel formation of the two nouns presents an
equivalence within their difference: abstracting from a state or disposition to
a quality, these two different states share a genealogy.

There are, then, ways in which rational, referential functions remain
present in the poetic processing of language. As noted above, there is no easy
distinction to be made between the referential function of a word and its
acoustic properties. The two are not separated to be reunited, but operate in
a total if not necessarily coherent fashion. The particular phoneme on which
I am concentrating my attention is heard against all the other acoustic-
referential facts of the poem. It sounds out clearly and distinctly against other
features, such as the richness of consonantal clusters and vowel-consonant
combinations occurring in some of the less common botanical language of
the poem: the 'waving glumes of marram grass' (p. 40) contrast acoustically
with the prominence of 'st' in the final stanza, quoted above.[13] One kind of
precise vocabulary is set against another, with the botanical precision characterised, in this poem, in this unique selection and organisation from and of
a language in constant systematic adaptation, by the 'gl' and the 'gr', the 'um'
and 'am' (labial and velar consonants produced by the tongue against the
soft palette or the lips), and the more reflective abstraction and precision of
the final stanza by the 'st' combination (produced by the front of the tongue
against the alveolar ridge at the front of the mouth).

Referential functions have acoustic properties in any poem, without the
expressivistic circularity of phonological universals being required. Likewise,
there is no need to presume that there is a universal relationship between 'st'
and some of the thematic emphases of the poem: their coexistence in this
unique poetic environment is all that needs to be noted. The phoneme and
its inversion defining the 'strict limits' which 'engage particulars' and bring a
'distance' in that same final stanza are, simply by so occurring, part of the play
of proximity and distance that constitutes being in an environment in this
poem, the play of being connected, more or less at a distance, to other things
that is a significant part of various sequences within the book. 'The Shape
Changer' records a set of transformations of the 'I' into animals, inanimate

objects, abstract mental states (pp. 55–60); longing is that which marks people out in their environment whilst at the same time marking them as of it:

> as longing stretches out
> and begins to detach itself from
> the initial object of longing
> it becomes present everywhere
> and can be found in everything
> forming and informing everything
> the weight of this stone is longing ('At Dusk & At Dawn', p. 79)

And again the particular combination 'st' is heard against another set of sounds, establishing their acoustico-referential value within the book.

There is no reason, of course, to suggest that relations between terms stand only for a particular poem: they can spread out across entire authorships, or entire reading experiences. But the means by which they are established remains the same: their simple co-presence in relation to one another. One moment at which the phoneme, in one of its most frequently occurring contexts, is heard against a broader poetical history is the following:

> sandpiper piping from a stone
>   lifting and lighting
> on the same stone
>   piping on alone (p. 21)

These lines recall the piping of the 'Introduction' to William Blake's *Songs of Innocence and of Experience*, and in particular the command of the child on a cloud to the speaker of the poem, 'Piper pipe that song again' (l. 7).[14] Some common-places concerning Blake's poem and the collection(s) from which it comes are highly relevant to Clark's book: the poet is encouraged to sing by a mysterious and uncanny childlike presence; the poet's songs are delightful and also saddening; they may have the effect of staining or darkening, as the poet stains the waters clear when starting to write; the poems explore the fundamental interrelatedness of simplicity and complexity, of attitudes and environments that might be described as innocent or experienced. Clark's directness and simplicity of statement clearly draws on Blake. Furthermore, the expert way in which Blake manages the phonological construction of his poems is an evident part of Clark's heritage, and I would like to turn to some recent writing on Blake and phonosymbolism to refine further my argument concerning the environmental significance of acoustico-visual equivalences in Clark's work.

Blake's 'The Tyger' is the subject of two sustained attempts to demonstrate the operation of phonosymbolism in poetic texts. The poet J. H. Prynne considers the poem as revealing a precise historical moment in the relation between elements of the language system regarded as either arbitrary or motivated. Prynne suggests the possibility of literature is dependent upon the layering of motivated or expressive and arbitrary functions of language materials, either sonic or graphic:

> For a language community to develop a literature, the cultural and significatory codes of the meaning process have to be extended in certain complex and distinctive ways. In particular, the mapping of sense on to sound and shape which is proposed by the strong version of the arbitrariness hypothesis has to be overwritten and re-mapped by a corpus of optional and variable connections secondarily imposed, so that literary motivation is essentially retrospective: precisely a reverse transcription.[15]

The precise nature of this interrelation is, then, historical, attesting to a certain moment in the history of a language, and that historical moment is not to be divorced from the total life of the society whose language is in question.

Recognising that echoes and recombinations of phonemes in the poem contribute at a high level to any sensible account of its meaning, Prynne contends that the tiger is figured as the product of modern industrial technology, exploiting the resources of furnaces fired by modern, de-localised fuel supplies, and representing the recombinatory power offered by this new technology. Seen in this way, the poem's phonosymbolic effects are also the product of the transformative power of energy upon the material of language:

> The cumulative shift from organic energy-sources to a mineral-based economy triggered into latent consciousness profound issues not unrelated to the arbitrariness question: was the concept of free convertible energy bound historically into the material forms which comprised its traditional sources, organically related to their characteristic locations in the geographical and industrial and social world-order; or could abstract 'force' and 'power' be allowed to break the moulds, as production pushed away from water-power and from wood and charcoal towards coal and coke and more radical transformations of matter and energy?

The forms of interrelation of motivated and arbitrary signification are here regarded in their full environmental and historical context. But this view does, crucially, depend on the notion of a historically prior moment of motivated expressivity in language that runs over a later arbitrary stage, a connection that can 'in intensely witty or language-conscious performance be recognised to run alternatingly back and forth, or even in both directions at once'.[16]

Háj Ross argues that the distribution of letters throughout Blake's poem produces effects of contrast and emphasis that he calls 'sore-thumbing', and which are not unlike the effect of Clark's poem.[17] Ross concentrates on an important question presented by the poem at the level of its semantic content: how can a god be conceived of who is capable of creating such diverse entities as the tiger and the lamb, or, at a slightly less literalistic level, how can such contrary spiritual characteristics of the universe be conceived? His discussion of the poem's phonemic structure suggests that contrary principles are intermingled at the acoustico-visual level, but he also suggests that the poem's fifth stanza is made to stand out: it lacks 'b' and 'f', and, in the case of its fourth line, 'r' and 't'; it adheres, in monosyllables, to an octosyllabic pattern around which the poem plays without otherwise conforming.[18] The introduction to the volume in which Ross's essay appears summarises the argument: 'the formal organization of the poem results . . . in just another way of "saying", in the language of poetry, the same coevocation that is found between items at the content level'.[19] The project of that volume is to explore various ways in which iconicity (non-arbitrary relations between signifiers and signifieds) operates within language, particularly poetic language. Again, the introduction states that

> quite a number of linguists believe that language might have had an iconic origin, repeating at the ontogenetic level that which happens at the phylogenetic level: it is a well known fact that iconicity plays a major role in children's language acquisition.[20]

Ross's argument, it seems to me, is strong precisely because it does not require an association of the ontogenetic and phylogenetic levels at which language can be described (as the possession of an individual, as a trans-individual historical system, respectively). Such an idea, that the stages of the development of an individual in some sense contain the development of the species, is not widely supported in evolutionary thinking, and leads, in linguistics, to various superstitions about language structure, as in Julia Kristeva's suggestion that individual language development and the history of poetic language recapitulate one another (see 'Measure: Robert Creeley'). I will return briefly to Julia Kristeva now to contrast her method of attending to equivalent phonemes with that which I propose here.

In *Revolution in Poetic Language*, Kristeva develops a method for reading the relationship between phonemes in the poems of Stéphane Mallarmé that draws on the work of Ivan Fonagy, the linguist referred to previously. Kristeva works with the idea that drives (of appetite and rejection) are associated with particular phonemes. Certain phonemes have an oral character, some an anal character, and so on. The semantic programme of the poem 'Prose' is complemented, equalled by a phonic programme.[21] The significance of the phonemes and their drive attributes does not remain phonic, but becomes semantic, participates in a process of semanticisation: the sound of a phoneme, by association with a drive, acquires semantic meaning (not just the expressive meaning of tone or colour). More than that, Kristeva's analysis proceeds on the basis that particular occurrences of phonemes relate to other occurrences of that phoneme, and share their meaning, whether attributed by semanticisation of drives, or in the traditional sense. Thus the three groups of sounds in the (French) word 'hyperbole' are said 'to semanticise themselves in order to designate the rejection of an authority': the elements 'per' (for 'père', 'father') and 'bole' (which appears in 'aboli', 'abolished') are related to their appearance in other works by Mallarmé in order to semanticise further the phonemes that make up the word.[22] This process of semanticisation proceeds by condensation and over-determination, terms from Freudian psychoanalysis. Kristeva's reading of the significance of phonemic equivalences, then, depends upon the attribution of an intrinsic drive character to the phoneme in question, and a further miscegenation of that drive character with any semantic content (traditionally understood) that the phoneme has or acquires from a relatively delimited set of contexts in which it occurs.[23] Kristeva goes on to develop a complex argument concerning the place of this particular form of poetic language in Mallarmé as a means of revolutionising the social, political, sexual and familial relations of late bourgeois society, in which the concept of the subject put in process or on trial by the operations of poetic language is central.

Clark's 'st' has no drive character, nor can it acquire, from a privileged set of contexts, a precise and more traditionally semantic meaning. As suggested above, the reader may experience a sense of semantic bleeding between terms in which the phoneme occurs, but this sensation has no grounds beyond the shared orthographic and acoustic structure of the words (even if this shared structure is sometimes derived from shared grammatical form, an iconicity or motivation interior to the structure of the language). I would be tempted to go still further and to say that 'st' does not even gain its peculiar significance in this poem because of a deviantly disproportionate frequency in relation to the language as a whole, the means by which Fonagy has recently attempted to explain the phenomenon of phonosemantics: he suggests that poems can acquire a phonetic dimension by 'transforming expressive articulatory deviances in deviant distributions of vowels and consonants in a line, a stanza, in a poem or a cycle of poems'.[24] One objection to such a view is that there is no known normal distribution of vowels and consonants, a point made forcefully by Donald Freeman:

Another difficulty in the work of the 'style as deviation' school of linguistic stylistics is its definition of the norm from which an author's style is supposed to differ in certain ways. For example, Bernard Bloch defines style as 'the message carried by the frequency distributions and transitional probabilities of [a discourse's] linguistic features, especially as they differ from those of the same features in the language as a whole.' This definition is a chimera. The 'frequency distributions and transitional probabilities' of natural language are not known and never will be, and even if they could be ascertained they would constitute no particularly revealing insight into either natural language or style.[25]

Whatever language is selected to provide a statistical norm is a selection from the written or spoken language, and not the entire language, nor representative of the entire language. All language uses are specific, and pertain to particular idiolects, dialects, generic conventions, and so on, that specify their properties. All language uses, that is, are particular, are deviant. One might search for norms against which to measure the occurrence of 'st' in 'Creag Liath', but where should one begin? With the language of Clark's place of birth (Greenock)? His total poetic output? The corpus of post-war British neo-pastoral poetry to which the book might be said to belong? Fonagy suggests that the sum of sonic and syntactical distortions is style, and expresses the personality of the poet, but the business of differentiation this seems to suggest is not possible, as there is no norm against which the poet can emerge.[26]

How, then, can this phoneme have the significance I am claiming for it? How can the series of equivalences in which it participates produce the effects of bleeding, of recapitulation, of sensitisation to neighbouring phenomena noted above? The connections between the equivalent items in the poem are made by the making of the poem: the poem itself makes them, makes its readers sensible to them. The phoneme does not emphasise some semantic feature of the poem from which all acoustico-visual properties have previously been separated. Rather, the things emphasised by the equivalences of the poem are simply what it is about: environment conceived as basic, as habitat, its crystallisation in detail, its distribution of those details, human perceptions of them, the relations of things perceived to one another and to the people who perceive them, their sometimes uncanny presentation of absence as qualitative (stillness, distance), their meaning. The phoneme, that is, becomes significant just as the world, the environment does, by people attending, relating, moving around, caring, finding shapes in emptinesses, and emptinesses in shapes. There is nothing behind these relations created by the unique text, the act of poetic utterance, but there could, by the same measure, hardly be anything more meaningful. The poem, then, and the book as a whole produce a meaningful environment not by drawing on phonological universals, or drive characters associated with phonemes, or deviant distributions of vowels and consonants, but by simultaneously inhabiting and adapting a system.

Notes

1. Thomas A. Clark, *Tormentil and Bleached Bones* (Edinburgh: Polygon, 1993), pp. 1–8, 23–30.
2. Ibid. pp. 31–3, 97–9.
3. Thomas A. Clark, *Creag Liath* (Cambridge: Peter Riley, 2003); Thomas A. Clark, *The Path to the Sea* (Todmorden: Arc, 2005). Further references to the latter will be given parenthetically by page number in the text.
4. I owe these last two points to private correspondence with Tom Clark, 7 March 2011.
5. Here is a list of every occurrence of the phoneme in the book, in sequence, without suppressing multiple appearances: unfasten, sandstone, stands, insistent, stonechat, stones, distances, stone, against, rusting, strewn, distances, stone, stone, constantly, stone, strong, stopped, lost, waste, stonechat, strand, stone, blast, gust, lost, first, strides, persisting, mist, stand, crystals, amethyst, strewn, against, east, west, stabilise, stone, stone, nest, strict, distance, distraction, crest, distance, sustained, distance, stone, twists, past, thrust, nest, stretches, least, gust, stepping, goldcrest, forest, stone, stillness, stillness, stripped, stand, stillness, stillness, almost, steady, mist, insistence, insist, mist, almost, distributed, undisturbed, substance, stands, last, stone, stone, listen, haste, stun, stillness, stand, distances, stretch, stretches, stone, rest, disturbing, stones, stones, rustling, mist, steep, stone, strange, steady, against, stillness, standing, gesture, stake, gesture, last, step, unfasten.
6. There are several pertinent recent discussions of phonosymbolic or other repetition effects that I am not referring to, such as Don Paterson, 'The Lyric Principle', available from his website at <http://www.donpaterson.com/arspoetica.htm> (last accessed 25 April 2011); Anna Christina Ribeiro, 'Intending to Repeat: A Definition of Poetry', *The Journal of Aesthetics and Art Criticism* 65:2 (Spring 2007), 189–201.
7. Reuven Tsur, *What Makes Sound Patterns Expressive: The Poetic Mode of Speech Perception* (Durham and London: Duke University Press, 1992), p. 136.
8. Ibid. pp. 49–50, 6–13, 24.
9. Ibid. p. 55. Tsur recapitulates his ideas in *Toward a Theory of Cognitive Poetics*, 2nd edn (Brighton: Sussex Academic Press, 2008), pp. 235–43.
10. Tsur, *What Makes Sound Patterns Expressive*, pp. 3–4.
11. Ibid, pp. 160, 74–5.
12. *Critique du rythme: Anthropologie historique du langage* (Lagrasse: Verdier, 1982), pp. 632–4.

13. Glume: 'One of the chaff-like bracts which form the calyx or outer envelope in the inflorescence of grasses and sedges; the husk of corn or other grain.' Marram grass: 'A grass of coastal dunes, *Ammophila arenaria*, native to western Europe and widely planted elsewhere, with long dense spikes and tough spreading rhizomes which help to bind and stabilize the sand; also called *sea-reed*' OED.

14. William Blake, *Songs of Innocence and of Experience*, ed. Geoffrey Keynes (Oxford: Clarendon Press, 1970), plate 4.

15. J. H. Prynne, *Stars, Tigers and the Shape of Words: The William Matthews Lectures 1992 Delivered at Birkbeck College, London* (London: Birkbeck College, 1993), p. 14.

16. Ibid. pp. 28, 32.

17. 'The Taoing of a Sound: Phonetic Drama in William Blake's "The Tyger"', in *Phonosymbolism and Poetic Language*, ed. Patrizia Violi (Turnhout: Brepols, 2000), pp. 99–145.

18. Ibid. pp. 111–15.

19. Patrizia Violi, 'Introduction', in *Phonosymbolism*, pp. 7–23 (p. 19).

20. Ibid. p. 9.

21. Julia Kristeva, *La révolution du langage poétique* (Paris: Seuil, 1974), pp. 241–2, 245–6. All translations from this text are my own unless otherwise stated.

22. Ibid. p. 243.

23. For a sceptical view of Kristeva's account see Adam Piette, *Remembering and the Sound of Words: Mallarmé, Proust, Joyce, Beckett* (Oxford: Oxford University Press, 1996), pp. 10–11.

24. 'Languages of Iconicity', in *Phonosymbolism*, pp. 57–83 (p. 59). It is Fonagy's piece that emphasises the relationship between ontogeny and phylogeny described in Violi's introduction.

25. Donald Freeman, 'Linguistic Approaches to Literature', in *Linguistics and Literary Style*, ed. Donald C. Freeman (New York: Holt, Rinehart and Winston, 1970), pp. 3–17 (pp. 5–6).

26. Fonagy, 'Languages of Iconicity', p. 68.

CHAPTER THIRTEEN

Epilogue: Deviance: Robert Creeley

Early in the introduction to this book I quoted the Czech structuralist Jan Mukařovský's itemisation of the supposed distinguishing formal features of poetic language, which came to the conclusion that, 'finally, not even *individuality*, the emphasized uniqueness of linguistic expression, characterizes poetic language in general'.[1] Whilst originality or uniqueness might characterise some instances of poetic language, only function will identify all instances. But some kind of qualification may be made to Mukařovský's assertion. It might not be the emphasised uniqueness of expression that makes the deployment of (for want of better terminology) a highly conventional phrase poetic, precisely because the poetry of the phrase is in its being conventional (as with the garden in the face of Campion's lady in 'Selection: Denise Riley'). But even in the deployment of 'conventional' language there is necessarily uniqueness: in even the most banal number series (1, 1, 1, 1, . . .) each 1 is different, as it occupies a different position in the series. Context and purpose distinguish all language uses from one another, even those in which the recurrence of a linguistic form is complete.[2] The deployment of a convention is always a unique gesture, and one that marks the participation of an utterance in a kind, at the same time as marking it as a new utterance, even if the newness is just a new set of circumstances (the same poem performed in a new moment). Uniqueness of this kind (obligatory uniqueness) is a fact about language, an interesting fact because it reveals language to be a certain kind of institution, one in permanent evolution. I have suggested that thinking of language as this kind of institution helps us to understand something about being human, at least in as much as being human is considered as being largely coterminous with using languages of one kind or another. Poetic language makes us conscious of language, not just as an institution, but as this kind of institution.

In some sense, then, poetic language might usefully be thought of as being characterised, if not by uniqueness of expression, then by a certain interplay between uniqueness and sameness. Such an interplay is observable, admittedly at an abstract level, in many of the themes explored in the chapters of this book, whether metre, figurative language, or any other common feature of poems. One theorist of poetic language has claimed that 'despite all complexities, a natural language is a sufficiently closed system so that a speaker can have unequivocal judgments about just what is normal in his language and what is deviant in varying degree'.[3] This kind of judgement places an improbable restriction on the capacity of natural languages to vary over time and space, not to mention the disputes about standard usage that can occur between 'well-informed' speakers, in the absence of an agreed ulterior authority. Some theorists of poetic language have underplayed the repeatability of utterances, their participation in genres of speech. Henri Meschonnic is one such writer, insisting that language is an unfolding present, rather than a series of acts tied to certain previous occurrences just as necessarily as they differ from those occurrences.[4] This view seems to me to unjustifiably relegate the systematic nature of language to a position of merely incidental relevance. Jacques Derrida has worked on the process of 'iteration', whereby particular speech instances transform the genre of act in which they participate, even to a highly destabilising degree. He suggests, for example, that the relation between the two meanings of the French word 'or' ('gold', 'now/therefore') is not merely one in which the uniqueness of each application of the word is confounded by its very repeatability, but a relation that challenges the very nature of what it is to be a word, to be a sign with a delimitable set of meanings.[5] What I am trying to draw attention to in poetic language is a similar phenomenon to that which Derrida identifies as the 'a-logical "logic" of the singular and iterable mark'.[6]

The emphasised uniqueness of a poetic work, even if that uniqueness is not definitive of poetry, but merely indicative, can also be seen in a more synchronic manner. Paul Celan's characterisation of modern poetry as slight, frail, absurd and close to silence is made in partially temporal terms. The 'poem takes its position at the edge of itself; in order to be able to exist, it without interruption calls and fetches itself from its now-no-longer back into its as-always'. But this character need not be understood strictly temporally, it may also be understood spatially, so that the image of the poem 'is perceived and to be perceived one time, one time over and over again, and only now and only here. And the poem would then be the place where all tropes and metaphors are developed ad absurdum.' The temporal moment of the poem is also a space, 'the place where strangeness was present, the place where a person succeeded in setting himself free'.[7] Relations between events in language are, of course, both synchronous and historical, paradigmatic and syntagmatic: they are sequential relations between a word or phrase and those with which it liaises, relations between words or phrases and their previous occurrences, and the relations between a word or phrase and other words and phrases that are like but also significantly unlike.

The following brief improvisatory lyric by Robert Creeley instantiates a poetic deviance both synchronous and historical, which develops absurd images, and which represents a step in which freedom is achieved:

She Went to Stay

Trying to chop mother down is like
hunting deer inside Russia
with phalangists for hat-pins
I couldn't.

This poem seems to exploit deliberate errors, selection or category errors.[8] In reading it we find ourselves comparing what is said to that which is not said, but which is like. The text points out some of its 'minus devices', things it might be expected to do, but does not do.[9] One reader of Creeley has recognised the connection between Creeley's poetic practice and the evocation of other, absent parts of a system: 'both numbers and language, perhaps even the human presence they help define, are essentially relational systems with each particular defined by the absent system of which it is a part. Creeley has always considered himself essentially a poet of relationships'.[10] 'She went to stay' is neither 'she went for good' nor 'she came to stay', but somewhere adjacent to both, so that the title of the poem is a blend of the inconsistent tones of initial optimism and terminal abandonment found in those two background phrases. But the phrase itself is not simply the declined possibility of those other phrases, nor even just holding them up together, but something in addition that suggests a relocation of the centre of the utterance in the 'she' who went, rather than the other (perhaps a 'he') to or from whom she comes or goes. The sense of those two other phrases having been declined suggests an independence, an independence that 'she' demonstrates.

The procedure this poem adopts, calling up a nearby phrase by deviating from it, is an evocation of the context of the poem, in the broad sense of 'all schemata, frames, scripts, systems and networks that we refer to when contrasting the units that actually occur in a piece of discourse, or can be inferred from it, with those units that do not occur'.[11] If a reader silently adjusts the category mistakes in the phrases, and then compares the phrase actually used with the phrase expected, a comparison emerges: one doesn't normally chop mother down, one chops trees down. Therefore mother is like trees, and a great deal of family romance might follow from that idea. Sometimes people cut one another down, in one sense by killing them, or in another by (verbally) humiliating them, cutting them down (to size). That mother is chopped down brings a definitive degree of violence to the phrase, but also suggests, by means of the Ovidian precedents for the transformation of women into trees, and the folkloric ambiance of the son who goes into the forest to chop down a tree that turns out not just to have human character-istics, but to be his mother, a mythological or parabolic means of explaining the potential complexities of mother-son relations. That chopping mother down is like hunting deer adds to the mythico-primitive air (the figure in the poem transgresses whilst hunting, as did Actaeon, but this transgression is against the mother rather than the goddess of chastity), whilst marking out the comparison ('is like') as decidedly absurd (deer don't stand still to be hunted), indeed marking comparisons in general as potentially absurd, because all things are conceivably alike in some respect (see the section of 'Figure: Tom Raworth' on Donald Davidson).

In a manner very like that seen in W. S. Graham (see 'Deviance: W. S. Graham'), the decision to employ an out of the way preposition calls up the more direct choice as an implicit comparison. 'In Russia' is neutral; 'inside Russia' is an instant link to Cold War, giving the country not just a border but an interior, one that is guarded against outsiders and which it is subver-sive and dangerous to penetrate. The connections made by the submerged metaphor (mother is a tree) and the patent simile (trying to chop her down is like hunting for deer) are also modified by the suggestion of a phrase, 'mother Russia', not evoked by any close formal parallel, but brought into presence simply by the tendency to give semantic unity to all parts of a sentence, par-ticularly where there is a challenge to 'plain' sense.[12] If mother is more like Russia than like the deer, hunting which is like chopping her down, then mother becomes both the ground and the figure, the scene and the action, in this sentence. The sentence that makes the poem up goes from being difficult to follow, and deliberately obscure in various pointed ways, to being more boldly absurd when it qualifies that the hunting is done with phalangists for hatpins. Phalangists are people, members of a right wing, national social-ist type party, particularly a fascist party in Civil War-era Spain, and the Lebanese militia founded after that model. On the whole, people make bad hatpins, but how should this absurd qualification be taken? Is it just the sound of the word that has appealed to Creeley here, or should the evocation of a Spanish Civil War context be read thematically in relation to the Cold War allusion? Creeley had, after all, served in Burma in the Second World War, and spent time in Majorca in the mid-1950s, and so was surely sensitive to both contexts.[13]

One could say that in just the two words 'Russia' and 'phalangist' the poem volunteers itself for consideration in relation to two confrontations that provide possible ideological orientations for the mid-twentieth century: the confrontation between fascism and socialism, and the confrontation between totalitarian communism and Western capitalism. But all the poem does is transform these confrontations into absurd scenes or stage properties for its oneiric utterance. The relegation of a context of this kind to the status of backdrop or sideshow is disarming and uncomfortable: if Creeley wanted to talk about wars, he should have done so with less indirection, and less risk of trivialising the world by making it no more than material for his own ingenious verbal performance. That is to say, the poem might be approached as attempting what, according to one commentator,

> poetry generally achieves: the production, by language-constructs differing from normal speech, or adumbrations of a metaphysical world in which the laws of science, causality, practicality, as we know them and need them in our workaday world, seem no longer to obtain and in which we vaguely come to visualize *other* laws.[14]

The poem might be thought to make 'Russia' and 'phalangists' mean something different, operate according to other laws; but the other laws can't displace the normal laws altogether (we never forget we're at the theatre). Rather, initiating discomfort by performing the transformation of the world into the ground for individual ingenuity, and doing so whilst maintaining an eye-catching levity of tone, is one of the achievements of the piece.

The poem is a kind of cheek, a getting away with it. The basis for the comparison between chopping mother down and hunting deer inside Russia is that the speaker couldn't do them: it is an absurdly open ground for comparison, because there are infinite things a speaker might not be able to do (hunt for mink inside Iran with bureaucrats for tiepins, and so on). What it is the poet couldn't do is also, in itself, absurd, impossible, other-worldly. But in saying what couldn't be done by the poet, and what, in all probability, could not be done at all, the poem seems to make that very impossibility possible, by giving representational form to it, by challenging the reader to imagine something that can't happen, and can't necessarily be imagined clearly (see Burke's remarks on Milton in 'Selection: William Cowper'). In doing so, the poem celebrates that capacity for deception that has resulted in sustained distrust and denigration of language by certain kinds of philosophers over the centuries. Creeley is playing with the capacity of language to make things which either have not been, or cannot be, nonetheless appear to be. The poem evokes an impossibility and acknowledges it as an impossibility, but in making the poem Creeley achieves that absurd, impossible, other-worldly thing – the poem itself.

The poem means things to us, nothing that could be rendered clear by even the fullest paraphrase, perhaps, but a specific yet changing range of tones, connections, attitudes, and affective responses. The poem can mean these things to us because we keep in mind what it doesn't say as well as what it does, because everything we say is connected to everything everybody ever says. These further contexts for the utterances that are not said in and yet impose themselves upon the poem are not neutral. They are shared between other contexts, all of which must be active in some way. As Michael Riffaterre says,

> while the poetic text is interpreted as a departure from a norm, that imaginary nonliterary norm is in effect deduced, or even retroactively fantasized, from the text perceived as departure. But no matter what the reader may think, there is no norm that is language as grammars and dictionaries may represent it: the poem is made up of texts, fragments of texts, integrated with or without conversion into a new system. This material (rather than norm) is not the raw stuff of language; it is already a stylistic structure, hot with intensified connotations, overloaded discourse.[15]

The phrases to which we compare what is in the poem are not neutral or normative, but phrases with their own determinate contexts and values. They are not neutral materials given a twist by the poem, but are already suggestive, indicative of value-laden orientations. Yury Lotman argues that this is a distinctive feature of verbal art, as 'language . . . constitutes a special matériel characterized by its high degree of social activeness even before the hand of the artist touches it'.[16] But it is tempting to say that audible and visual colours and textures also possess this high degree of social activity before the artist touches them: the red in the painting acquires its meaning in part through its presence in a practical, social world. That is not to say that its meaning is natural (absolute), that the red must always mean something particular that it draws with it from a definitive, ultimate context; but, on the contrary, to recognise that its natural or iconic signification is the combination of its most diffuse contexts (I try to argue something similar to Tom Clark's construction of an environment in which phonemes become significant in 'Equivalence: Thomas A. Clark').[17]

What Creeley's poem deviates from is not neutral, it is already a value-saturated language, inseparable from the sum of its contexts, because no purely formal language, without any context of utterance whatsoever, could possibly exist (see the discussion of Voloshinov in 'Spirit: Frank O'Hara'). The poem performs some improvisatory, unrepeatable gestures. These gestures evoke and at the same time mark themselves out as different from related terms and utterances: they possess an emphasised uniqueness. But that uniqueness is not what makes this poem a poem, because all utterances work in the same way, being unique, but drawing on types of speech that have histories. The tones, associations and attitudes brought into play in the poem could not have been made in any other way, and are at once a step beyond the particular system of the language and its history, when regarded from the perspective of an open future and an active present, and precisely the next and necessary step in that history, when regarded after the fact. The poem is a moment, then, at which value is produced, a moment at which the repertoire of what people can say and think is extended in an unpredictable but necessary manner. The uniqueness of the language of the poem is emphasised, in such a way as to reflect upon this production of values that are contingent and yet necessary.

Notes

1. Jan Mukařovský, 'On Poetic Language', in *The Word and Verbal Art: Selected Essays by Jan Mukařovský*, trans. and ed. John Burbank and Peter Steiner, foreword by René Wellek (New Haven and London: Yale University Press, 1977), pp. 1–64 (p. 3).
2. Henri Lefebvre, *Rhythmanalysis: Space, Time and Everyday Life*, trans. Stuart Elden and Gerald Moore, intro. by Stuart Elden (London and New York: Continuum, 2004), p. 7; Yury Lotman, *Analysis of the Poetic Text*, ed. and trans. D. Barton Johnson (Ann Arbor: Ardis, 1976), p. 39.
3. Manfred Bierwisch, 'Poetics and Linguistics', trans. Peter H. Salus, in *Linguistics and Literary Style*, ed. Donald C. Freeman (New York: Holt, Rinehart and Winston, 1970), pp. 96–115 (p. 108).
4. Henri Meschonnic, *Critique du rythme: Anthropologie historique du langage* (Paris: Verdier, 1982), p. 27, insists that all discourse and expression are historical. His argument is that the phenomena of language must be conceived historically, not as cognitive capacities, nor as systems, elements of which can be reproduced in the same form at different times. On this aspect of Meschonnic's thought see Marko Pajević, 'Beyond the Sign. Henri Meschonnic's Poetics of the Continuum and of Rhythm: Towards an Anthropological Theory of Language', *Forum for Modern Language Studies* 47:3 (July 2011), 304–18.
5. Jacques Derrida, 'Mallarmé', in *Acts of Literature*, ed. Derek Attridge (London: Routledge, 1992), pp. 110–26 (p. 125).
6. '"This Strange Institution Called Literature": An Interview with Jacques Derrida', in *Acts of Literature*, pp. 33–75 (p. 66).
7. Paul Celan, 'The Meridian' (1960), trans. Jerry Glen, in Jacques Derrida, *Sovereignties in Question: The Poetics of Paul Celan*, ed. Thomas Dutoit and Outi Pasanen (New York: Fordham University Press, 2005), pp. 173–85 (pp. 181, 183, 179).
8. *The Collected Poems of Robert Creeley, 1945–75* (Berkeley and Los Angeles: University of California Press, 1982; repr. 2006), p. 171. The oddities of this poem being, largely, semantic, it falls outside of the category of nonsense considered by Roger Fowler, 'On the Interpretation of Nonsense Strings', *Journal of Linguistics* 5:1 (April 1969), 75–83.
9. See Lotman, *Analysis of the Poetic Text*, pp. 29–30, for minus devices as a distinctive feature of artistic texts.

10. Charles Altieri, 'The Unsure Egoist: Robert Creeley and the Theme of Nothingness', *Contemporary Literature* 13:2 (Spring 1972), 162–85 (p. 181).

11. Nils Erik Enkvist, 'Context', in *Literature and the New Interdisciplinarity: Poetics, Linguistics, History*, ed. Roger D. Sell and Peter Verdonk (Amsterdam: Rodopi, 1994), pp. 45–60 (p. 50). Bob Perelman, 'Sense', in *Writing/Talks*, ed. Bob Perelman (Carbondale and Edwardsville: Southern Illinois University Press, 1985), pp. 63–86 (p. 76), suggests that many 'meaningless' sentences can be perceived as meaningful given a sufficiently imaginative attitude to the provision of context. In demonstration he interprets Bertrand Russell's example of a meaningless sentence, 'procrastination drinks consanguinity', as if it were a line from a play by Eugene O'Neill.

12. I have addressed this subject in 'Andrea Brady's Elections', in *Complicities: British Poetry 1945–2007*, ed. Sam Ladkin and Robin Purves (Prague: Litteraria Pragensia, 2007), pp. 238–52.

13. Ekbert Faas with Maria Trombacco, *Robert Creeley: A Biography* (Montreal and Kingston: McGill-Queens University Press, 2001), pp. 38–47, 123–2, 171–8.

14. Leo Spitzer, 'Language of Poetry', in *Language: An Enquiry into its Meaning and Function*, ed. by Ruth Nanda Anshen (New York: Harper and Bros, 1957), pp. 201–31 (pp. 209–10).

15. Michael Riffaterre, *Semiotics of Poetry* (London: Methuen, 1980), p. 164. This suggestion does not prevent Riffaterre talking about poetry, throughout his study, as if it deviated from a measurable linguistic norm.

16. Lotman, *Analysis of the Poetic Text*, p. 17.

17. For two accounts of the kinds of meaning colour might have, both of which emphasise the impossibility of there being a paradigmatic colour that exists independently of human perceptual and linguistic capacities, see Ludwig Wittgenstein, *Philosophical Investigations*, trans. G. E. M. Anscombe, P. M. S. Hacker and Joachim Schulte, rev. 4th edn by P. M. S. Hacker and Joachim Schulte (Oxford: Blackwell, 2009), pp. 28e–32e, Nos. 50–7 and Maurice Merleau-Ponty, *Phenomenology of Perception*, trans. Colin Smith (London: Routledge, 1962), pp. 221–6, whose argument tends towards the following question and answer (p. 225): 'What then does language express, if it does not express thoughts? It presents or rather it *is* the subject's taking up of a position in the world of his meanings.'

Further Reading

These suggestions, in roughly chronological order, are designed to supplement the texts on the theory of poetic language cited in the notes to each chapter. The first two paragraphs give some classical and mediaeval background. The later paragraphs present twentieth-century works, loosely organised by tendency and geographical situation.

Plato's *Ion* deals with the nature of poetic inspiration, and whether the *rhetor* may be regarded as knowing that of which he speaks when he is inspired. Aristotle's *Poetics*, though largely a treatise on the plot structure of tragic drama, advises a diction that combines ordinary and unusual ways of designating objects, which, together with his model of metaphor, is of the greatest importance in the history of thinking about literary language. Michael Davis, *The Poetry of Philosophy: On Aristotle's Poetics* (South Bend, IN: St Augustine's Press, 1999) is a good guide to the interrelation of the strange and the ordinary in Aristotle's theory of diction. *On the Sublime*, a text commonly attributed to Longinus, again testifies to the strong relationship between ordinary and exceptional language in classical literary thought, and is vital for understanding later thinking that posits literature as the category that avoids or exceeds categorisation. All three of these texts are available in *Classical Literary Criticism*, trans. by Penelope Murray and T. S. Dorsch (Harmondsworth: Penguin, 2000).

In later antiquity, St Augustine's writings include various remarks on the process of signification and the role of symbolism in language, including literary language, as evidenced in the selections in *The Norton Anthology of Theory and Criticism*, ed. Vincent B. Leitch *et al.* (New York: Norton, 2001). His treatise on music, *De musica*, relates the numerosity and harmony of versification to the perfectly harmonious nature of God, and accounts for the pleasure of measured language by reference to the physiological states of the body involved in perceiving different phenomena. A full translation by Robert Catesby Taliafero is available in *Writings of St Augustine (Volume 2)* (New York: CIMA, 1947), pp. 153–379, but, whilst still giving a strong outline of the argument, the English of W. F. Jackson Knight, *St Augustine's De Musica:*

A *Synopsis* (London: The Orthological Institute, ND), is much more accessible. One mediaeval treatise describing the art of the poet as the production of graceful utterance that plays its features, such as metre and diction, against one another, modulating the expected with the unexpected, is Matthew of Vendôme, *Ars Versificatoria (The Art of the Versemaker)*, trans. and intro. by Roger P. Parr (Milwaukee: Marquette University Press, 1981). The approach adopted by Geoffrey of Vinsauf, trans. by Roger P. Parr, *Documentum de Modo et Arte Dicandi et Versificandi (Instruction in the Method and Art of Speaking and Versifying)* (Milwaukee: Marquette University Press, 1968) offers technical advice on the transformation of parts of speech to produce poetic discourse.

A consideration of what it is to use the best form of the vernacular paying great attention to the stratification of speech according to social class and function, as well as practical advice on the mixture of different types of diction, is found in Dante, *De vulgari eloquentia*, ed. and trans. by Steven Botterill (Cambridge: Cambridge University Press, 1996). John M. Fyler, *Language and the Declining World in Chaucer, Dante, and Jean de Meun* (Cambridge: Cambridge University Press, 2007), helps to contextualise Dante's thought on divisions between speakers of the same language. Angelo Mazzocco, *Linguistic Theories in Dante and the Humanists: Studies of Language and Intellectual History in Late Medieval and Early Renaissance Italy* (Leiden, New York and Koeln: E.J. Brill, 1993) shows how Dante's thinking relates to questions of nature and artifice in language (see 'Figure: Walter Ralegh'), and to the tension between the common and the literary as standards for linguistic excellence (see 'Measure: William Wordsworth').

Desiderius Erasmus of Rotterdam, *On Copia of Words and Ideas*, trans. and intro. by Donald B. King and H. David Rix (Milwaukee, WI: Marquette University Press, 1963) offers similar guidance to Geoffrey of Vinsauf, acknowledging that some of his recommendations for developing a copious style are as fit for poetry as prose. Texts by Samuel Daniel and Thomas Campion included in *Sidney's 'The Defence of Poetry' and Selected Renaissance Literary Criticism*, ed. Gavin Alexander (Harmondsworth: Penguin, 2004) provide much insight into thinking about measure and proportion in English renaissance verse. The 'Preface' to Abraham Cowley's 'Pindarique Odes', in *The Poems of Abraham Cowley*, ed. A. R. Waller (Cambridge: Cambridge University Press, 1905), pp. 105–6 suggests another way in which the language of poetry at the time of Milton might justify its eccentricity. 'Selection: William Cowper' sets out the broad outlines of the theory of poetic diction in the eighteenth century, but other aspects of literary criticism in the earlier eighteenth century are revealed in David Womersley, ed., *Augustan Literary Criticism* (Harmondsworth: Penguin, 1997). Moving into the romantic period, Leigh Hunt, 'An Answer to the Question, "What is Poetry?" Including Remarks on Versification', in *The Selected Writings of Leigh Hunt*,

IV (2003) *Later Literary Essays*, ed. Charles Mahoney (London: Pickering and Chatto, 2003), pp. 5–41 may be related to the terminology of Wordsworth and Coleridge, offering a criterion for poetic language in the principle of variety in uniformity. Percy Bysshe Shelley's 'A Defence of Poetry' (available in the *Norton Anthology* cited above) develops an argument for seeing poetry as measured language, and as intrinsically connected to the origin and development of social life, and does so from a progressive, egalitarian perspective. Amongst Victorian contributions to the theory of poetic language not discussed in 'Equivalence: Gerard Manley Hopkins' and 'Spirit: Wallace Stevens', Coventry Patmore's 'Essay on English Metrical Law', in *Poems*, 2 vols (London: George Bell, 1886; second collective edition), II, 215–67 is remarkable. He proposes a theory of metre in which units of equivalent duration (not necessarily determined numbers of syllables) are marked by an accent, and in which the deformation metre enforces upon other parts of language are its beauties (see remarks on Yuri Tynianov in 'Measure: Robert Creeley').

Structuralist approaches to poetic language deeply inform the argument of this book. Roman Jakobson's work on poetry is available (in addition to the collection cited in 'Equivalence: Gerard Manley Hopkins' and elsewhere) in *Verbal Art, Verbal Sign, Verbal Time*, ed. Krystyna Pomorska *et al.* (Oxford: Blackwell, 1985) and *Poetry of Grammar and Grammar of Poetry*, ed. Stephen Rudy, *Selected Writings of Roman Jakobson*, ed. Stephen Rudy, III (The Hague, Berlin: Mouton, 1981). In collaboration with Linda R. Waugh, Jakobson wrote *The Sound Shape of Language*, 3rd edn (Berlin: Mouton de Gruyter, 2002), a significant contribution to discussions of phonosymbolism. Historical and critical studies of structuralism include Frederic Jameson, *The Prison-House of Language: A Critical Account of Structuralism and Russian Formalism* (Princeton: Princeton University Press, 1972) and Jurij Striedter, *Literary Structure, Evolution and Value: Russian Formalism and Czech Structuralism Reconsidered* (Cambridge, MA: Harvard University Press, 1989). The former links Saussure, Russian formalism, and French post-structuralism; the latter pays more attention to the tradition of Czech structuralism, including the domain of literary history. The influence of Slavic studies on structuralist poetics is evident in such works as Michael Shapiro, *Asymmetry: An Inquiry into the Linguistic Structure of Poetry* (Amsterdam, New York, Oxford: North Holland, 1976), which focuses on the markedness of opposed items in any language system or sub-system, such as rhyme.

The Francophone tradition of structuralist work on poetic language builds on Ferdinand de Saussure, with important essays such as Émile Benveniste, 'La notion de «rythme» dans son expression linguistique', in *Problèmes de linguistique générale* (Paris: Gallimard, 1966), pp. 327–36. For the writings of a poet that have stimulated and provided examples for French (and English) writing on poetic language, see Paul Valéry, *The Art of Poetry*, trans. Denise Folliot, intro. by T. S. Eliot, *The Collected Works of Paul Valéry*, ed. Jackson Matthews, VII (Princeton: Princeton University Press, 1958). The period in which Julia Kristeva composed *Revolution in Poetic Language* (see 'Spirit: Frank O'Hara', 'Measure: Robert Creeley' and 'Equivalence: Thomas A. Clark') is rich in discussions of the deviant and deformational power of language in the structuralist tradition such as Jean Cohen, *Structure du langage poétique* (Paris: Flammarion, 1966), and A. Kibédi Varga, *Les Constantes du poème: Analyse du langage poétique* (Paris: Picard, 1977). These texts often take nineteenth-century French poems as exemplary material, as does the English writer Elizabeth Sewell, in *The Structure of Poetry* (London: Routledge and Kegan Paul, 1951), though her emphasis is more on equilibrium than disruption.

Perhaps the single most comprehensive summation and criticism of the structuralist approach to literary, including poetic, texts remains Jonathan Culler, *Structuralist Poetics: Structuralism, Linguistics and the Study of Literature* (London: Routledge, 1975). The influence of structuralist linguistics on Anglophone literary criticism is evident in many of the collections of essays cited throughout this book, and others such as *Essays on Style and Language: Linguistic and Critical Approaches to Literary Style*, ed. Roger Fowler (London: Routledge and Kegan Paul, 1966). Work in the tradition of generative grammar such as Jean Boase-Beier, *Poetic Compounds: The Principles of Poetic Language in Modern English Poetry* (Tuebingen: Max Niemeyer Verlag, 1987), in addition to those cited in 'Selection: Denise Riley', could be taken as part of the same broad enterprise bringing linguistics and literary criticism together. So too, but from a more determinedly poetic point of view, could the work of John Hollander, in books such as *Melodious Guile: Fictive Pattern in Poetic Language* (New Haven and London: Yale University Press, 1988), which represents an attempt to find meaning and humanistic value in the reflexive nature of poetic language, and indeed in its instability.

The transition to post-structuralist poetics is fluid, with a text such as Gérard Genette, *Fiction and Diction*, trans. Catherine Porter (Ithaca and London: Cornell University Press, 1993) employing structural terminology, yet taking a more extensive view that identifies two different regimes of the literary: writing about things that didn't happen (fiction); using a certain kind of language (diction). Still in the Francophone tradition, a variety of influences, from phenomenology and psychoanalysis, are felt in texts such as Nicolas Abraham, *Rhythms: On the Work, Translation, and Psychoanalysis*, trans. Benjamin Thigpen and Nicholas T. Rand (Stanford: Stanford University Press, 1995), which offers an account of poetic and rhythmic consciousness as active mental states producing physical realities (through muscular anticipation, for example). Emmanuel Levinas, *Proper Names*, trans. Michael B. Smith (London: The Athlone Press, 1996) emphasises the openness of the process of poetic signification as a model for the human spirit after the Holocaust, which is understood in part as the perverse triumph of certain forms of rationality. Challenges which suggest that consciousness is as much rhythmic-poetic as semantic-rational are also to be found in *Between Philosophy and Poetry: Writing, Rhythm, History*, ed. Massimo Verdicchio and Robert Burch (New York and London: Continuum, 2002), with the ideas of one contributor developed at greater length in Amittai F. Aviram, *Telling Rhythm: Body and Meaning in Poetry* (Ann Arbor: The University of Michigan Press, 1994), a book that strikingly, if not convincingly, gives a politicised, post-structural account of the subject as rhythmic and reads it into texts from popular culture.

Discussions of poetic language in North America in the twentieth century are of course open to the tendencies sketched above, but they also have a certain internal logic. At mid-century R. P. Blackmur, *Language as Gesture: Essays in Poetry* (New York: Harcourt, Brace and Company, ND [1952]) registers a pragmatic inheritance, but also makes connections to early theorists such as St Augustine. Since the 1970s L=A=N=G=U=A=G=E poetry has done something to polarise debate, with Aviram (see above) opposed to the avant-gardist (and hence, he contends, elitist) stance. In addition to works cited in 'Deviance: W. S. Graham', theoretical writings associated with the L=A=N=G=U=A=G=E group are collected in *Artifice and Indeterminacy: An Anthology of New Poetics*, ed. Christopher Beach (Tuscaloosa and London: The University of Alabama Press, 1998) amongst others. A slightly sceptical account of the politics of writing and reading in the L=A=N=G=U=A=G=E group is given by Gerald Burns, 'How to Nonread', in *A Thing About Language*, foreword by Robert Creeley (Carbondale and Edwardsville: Southern Illinois University Press, 1990), pp. 58–61. Questions of deviance and strangeness figure prominently even in the theorising of poets who disrupt language less, and make fewer claims for their disruptions, such as Alice Fulton, *Feeling as a Foreign Language: The Good Strangeness of Poetry* (Saint Paul, MN: Gray Wolf, 1999).

The field of English poetry in the UK and Ireland over the last fifty years is characterised by a wide variety of different practices often sorted into two tendencies, the mainstream and the innovative. Helpful orientations in this field are provided by Keith Tuma and Nate Dorward, 'Modernism and Anti-Modernism in British Poetry' and Peter Middleton, 'Poetry after 1970', in *The Cambridge History of Twentieth-Century Literature*, ed. Laura Marcus and Peter Nicholls (Cambridge: Cambridge University Press, 2004), pp. 510–27 and pp. 768–86. Middleton calls the mainstream tendency postmodern and the innovative modern. This book focuses on poets who are innovative or modern. *Strong Words: Modern Poets on Modern Poetry*, ed. W. N. Herbert and Matthew Hollis (Tarset: Bloodaxe, 2000) presents a number of reflections by contemporary British and Irish poets from mainstream traditions, and does so in the context of selections from the theoretical writings of British, Irish and American modern and modernist poets. David Constantine, a poet featured in that anthology, presents sustained reflections on many of the themes raised in this book (poetic spirit, identity and difference, the politics of poetic utterance) in *A Living Language* (Tarset: School of English Literary and Linguistic Studies, University of Newcastle in association with Bloodaxe, 2004).

Notes on Poets

Walter Ralegh (1554–1618)

Ralegh, from a Devon family, studied at Oriel College, Oxford, and the Middle Temple (one of the law schools in London). He became a courtier, and an extremely successful naval officer. He participated in the brutal English military campaigns in Ireland of 1580–81. Having established himself as a favourite of Elizabeth I, his marriage to Elizabeth Throckmorton saw them both imprisoned. Although released, Ralegh was accused of involvement in Lord Essex's plot against Elizabeth, and was imprisoned by James I when he came to the throne in 1603. During this long imprisonment Ralegh wrote *The History of the World*. He was released to perform a last naval expedition, but was executed as a result of its mismanagement. The canon of his poetry is slight and of uncertain attribution. Many of the poems are answers to other poems, or are commendatory verses for other poets, attesting to an intensely social writing practice.

Stephen J. Greenblatt, *Sir Walter Ralegh: The Renaissance Man and his Roles* (New Haven and London: Yale University Press, 1973)
Steven W. May, *Sir Walter Ralegh* (Boston: Twayne, 1989)

William Cowper (1731–1800)

Cowper was educated at Westminster School in London. A possible career in public service was stalled by his panic before the interview. Throughout his life he experienced severe bouts of depression and, in his younger days, made several suicide attempts. He experienced a religious epiphany, and spent much time in a small circle of friends in quiet rural locations such as Olney. His hymn writing connects him to figures such as Isaac Watts, the Wesleys and Christopher Smart, and his brilliantly ironic and self-ironising social poems (such as 'On the Death of Mrs Throckmorton's Bullfinch') to Thomas Gray. His six-book poem in a mixed or composite genre, *The Task*, ties him more closely to Wordsworth than any other contemporary. One of Cowper's last major projects was a translation of Homer, conceived directly as competing with the earlier translation by Alexander Pope.

Vincent Newey, *Cowper's Poetry* (Liverpool: Liverpool University Press, 1982)
Martin Priestman, *Cowper's* Task: *Structure and Influence* (Cambridge: Cambridge University Press, 1983)

William Wordsworth (1770–1850)

Born and, for the majority of his life, resident in the Lake District, Wordsworth was educated at St John's College, Cambridge, graduating in 1787. He spent some time in France in the early stages of the revolutionary period, and toured Germany with his sister Dorothy and Samuel Taylor Coleridge in 1798–9. Coleridge and Wordsworth collaborated on *Lyrical Ballads*, but expressed divergent views on many literary subjects throughout their lives. Before becoming poet laureate in 1843, Wordsworth was sustained financially by a post as a customs officer. Wordsworth's political views are sometimes taken as a paradigm of early radicalism giving way to later conservatism. His contributions to *Lyrical Ballads* were self-consciously experimental. *The Prelude* and *The Excursion* represent the surviving elements of a monumental philosophical poem.

Frances Ferguson, *Wordsworth: Language as Counter-Spirit* (New Haven, CT: Yale University Press, 1977)
Keith Hanley, 'Wordsworth's Revolution in Poetic Language', *Romanticism On the Net* 9 (February 1998)
Geoffrey H. Hartman, *The Unremarkable Wordsworth* (London: Methuen, 1987)

Gerard Manley Hopkins (1844–89)

Educated in classics at Balliol College, Oxford, Hopkins converted to Roman Catholicism in 1866 and went on to join the Society of Jesus, burning his poems before he did so. He taught in various places in England, Wales, Scotland and Ireland, including as Professor of Greek and Latin at University College, Dublin, where he died. His poems were published posthumously by his friend Robert Bridges, with whom Hopkins sustained a long correspondence on poetic matters. Hopkins's thinking about poetics is famously idiosyncratic, particularly his writing on sprung rhythm. His poetic practice has few very close contemporary parallels, though he has been claimed as an important precursor by poets such as Seamus Heaney.

Joseph J. Feeney, *The Playfulness of Gerard Manley Hopkins* (Aldershot: Ashgate, 2008)

Michael Sprinker, *A Counterpoint of Dissonance: The Aesthetics and Poetry of Gerard Manley Hopkins* (Baltimore: Johns Hopkins University Press, 1980)

Wallace Stevens (1879–1955)

Born in Reading, Pennsylvania, educated at Harvard and New York Law School, Stevens lived for most of his life in Hartford, Connecticut and worked as a lawyer and insurance executive, as well as being a poet. His first book, *Harmonium* (1923), was not particularly well received, but towards the end of his life he was awarded the Pulitzer Prize for Poetry. Stevens represents an alternative to other modernistic strands in American poetry, such as the agonised historical consciousness of Ezra Pound or T. S. Eliot, or the pragmatic objectivity of William Carlos Williams. Stevens demonstrates a great interest in the inter-related unfolding of material reality, consciousness and language. Some of his earlier poems make evident play with the phonetic structure of language at the same time as developing absurd or surreal re-imaginings of human roles and relationships. Stevens is a meditative, phenomenological poet whose relationship to American and European romanticism has frequently been noted.

Beverly Maeder, *Wallace Stevens' Experimental Language: The Lion in the Lute* (Houndmills, Basingstoke: Macmillan, 1999)

Eleanor Cook, *Poetry, Word-Play, and Word-War in Wallace Stevens* (Princeton: Princeton University Press, 1988)

Anca Rosu, *The Metaphysics of Sound in Wallace Stevens* (Tuscaloosa: University of Alabama Press, 1995)

W. S. Graham (1918–86)

After briefly working on the Clyde docks as an engineer, Graham studied at Newbattle Abbey College, and began a career as a poet in 1942 with *Cage without Grievance*, a collection often associated with the style of Dylan Thomas. Graham's work is often said to have entered a new phase in 1955 with *The Nightfishing*, and from that point concerns with the landscape (of North Cornwall, where he had relocated, and behind it the Clyde), language, and human intimacy never left his work. His time in Cornwall saw him associate with painters of the St Ives school, notably Peter Lanyon and Michael Snow. Graham has long attracted the attention and admiration of other poets, themselves from various different tendencies, such as Douglas Dunn and Tony Lopez, and is newly the focus of increased scholarly and critical attention.

Matthew Francis, *Where People Are: Language and Community in the Poetry of W. S. Graham* (Cambridge: Salt, 2004)

Frank O'Hara (1926–66)

Having been brought up in Massachusetts, served for two years in the US navy, and graduated in English from Harvard, O'Hara spent most of his adult life in New York, where his intellectual and artistic sociability were expressed in intimate relationships with the poets John Ashbery, Kenneth Coke and Bill Berkson, and the painters Larry Rivers, Willem de Kooning, Helen Frankenthaler and many others (O'Hara's professional life was in the gallery world, and he produced a substantial body of art criticism). These friendships become the substance of many of O'Hara's poems, which often depart from particular personal or artistic connections to engage in improvisatory and meditative reflections on, or diversions from, those points of departure. He published little of his work during his lifetime, with collections of poems of a certain type (*Lunch Poems*, notionally written immediately after lunch-hour excursions, or *Odes*), but the posthumous collections of his poetry demonstrate an enormous and often challenging expressive range and set of influences (from early twentieth-century French and Russian poetry, to classical music, to Hollywood movies).

Micah Mattix, *Frank O'Hara and the Poetics of saying 'I'* (Madison, NJ: Fairleigh Dickinson University Press, 2011)
Marjorie Perloff, *Frank O'Hara: Poet Among the Painters: With a New Introduction* (Chicago: University of Chicago Press, 1998)

Robert Creeley (1926–2005)

Creeley corresponded with major figures of early and mid twentieth-century experiment, such as Ezra Pound, William Carlos Williams and Charles Olson (the theorist of projective verse and author of the *Maximus* poems). After serving in the Second World War as an ambulance driver, dropping out of a degree at Harvard, living in France and Majorca and teaching at Black Mountain College (the innovative American liberal arts college in North Carolina at which Olson was a Dean), Creeley taught at Universities in New Mexico and in New York state. His first publications were in the later 1940s, with major recognition from the earlier 1960s, after the publication of the selection of his earlier work *For Love*. His writing is associated with the Black Mountain School, manifesting an interest in language as a material, and commitments to experimentation in open form and the reclamation of the quotidian. He was also preoccupied by questions of human intimacy and community.

Stephen Fredman and Steve McCaffrey, ed., *Form, Power, and Person in Robert Creeley's Life and Work* (Iowa City: University of Iowa Press, 2010)
John Wilson (ed.), *Robert Creeley's Life and Work: A Sense of Increment* (Ann Arbor: University of Michigan Press, 1987)

Tom Raworth (1938–)

Raworth left school at age sixteen and worked in a variety of jobs before graduating from the University of Essex in 1970. He is a co-founder of Goliard Press, which published avant-garde poetry. He spent a number of years in the United States in the 1970s, and shares the immediacy or willingness to incorporate elliptical, transient verbal formulations from daily life into his poetry also seen in some strands of mid-century American poetry. Raworth has been anthologised in *A Various Art*, and is a major figure for the last two generations of British, Irish and American poets often grouped together as experimental or innovative.

Andrea Brady, 'On Poetry and Public Pleasure: A Reading of Tom Raworth', in *Poetry and Public Language*, ed. Tony Lopez (Exeter: Shearsman, 2007), pp. 25–37
Nate Dorward (ed.), *Removed for Further Study: The Poetry of Tom Raworth* (Toronto: The Gig, 2003)

Denise Riley (1948–)

Riley's work as a poet, in significant collections such as *Dry Air* and *Mop Mop Georgette*, represents a careful scrutiny of the very language and interior states that might be said to constitute the life of a female poet in late twentieth-century Britain. In that sense, her poetry and scholarly/philosophical work are closely allied, her early study *Am I that Name?* rejecting a trans-historical and universalising category of woman as a means of political containment, and her more recent work on the linguistic construction of subjectivity and inner voices (particularly in relation to poetry), noting the ideological power of inner voices, and the liberating potential of irony. These theoretical works might be considered alongside the study of language, gender and performance with which Judith Butler is so strongly associated. Riley's poetry is highly regarded by more recent poets from across the range of poetic practices. She has taught and researched at numerous universities in the United States and the United Kingdom.

Andrea Brady, 'Echo, Irony, and Repetition in the Writings of Denise Riley',
   Contemporary Women's Writing, forthcoming 2012
Simon Perrill (ed.), *The Salt Companion to Denise Riley* (Cambridge: Salt,
   2007)

Thomas A. Clark (1944–)

Having worked in collaboration with his wife Laurie Clark as a gallerist,
curator, publisher (at their Moschatel press) and maker, Clark's work bears
comparison to the recent visual art traditions of minimalism, geometrical
abstraction and land art. He has produced poems that work with a deliberately limited set of linguistic resources, explored the construction of page
space, and used walking as an integral part of composition. His work most
clearly relates to that of Ian Hamilton Finlay, the avant-garde poet and visual
artist, with whom Clark was friendly, but the impact on his work of concrete poetry, and experimental poetry from North America and Britain and
Ireland is also clear. He has recently been anthologized by Harriet Tarlo in
The Ground Aslant: An Anthology of Radical Landscape Poetry. His texts have
been installed in various locations, most recently New Stobhill Hospital in
Glasgow.

Peter Dent (ed.), *Candid Fields: Essays and Reflections on the Work of Thomas
   A. Clark* (Budleigh Salterton: Interim, 1987)
Tony Lopez, 'Thomas A. Clark, Nationality, Modernism', *Scottish Literary
   Review* 20:2 (November 1993), 75–85

Glossary

The glosses provided below are designed to help readers comprehend the use of particular terms in this book: they relate to questions of poetic language only, and do not attempt general definitions of complex terms such as post-structuralism.

Cognitive poetics: a relatively new tendency in literary study, attempting to integrate the study of texts into a model of the human mind as embodied and evolved. The tendency of cognitive poetics is to move from particular literary texts to underlying cognitive processes that have been identified through more or less rigorous experimental research. It is perhaps in the areas of metaphor (in relation to poetry) and discourse-worlds (in relation to fiction) that cognitive poetics has become most current.

Context: broadly, any information that is required to interpret, or to improve an interpretation of, a particular utterance or text. Such information can take a variety of forms: linguistic – knowing (well) the rest of the language in which an utterance is made; historical – knowing the history of the language, or the history of the culture to which a particular text pertains; pragmatic – having a sense of what the speaker/author is attempting to achieve in speaking/writing; world knowledge – knowing how the things or situations that are being talked about normally behave.

Deformation: the definitive characteristic of poetic language as proposed by some formalist and structuralist theorists. Viktor Shklovsky suggests that poetic language deforms ordinary language in order to elongate and deautomatise the experience of perception. Yuri Tynianov suggests that verse is the characteristic feature of poetic language, as it is allowed to deform other aspects (by altering expected word order for the purposes of metrical conformity, for example).

Deviance: the departure from a norm of language for poetic effect, whether that norm is established in a particular text, or is taken from the language as a whole. Scepticism has been expressed about the theory of style as deviance, given the difficulty of establishing norms for any aspect of language (phoneme frequency, for example).

Diction: the specific words chosen from a total vocabulary for a particular utterance or set of utterances. In relation to poetry, a register believed appropriate to poetic expression.

Domain: in cognitive psychology, the discrete body of knowledge (in the practical sense of how things behave or respond, and taking the form of scripts, schema, parables and so on), that people have about any particular set of concepts. Concepts can belong to more than one domain (the arrow to flying objects or weapons, for example).

Drive: in Julia Kristeva's work, the appetites and urges of the infant, such as the oral and anal drives, that survive in adult psychology and express themselves in the patterns of rhythmic language.

Generative grammar: a theory of grammar inaugurated by Noam Chomsky, focusing on the way in which kernel sentences (simple declaratives) undergo transformations in order to produce any other sentence. Since the 1950s, as the domain has expanded, generative or transformational grammar has focused more on language universals; those cognitive capacities underlying any particular language use.

L=A=N=G=U=A=G=E poetry: this loosely constituted group of poet-theorists has been active in North American cities, notably San Francisco, New York and Vancouver, since the 1970s. Bringing the radical politics of language characteristic of French post-structuralist thought into American poetic practice, they have engaged in sustained scrutiny of the socio-political consequences of naturalising language, grammar, syntax and poetic forms of speech such as the confessional lyric. There is a high degree of confluence between the theoretical and poetic aspects of the various projects.

Phonosymbolism: the appearance of a relationship between properties of the phonetic material of a word and properties of its referent; or the same relationship between an utterance (such as a poem) and its theme or subject. Phonosymbolism can be caught up in the continuing debate over the arbitrariness or motivation of the relationship between the material (sound or orthographic) form of words and their conceptual or referential content. Plato's dialogue *Cratylus* is at the root of this debate, and its participants express opposing views. Whilst most students of language are now cautious of stating that the origins of language are phonosymbolic (derived from deep correspondences between certain phonemes and properties of objects), there is general recognition that readers of poetry experience phonosymbolic effects.

Poetic function: in the work of structuralist poeticians such as Jan Mukařovský and Roman Jakobson, the means of identifying poetic language, in specific opposition to the idea that any formal feature of the utterance (such as its grammar) might do so. All language uses have a function directing the attention of the participants in the speech situation to one or another element of that situation. The poetic function is the direction of attention to the message itself, the utterance produced in the speech situation.

Post-structuralism: structuralist linguistics suggests that signs operate differentially within a system, that they acquire their meaning not by individual correspondences between the material form of a sign and its mental contents, but by those two inseparable elements of any sign standing in a relation of non-identity with every other sign in the system. Post-structuralist approaches to language suggest various ways in which that differentiality is unstable. They may focus on reading as an active process of establishing these differential relationships, advocating reading practices that are curious, investigative, and sceptical, and which locate radical uncertainties in the relationships between concepts previously taken to stand in a natural, stable order of priority and value. An interest in destabilising the implicit ideological orientation of language systems unites the work of the post-structuralist writers featured in this book (Julia Kristeva, Jacques Derrida, Paul de Man).

Re-accentuation: in Michael Bakhtin's theory of 'speech genres', the emphasis given by any speaker to words already spoken by some other speaker; a means of identifying the uniqueness of utterances at the same time as their participation in a historically delimited series. Speakers always use the language that has gone before them, but they give it new emphases that relate to their own social and ideological position.

Semiotic: having to do with signs; in Julia Kristeva's work on language, the aspect of language relating to the drives and appetites of the body, conceived as an ensemble, and in opposition to the symbolic aspects of language.

Sociolect: the form of speech characteristic of a particular community (given the important caveat that anyone can and probably does belong to more than one community).

Speech-act theory: a branch of the philosophy of language developed from the work of J. L. Austin in which the performance of certain actions, rather than the reporting of certain states of affairs, is regarded as a primary function of language. Austin identified various acts that are achieved primarily in and through language, such as promising, and for which discriminations based on truth or falsehood were therefore irrelevant. Austin suggested that such acts could be happy or unhappy, that they could succeed or misfire. Some writers after Austin have sought to codify the conditions under which certain speech acts could be said to have taken place (John Searle, Paul Grice). Others (Shoshana Felman, Judith Butler) emphasise the slipperiness of knowing what acts are taking place in which circumstances, focusing on literary and legal issues.

Speech genre: in Bakhtin's thoughts on language all utterances are utterances of a certain kind, they fall into genres. So utterances such as haggling or declaring love are types, with common attributes. That Bakhtin took participation in such genres to be fluid and historical is evident from his writing on re-accentuation, the process by which individual utterances contribute to the evolution of the genre.

Structuralism: in linguistics, the focus on synchronic study of language (the language as it exists at one historical moment), emphasising the arbitrariness of the relationship between the two inseparable parts of the sign, signifier (sound or orthographic form) and signified (conceptual content), and insisting that languages work not by a set of discrete relationships between individual signs and their referents, but by a process of negative differentiation between all signs in the system ('cat' does not have a meaning because a person or persons establish the relationship between the word and the object, but because there are numerous conceptual-verbal distinctions between signs in a system whereby 'cat' is not 'mat', nor 'dog', nor 'sat' and so on). Structuralism studies these negative differential relationships in order to understand the operation of a system, and has been applied to systems of myth in anthropology, to the literary market place in sociology, and many other fields. Structuralism makes a very significant contribution to the study of poetic language, with texts studied as systems, participating in various higher order systems such as genres, and ultimately in the language of their composition and the broadest possible set of systems (economic, ecological and so on). Work on poetic function, the tendency of poetic language to focus attention on itself, comes from the structuralist tradition. Many later twentieth-century students of poetic language have criticised structuralist poetics for a focus that excludes anything that falls beyond the linguistic system (Mary Louise Pratt, Derek Attridge), but structuralist poeticians understood themselves to be operating within a science of all human behaviour, in which the interaction of linguistic and poetic systems with other systems was paramount.

Symbolic: generally, the quality of representing something else; in Julia Kristeva's work on language, the aspect of language that differentiates and names objects in the phenomenal world of speakers, and at the same time makes propositional statements about them (even at an implicit level of propositions about existence or relation to the speaker). In this same line of thinking, the symbolic aspect of language is inaugurated by the thetic moment.

Thetic: from the Greek θεσις (thesis) for 'setting' or 'placing'; in Julia Kristeva's work on language, the moment at which a subject differentiates herself from her mother's body by placing herself in a phenomenal world, recognising distinct objects. This moment in language acquisition also has a corollary for Kristeva in qualities of utterances: any utterances that firmly place the subject in relation to a world may be called thetic. It is against this thetic quality that avant-garde literary activity strives.

Index